The Miss America™ Cookbook

Ann-Marie Bivans

WITH RECIPES EDITED BY BILL CALIGARI
NATIONAL PRODUCTION MANAGER
THE MISS AMERICA ORGANIZATION

INTRODUCTION BY Phyllis George
MISS AMERICA 1971

FOREWORD BY LEONARD C. HORN
PRESIDENT AND CHIEF EXECUTIVE OFFICER
THE MISS AMERICA ORGANIZATION

RUTLEDGE HILL PRESS

NASHVILLE, TENNESSEE

Published in Nashville, Tennessee, by Rutledge Hill Press, 211 Seventh Avenue North, Nashville, Tennessee 37219. Distributed in Canada by H. B. Fenn & Company Ltd., Mississauga, Ontario L5S 1R7.

Typography by D&T/Bailey Typesetting, Inc., Nashville, Tennessee
Design by Harriette Bateman

Library of Congress Cataloging-in-Publication Data

Bivans, Ann-Marie.
The Miss America cookbook / Ann-Marie Bivans, with recipes edited by Bill Caligari : introduction by Phyllis George : foreword by Leonard C. Horn.
p. cm.
Includes index.
ISBN 1-55853-328-1 (hardcover)
1. Cookery. American. 2. Beauty contests—United States—History. 3. Miss America Pageant. Atlantic City, N.J. I. Caligari, Bill. II. Title.
TX715.84996 1995
641.5973—dc20 95-8101
CIP

Printed in the United States of America
1 2 3 4 5 6 7 8 9 — 99 98 97 96 95

Contents

Recipes

Introduction

Phyllis George
Miss America, 1971

For seventy-five years the Miss America Pageant has mirrored the nation's attitude about women and our society's values. In the process, Miss America has gone from being a "bathing beauty" on the beaches of Atlantic City to being an advocate for AIDS awareness and prevention, to Heather Whitestone's platform that "Anything Is Possible." But always the Miss America contestants have stood out as the favorite of their home states. And then one contestant becomes the nation's favorite.

(Dick Zimmerman)

Miss Americas have become lawyers, doctors, public speakers, homemakers, entrepreneurs, television talk show hostesses, and actresses (to mention just a few of their many notable achievements). And we have always been in the public eye, entertaining and being entertained. A large part of that—both in public and in our homes with our families—is cooking. To celebrate the 75th anniversary of the Miss America Pageant, the women who have participated in and won the Pageant have contributed their favorite recipes, representing all fifty states, to *The Miss America Cookbook.*

Many of the recipes included in this book are family favorites—recipes we have inherited from our mothers, grandmothers, or favorite aunts. Others are regional favorites—recipes associated with the part of the country and the state we represented during our years of service. Still others are recipes we discovered while traveling as Miss America. And many of the recipes focus on healthy eating. *The Miss America Cookbook* contains a delightful assortment of recipes and, in addition, is a beautiful keepsake volume filled with nostalgic remembrances by Miss Americas of the well-traveled road to pursuing the crown, an account of the Miss America experience itself, and the rewards of being a titleholder—career stepping-stones, professional contacts, and scholarships. All Miss Americas—from the first in 1921 to Miss America 1995—are portrayed in "Miss Americas In Review."

This is a wonderful history of the Pageant with factual sidebars and fascinating and often humorous behind-the-scenes stories. It is a classic collection of all that is involved in achieving the Miss America dream.

In my own experience, I found the transition from Miss America to the role of wife, mother, and businesswoman to be filled with challenges. As wife of the governor of the state of Kentucky, I was hostess at many events. We entertained frequently at social gatherings, and planning menus was often on my agenda. Like other Miss Americas, I have been challenged with changing my family's eating habits to a more healthy diet.

Miss Americas have something in common. There is a camaraderie, a depth of feeling and understanding. We have been down the marathon road Ann-Marie Bivans writes about and we've come out winners. The American public is so receptive and responsive, warm and loving. This book is something of a 75th anniversary gift from us to you. It is one way of showing our gratitude to you for cheering us on. Enjoy it. And when you prepare these recipes and share them with friends and family, you just might find yourself saying, "This is one of Miss America's favorite recipes. . . ."

Phyllis George

Foreword

Leonard C. Horn
President, CEO
The Miss America Organization

This book, in a unique way, captures the essence of what has made Miss Americas and contestants so very special for seventy-five years. These women have brought their diversity and backgrounds from every state in the union—reflecting the host of nationalities, customs and traditions which make up our country. Miss America participants have always reflected the heartland of our great nation.

The *Miss America Cookbook* memorializes their time spent in the kitchen with parents and grandparents. It offers you passage into a collection of their fondest memories: Thanksgiving on a Vermont farm, summer barbecues in the mountains of Oregon, after-school cookie-baking in a Chicago flat. Each contestant brought that part of herself to Atlantic City, and regardless of her ambition, occupation and career choice, it remains part of each of them today. These recipes are not only traditions; they are commemorations.

In addition, Ann-Marie Bivans has captured the prestige and excitement, the hard work and effort, surrounding each contestant who earns her way down the path to Atlantic City. This is wonderful reading, providing many reflections on a tradition as American as apple pie.

As I often say, the Miss America Organization exists, in part, to recognize the capabilities of young women. It provides them with a support system through which they can develop their talents and obtain the skills of leadership. They emerge as role models—educated, confident, yet always reflecting the positive traditions of their youth. *The Miss America Cookbook* presents all of this.

Enjoy it in good health.

The Miss America™ Cookbook

The Road to Miss America

"It's really the only Cinderella story left in America today."
Mary Ann Mobley, Miss America 1959

"And our new Miss America is. . . ." Since 1921, when the first Miss America was crowned, those words have launched the climactic moment when one astonished young woman hears her name announced as American royalty and accepts the glittering crown and scepter. It is a scene that has fascinated generations of fans—and inspired legions of aspiring pint-sized hopefuls. "I think every little girl dreams of being Miss America," says Jacquelyn Mayer, Miss America 1963. "Winning is the fulfillment of a *dream.*" A life-changing dream. Being named Miss America is the ultimate modern-day fairy tale, when in one magical moment, a previously unknown young woman is elevated from obscurity to national celebrity. "To think that some little girl who is right in our midst somewhere is going to be Miss America next year!" enthuses Kenn Berry, a pageant volunteer for four decades. "You know, she can come from the poorest, unknown area in the United States—and next year be a celebrity. It is a Cinderella story!"

Kaye Lani Rae Rafko, moments after being crowned Miss America 1988. (Irv Kaar)

What makes this particular fantasy so timeless is that it is a dream with a tantalizing twist—it is *achievable!* Consider Kaye Lani Rae Rafko. An oncology nurse and the daughter of a used auto parts dealer, she hardly grew up with a silver spoon in her mouth and a closet full of debutante gowns. She was just another middle-class working girl, who, like millions of her counterparts, assumed that winning Miss America was a nifty fantasy—but something that happened to somebody else. That is, until she was crowned Miss America 1988. "I never thought that I could *be* in that position," she admits, wonder still evident in her voice. "I was just the girl-next-door, just like everyone dreams about . . . I wanted people to realize that it can happen to *anyone*—and I am an example that it *does* happen to anyone."

The life of the young woman who achieves that distinction will be instantly and dramatically changed. In one moment she will be vaulted from the privacy of campus life into the enviable media coverage and public appearances synonymous with national celebrity. As Eva Gabor observed while judging the 1989 Miss America Pageant, "The young lady who wins Miss America in a moment will become a celebrity such as all of us on this judges panel have worked our whole lives for." As the winner glides down the illuminated runway, smiling tearfully and waving at the crowd, she will be on her way to far more than instant celebrity status. Miss America will waltz off with a $35,000 scholarship (in addition to whatever she has won previously), a new sports car, a luxurious four-season wardrobe by American designers, 200,000–250,000 miles of free travel across the United States, and $150,000–$200,000 in appearance income.

That's only the beginning. The last few Miss Americas discovered that their famous title instantly launched lucrative and glamorous careers. Even before crowning a successor, Kaye Lani Rae Rafko (1988) was booked solid for a year traveling around the world as a spokesperson on medical issues; Carolyn Sapp (1992) starred in a television movie on her life, *Miss America: Behind the Crown,* and Leanza Cornett (1993) was offered a lead role on Broadway and signed a four-year co-hosting contract with *Entertainment Tonight.* Not bad for young women who were unknown college kids just a year earlier.

The Road to the Crown Begins in Your Backyard

The realization of the dramatic effect the title could have upon their lives is so magnetic that 50,000–80,000 contestants pursue that privilege every year, each hoping that she will be the lucky candidate to emerge from the crowd to take that heart-stirring walk down the runway into fame and fortune. Indeed, before the year is out, someone in their midst will wear the coveted Miss America crown. Her road to victory will begin right in her backyard, for Miss Americas—like NFL heroes and Hollywood stars—begin their quest for fame in grassroots America. Whether it is in a school auditorium in Powdersville, South Carolina, or in a sophisticated amphitheater in Miami, Florida—the local pageant stage is where the public catches its first glimpse of the hometown girl who will soon wear the coveted national crown. "A local winner is going to be the state winner," says Tom Hensley, chairman of the Miss Tennessee Pageant, which produced Miss America 1987, Kellye Cash. "Once the contestants start in the program, someone who wins a local pageant is going to be Miss America. One of them—*somewhere!* It's just a sifting, shaking-out process."

But the local pageant isn't merely about discovering a future Miss America. The Miss America program is a respected per-

The Miss America title can dramatically change a young woman's life. In one year, Leanza Cornett, shown during the 1992 Miss Florida Pageant with emcee Jennifer Sauder, went from being an unknown college student, to Miss America 1993, to Entertainment Tonight *co-host.* (Ann-Marie Bivans)

sonal development program and the world's largest private scholarship program for women, making available more than $24 million in scholarships and grants annually. The program includes approximately 2,000 local pageants, called "preliminaries," held nationwide, from Miss Cottage Grove to Miss University of Miami. These local pageants are not-for-profit programs operated by civic organizations or colleges and run entirely by volunteers, an estimated 300,000 nationwide. To assure a uniform standard of quality from the local to national levels, every pageant must abide by identical regulations, operational procedures, and judging criteria established by the Miss America Organization.

As a women's scholarship and personal development program, the competitions are intended to be enjoyable and beneficial experiences that provide opportunities for girls to "test their wings" with some new challenges, practice interviewing and public speaking, develop their stage talents, earn some money for college, make career contacts, bask in the spotlight of public recognition, make new friends—and have *fun!* A contestant's first experience should be an enjoyable one, according to Anne St. Pierre, a Florida regional director and pageant volunteer for twenty-four years. "I always tell a first-time contestant to go in with the idea of *learning*. Enjoy it. Let it be a learning experience. Don't go in with the idea, 'I've got to win!' because if you do that, you're not going to enjoy the experience."

Most contestants find that participating in a local pageant is a lot more fun than they expected. "I never would have thought on my own of going into a pageant," admits Jill St. Pierre (no relation to Anne), who later won a string of impressive titles and placed as first runner-up to Miss Florida. "My dad suggested it to me after he saw an ad for the Miss Monroe County Pageant. I thought he was kidding. At that age, we thought that girls who did pageants were stuck up. He mentioned it again a few months later, and I don't know what made me, but I went to their first meeting and I found that the other girls were very nice, normal, not stuck up,

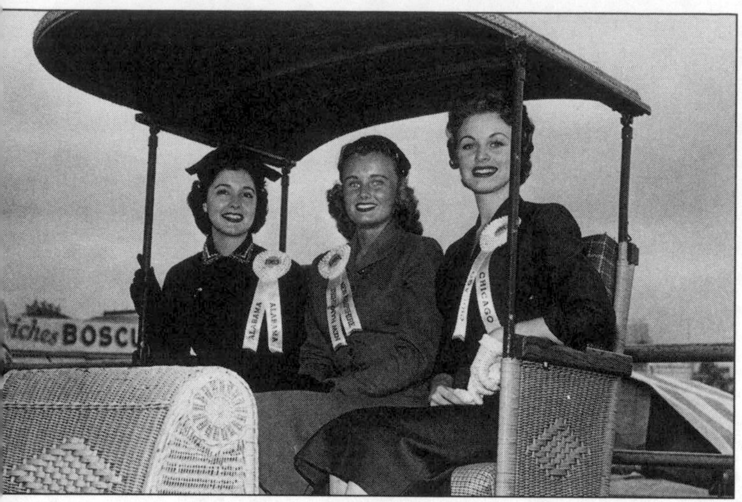

Miss Chicago (right) enjoys the Boardwalk before the 1953 Pageant with Miss Alabama and Miss New Hampshire. Before 1959, not every state was represented every year and cities as well as states sent contestants. Barbara Jo Walker, for instance, successfully competed for the Miss America 1947 title as Miss Memphis and Bess Myerson became Miss America 1945 representing New York City. (Fred Hess & Son)

and I fit in real well. I continued with the pageant, had a great time, and I ended up winning that local on my first try! It was just great because I had never won at something. You know, I was never straight A's at school, I was never best on the track team, I didn't have the best splits as a cheerleader...but I finally *won* something—and that changed my whole attitude!" she admits, chuckling. "It got into my blood!"

While a young woman's initial introduction to the world of Miss America competition is a fun experience of youth, it often leads to a more significant role in her life. "It was something I've watched since I was little," says Melissa Aggeles, Miss Florida 1988. "You dream about it, but you never think you're capable of actually accomplishing that. I saw the girls who had competed and they were much older. I was only nineteen and in awe of Miss Florida. Winning that seemed unreachable. But each year I got closer and closer. It's wonderful to think how far I've come—from not making the top ten the first year—to *winning* five years later!" Melissa not only managed to become Miss Florida, she won the national swimsuit competition, and made the top ten at Miss America. So much for little girls' "unachievable" dreams.

As each new generation of entrants watches the contestants before them evolve and move from the local competition, to the state title, to the Miss America stage, they begin to realize that they, too, can actively pursue the crown. "Winning Miss America is a fantasy," says Kris Beasley, Miss Tennessee 1986. "We all grew up watching the Miss America Pageant and wondering how in the world the girls got up there, what they had to do to get there, and how it all comes together. Then, all of a sudden, you learn how it happens. It's a step-by-step process. The bug bites you, and once it bites you—it's there!" Then, she explains, the childhood fantasy matures into an adult goal backed by the decision, "Okay, I'll pay the price!"

Paying the price is simply a matter of a young woman's committing to investing the time, effort, and determination to achieve her personal best. The crown ultimately becomes a byproduct of those efforts. "The girl who wins Miss America is just like you or me, just a girl next door," says Jill St. Pierre, who as Miss Monroe County, awarded Kaye Lani Rae Rafko,

Miss America 1988, her first-ever local pageant crown. "But with all the polish, the makeup, the hair, the gowns, the lights, and the adrenaline that night—that girl fulfills her dream. It's intimidating to sit back as a little girl or a teenager and watch that girl win, but it's important to realize that no matter how gorgeous, talented, and smart the girl who wins that night may appear, she is *just like them.* Yes, she has all these wonderful qualities—but so do they. They just need to be *developed.*" The local and state pageants are where that process of development occurs.

But whether the contestant is a first-timer seeking a bit of adventure, or a more advanced contestant hoping to make it to the national runway, the local pageant is her entrée. Most preliminaries are held between November and April, with a typical schedule including a get-acquainted party, rehearsals, perhaps a group public appearance, and a dress rehearsal. On pageant day, the private interviews with judges are held in the morning, with the evening wear, fitness in swimsuit, and talent competitions conducted on-stage later that night. It's all topped off with the big moment—the crowning of the young woman who will wear the local crown and represent her community at the state pageant.

While participating in the pageant is, and should be, an exciting, rather glamorous experience, actually serving as a local titleholder is a responsibility. Thrilling, glamorous, and fun—but a responsibility all the same. A local titleholder doesn't simply take the crown and go home. She is a representative of her community and the Miss America program. "She has to realize that if she is the winner she has a big responsibility ahead of her," notes Jeff Bell, a veteran local pageant director, "and she has to uphold the values and morals of that particular crown." During a titleholder's year of service she will make appearances in her area promoting the pageant's scholarship program, her "platform" (a worthy cause or charity), and the pageant's generous sponsors. Often she will be invited to address elementary and high school students, meet city leaders at public functions, visit nursing homes and hospitals, and interview with local newspaper, radio, and television reporters. In essence, a local winner serves as a role model for her community and future contestants. "When you enter a pageant and win a title, you have a responsibility," explains Dr. Sandra Adamson Fryhofer, a former Miss Georgia. "I mean, I set precedents for the women who followed me, just as the women who held the title before me set precedents."

In addition to the responsibilities, there's the exciting, although tiring, process of preparing for the state pageant, usually held in June or July. The exciting weeks preceding the state competition are filled with public appearances, speeches, press interviews, talent rehearsals, mock interviews, exercise sessions, shopping for a competition wardrobe, fittings, appointments with hairstylists and makeup artists, practice, and packing. When the Big Day finally arrives, the local pageant committee and supporters, and the contestant's family and friends gather to wish her success and send her off to the state pageant with her traveling companion. Everyone present realizes that there is the thrilling possibility that when she returns, her luggage may include a state crown—and a coveted ticket to the Miss America Pageant. "This is where she first realizes," says former Miss America Mary Ann Mobley, "that if she wins the state title, there is a real chance that she might become the next Miss America!"

The People Behind the Contestants

The contestants are not alone in their high hopes to make their way to the national runway. Behind each contestant is a small army of local and state directors and volunteers, 300,000 nationwide. These tireless volunteers devote hundreds and hundreds of hours annually to plan and produce their pageants, raise scholarship money and prize packages, choreograph production numbers, hold rehearsals, coordinate chaperons, dancers, hotel rooms, and drivers, build stage sets, prepare judges, write cue cards . . . and work until they drop from exhaustion. Once the pageant is over and the judges have given them a titleholder, they invest hundreds more hours preparing her for the next level of competition, helping her refine her interview skills, finding her the right talent coach or fitness trainer, and shopping to compile a wardrobe for pageant week. All of which is done on a volunteer basis after they've put in a full week at work and tucked the kids into bed. "They are professional people who *give* to their communities," says Robert Arnhym, longtime president/CEO of the Miss California Pageant, "people who work in constructive ways to do things for others, and who are proud that they have been able to make a contribution to young lives and to work with the largest women's scholarship program in the world."

With so much heart, soul, and backbreaking effort invested in their pageants and titleholders, can anyone begrudge pageant volunteers for being nearly as competitive as the young women on the runway? "As far as I'm concerned, we're going to keep fighting to win until somebody else has the crown—and then we'll try to get it the *next* year," declares Robert Zettler, retired executive director of the Miss Ohio Pageant. "We don't go there to come in second. We go there to do the very best we can, thinking that we have a super chance to win. But we don't come out crying if we don't win. Well, I guess some of our people have," he admits, grinning, "but not for long."

Contestants' families and friends, who are often newcomers to the pressures of pageantry, tend to be more nervous than competitive. By pageant day, when their daughter or sister is standing on-stage vying for a title that could make them "first family" of their state, relatives are as nervous as the contestants. Parents, grandparents, siblings, and friends proudly wearing photobuttons of "their girl" nervously scurry throughout the auditorium visiting with excited local and regional directors and studying the program book to size up the competition. The back of the room often resembles a maternity waiting room, with clusters of camera-laden dads trying to conceal their jitters. "My father was pacing the floor!" says Kylene Barker, Miss America 1979. "They told me later that he was more nervous at the Miss Virginia Pageant than he was the night I was born!" Who can blame them? After all, it's not every day that a loved one battles to represent her state at the Miss America Pageant.

The Marathon toward the Crown Continues

As the competition gets underway, the auditorium becomes a sea of camera flashes and waves of applause. Despite the loyalty evident as different sections of the audience cheer their own contestants, newcomers are often surprised to find that such partial audiences demonstrate the goodwill to applaud the efforts of *every* woman on-stage. By the end of the evening when the emcee tears open the auditor's envelope containing the judges' decision, the tension is as sharp as the prongs on the rhinestone crown. Suddenly, the emcee turns toward the crowd and dramatically announces, *"And the winner is...."* Instantly, the audience roars with approval as one stunned young woman on-stage gasps in shock at the realization that her dream has just become reality. "I felt like I went through the ceiling, back down, and through the ceiling again," exclaims former Miss New Jersey Christina Chriscione. "I was floating and I didn't come down for days. It was one of the most exciting, thrilling moments of my life. I will never forget that feeling—never!"

The audience roars with approval as Tami Elliott realizes that her dream has just become reality when she is crowned Miss Virginia 1989 by April Fleming, Miss Virginia 1988. (Doug Rumburg)

The winner's family and pageant supporters are equally ecstatic, appreciating that the young lady they have encouraged, worked with, and supported through years of losses and victories, has earned one of only fifty coveted tickets to the Miss America stage. "When the final announcement came and I realized that she had *won*, I screamed, I cried, I prayed," recalls Elizabeth Aggeles, mother of Melissa Aggeles, Miss Florida 1988. "I was totally elated, and so proud...so very, very proud!"

The hours after the crowning are a blur of activities. "After you take the runway

The hours after a state titleholder's crowning are a blur of activities as she embarks on the most exciting year of her life. The morning headlines tell Anna Graham Reynolds that her victory as Miss South Carolina 1988 was not a dream. (Irv Kaar)

walk you're congratulated by all the contestants at once, which is really fun," says Sarah Evans, Miss Ohio 1988. "Then they keep you really, really busy!" The new titleholder is ushered aside for interviews with local television crews, then photographed on-stage alone, with her runners-up, with her family, and with the judges. Sponsors present her with some of the many generous gifts she will receive, from diamond jewelry, to fur coats, to keys to a sports car for a year. Following the on-stage ceremonies, the winner is whisked away for her first press conference. She then returns to her hotel room to catch her breath and freshen up. At last, she is escorted to the state reception where she is officially introduced to the public as the state titleholder, gives her acceptance speech, greets guests, signs autographs, and poses for snapshots. Despite the thrills of victory and celebration, Evans recalls, "That was a *long* night. I finally got to bed about 4:30!"

That's only a taste of the year ahead. A popular state titleholder quickly finds herself caught up in a whirlwind year in the public spotlight. Her days are packed with appearances for sponsors, stores and malls, performances at charity fundraisers, speeches before clubs and churches, motivational talks at schools across her state, and media interviews and local talk shows wherever she travels. "We try to get her very active in the appearance field with media appearances, fairs, festivals, corporate appearances," says Robert Zettler. "It helps prepare her for the Miss America Pageant's tough grind—and to understand the pressures of her job if she becomes Miss America." That means early hours, nonstop travel, red-eye flights, and constantly being in the public eye. "I did 300 appearances that year," recalls former Miss Florida Kim Boyce. "I mean, there were days when I was doing five or six things in a day! I don't remember having more than a three-day stretch that year when I wasn't doing something. It was a real hectic year." Despite its brisk schedule, serving as a state titleholder is a thrilling opportunity and privilege that thousands of young women dream of experiencing.

Preparing for the Miss America Pageant

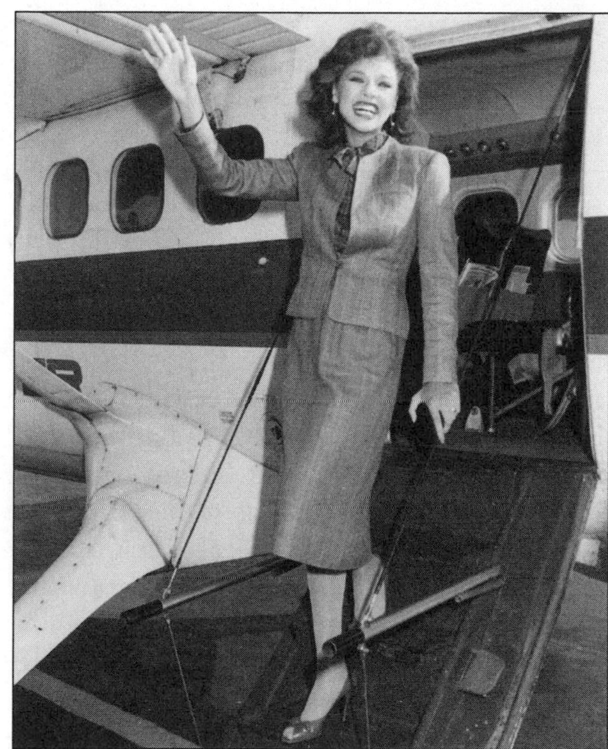

Contestants arrive in Atlantic City, aware that the week ahead could change their lives. In 1983, future recording star Vanessa Williams arrived as Miss New York. She left as Miss America 1984. (Irv Kaar)

In addition to such rigors and rewards of her victory, the highlight of any winner's year of service is her trip to the national competition. Brimming with enthusiasm, determination, and high hopes, the fifty newly crowned state titleholders begin their preparations for the upcoming Miss America Pageant. "Our girl lives, eats, and breathes nothing but preparation for Atlantic City," asserts Joseph Sanders III, president and chairman of the Miss South Carolina Pageant which produced Miss America 1994, Kimberly Aiken. "We call it 'having our act together.'"

It's what every contestant strives to achieve. With a state representative allowed only one shot at the national title, that final round of preparation is intense: public appearances to strengthen their confidence, media interviews for advance publicity, hours of fitness training daily to perfect their figures, studying newspapers and magazines to keep abreast of current events, practice interviews with mock panels of judges to strengthen their verbal skills, consultations with talent experts to refine their talent performances, consultations with hairstylists and makeup artists, wardrobe fittings, and shopping to acquire and accessorize a sufficient wardrobe for two weeks of appearances, rehearsals, and on-stage competitions. "It's almost like preparing for the Olympics," observes Donna Axum Whitworth, a former Miss America and national judge. "It's mental, physical, and emotional training."

Yet, that's what it requires. Unlike the public's perception of Miss America being a magical "dream come true" that somehow *happens*, transforming that dream into reality takes far more than just fantasizing about becoming Miss America. The national title is *earned*. "I think it is viewed as a fairy tale by young girls," acknowledges Karen Aarons, the Organization's executive vice president. "When they don't know all the hard work that has gone into getting up to that point, I think they can view Miss America as being *anointed*, rather than as part of an arduous selection process and competition. When in the space of two hours, someone who is unknown goes to being Miss America, it *does* appear to be a Cinderella story. I think that what is not really known is all the hard work that leads up to it."

But what motivates contestants to invest the thousands of hours of hard work and faith to pursue the national crown? Usually it is the same drive for accomplishment that motivates an actor to strive for the Oscar or an Olympian to reach for the gold—good old American ambition. "I wanted to have an extraordinary destiny . . . something very special in life," explains Laurel Schaefer, Miss America 1972. "It wasn't that I had the dream of being Miss America—I just wanted to become all that my potential enabled me to be. We are all responsible for establishing our priorities and values. If you seek a life that is *extra*ordinary, you've got to live an exemplary life!" That commitment to investing hard work and persistence is unquestionably the key to the title. And in those last crucial weeks leading up to the Miss America Pageant, each state titleholder gives her best, fully appreciating that her performance in the days to come may very well change her life forever. "It's only a one-shot deal," says Kaye Lani Rae Rafko. "You only can go to the Miss America Pageant once. I didn't want to come back home to Michigan wishing that I could have done something differently, or that I could have tried just a little harder," she admits. "I gave it everything I had—and it paid off for me!"

With such self-imposed expectations weighing upon their young shoulders, approaching the national competition with a healthy attitude is critical. "I didn't go to Atlantic City saying to myself, 'I'm going to be the next Miss America!'" says Kylene Barker, Miss America 1979. "With some state winners, everybody has them so pumped up saying, 'You're gonna win, you're gonna win!' that it's the worst disappointment in the world if they *don't*. I feel that you have to go to Atlantic City—and this is the way I went—saying to yourself, 'If I win, okay . . . If I lose, okay—but I'm just going to do my best. I have worked to achieve my personal best, and that's the best I can do. You know, if the judges like it—fine; if they don't like it—fine. But I've done my best."

For the fifty young women whose dreams and determination have earned them local and state titles, the first two contests on the road to the crown are behind them. Now they face the all-important third, and final, sprint toward the national title. They are in for the experience of a lifetime—the thrilling opportunity to compete in the famous Miss America Pageant, where, in a magical moment they have all dreamed about, someone in their midst will be singled out to wear the most coveted crown of them all . . . *Miss America.*

On to the Miss America Pageant

"I just kept thinking, 'This is it! Girls dream about doing this their whole lives, so let's just have a good time and enjoy it.' "
Kim Boyce, Miss Florida 1983, national semi-finalist

In early September, the fifty women who would be Miss America leave for Atlantic City, breathlessly awaiting the moment they will finally step onto that famous Convention Hall stage and compete for the most coveted crown in the country. While millions of viewers will watch the televised crowning, what they won't see is the grueling two weeks of dawn-to-midnight activities and pressure that lead up to that thrilling finale.

A highlight of Pageant week is the Miss America Parade when 200,000 people jam Atlantic City to cheer the contestants. (Irv Kaar)

The first leg of the contestants' adventure is the Pageant's "field trip," a mini-vacation and public relations blitz that allows them to get to know each other before the pressures of competition begin. Traditionally, the fifty titleholders have met in Philadelphia for a tour of historic sights by horse-drawn carriage. More recently they have been VIP guests of Disney's Magic Kingdom and MGM Studio for several days of fun, frolicking, and media hype before leaving for the national finals via a chartered plane, the "Miss America Special."

When the young women finally arrive in Atlantic City, they pinch themselves to make sure it's not a dream. After all, this is the home of the world-famous Miss America Pageant—where "the dreams of a million girls" will become one young woman's reality. "It's a feeling of elation," says former Miss America Mary Ann Mobley, "that all the hard work has paid off and you are finally in Atlantic City." Upon arrival, contestants are greeted by city dignitaries, pageant officials, and reporters before they

The first part of the contestants' adventure is the pageant's "field trip," a mini-vacation and media blitz that allows them to get to know each other before the pressures of competition begin. In 1992 the contestants toured historic Philadelphia. (J.M. Frank/C P News)

begin a week packed with glamour, suspense, and publicity any celebrity would envy. "We encourage them to enjoy the week to its fullest," says pageant CEO Leonard C. Horn, "because it's going to be something they're going to look back on for a long time as a high point of their lives."

During their stay, the young women and their official traveling companions are guests of the glamorous casino hotels along the Boardwalk, where they are protected by special security and barraged with gift baskets and flowers from the hotels, sponsors, family, and friends. Once the young ladies have a chance to unpack and unwind, they are escorted to the nearby Convention Center, home to the pageant since 1940. There they register, autograph their state on a wall-sized map of America, interview with reporters, pose for photographers, and tour backstage. Taking their first steps on the massive stage is always a nostalgic moment. After all, this is the hallowed ground where half a century of Miss Americas have earned their crowns. "When we first walked down the hall, we just kind of peeked in through the door," recalls Sophia Symko, Miss Utah 1988. "You see this stage and you think, 'Oh my gosh, this is it. I am really *here!*'" A few bone-tiring rehearsals quickly diminish some of the mystique. "Once you've been on it practicing," she admits, "it shrinks and doesn't seem *quite* as overwhelming as it was."

To assure their safety and well-being, contestants are surrounded by a small army of attendants. Each young woman brings along a state traveling companion who rooms with her and helps her throughout the week. A second group of attendants, the national hostess committee, oversees every other aspect of contestants' lives that week: transportation, meals, press interviews, the dressing room, emergencies, and so on. "They are supervised about as well as you are in the army!" Bert Parks once quipped. Indeed, the hostesses have the responsibility to make the experience as positive as possible for their young charges. "I think the hostesses do a very good job of helping contestants to know what to expect, to measure their time, and to enjoy the week to its fullest," says Leonard C. Horn.

With the hostesses in such constant contact with the contestants over the week, close bonds of affection develop—sometimes leading to comical situations. One of the funniest involved a hostess-trainee who was assigned to Miss Arkansas 1983, Regina Hopper. As Regina walked on-stage for the swimsuit competition, the Arkansas delegation roared the state's famous razorback "hog call" in support, "*Whoooo piiiiggg sooeeeyyy!*" "I laughed and everybody else laughed," says Regina. Everybody except the new hostess who rushed to Miss Arkansas's side the moment she made it backstage and tearfully reassured her, "Honey, you are *not* fat. You are not a pig. I don't know who those people are calling you a fat pig! I think that's just terrible!" "I still laugh at that," Regina admits, smiling. Unusual as it is, the story illustrates the affection that develops between the women who would be Miss America and the hostesses who would love to see them accomplish that dream.

After contestants arrive at the Miss America Pageant, they autograph their state on the wall-sized map of America, as Kathy Manning, Miss Mississippi 1984, did. (Irv Kaar)

The moment when the candidates for the title come face to face for the first time is always a memorable—and unsettling—occasion. "I can remember the first time I met the other contestants, I thought, 'What am I doing here?'" former Miss Rhode Island Michele Passarelli admits, chuckling at the memory. "I became more overwhelmed by the minute." Finally, she told her state traveling companion, "Louanne, take me home. Tell them I have pneumonia. We're leaving!" Louanne managed to pick up her contestant's spirits—until the next day when tiny Miss Rhode Island rounded a gown rack backstage and ran headlong into Miss Texas's midriff. "She was probably five-foot-eight," Michele recalls, "and to five-foot-three, it looked like New York City! Well, she patted me on the head, introduced herself, and said, 'I know you. You're Miss Rhode Island. Aren't you the *cuuutest* little thing!'" Michele looked up at the statuesque beauty and sighed, "And I know you too. You're gorgeous and wonderful Miss Texas!" Despite her initial reservations, which she finds amusing in retrospect, Michele went on to have a wonderful experience at the Pageant that inspired her to become a local pageant director.

Even the most confident of souls discover that meeting the other contestants evokes an unnerving blend of emotions—admiration for the impressive quality of the national representatives tinged with nervousness at having to compete with them. "I realized that there were a lot of very pretty, intelligent, talented young women in the United States," says former Miss Georgia, Dr. Sandra Adamson Fryhofer, "and *fifty* of them were there!"

The Demanding Schedule

The days following the contestants' arrival are a whirlwind of activities: early morning pickups, marathon rehearsals, press interviews, photo shoots, a formal hospital fundraiser, a picnic, lunch with Miss America, the Parents' Reception, topped off with after-dinner rehearsals. "Life is not a continuing pageant," observes former Miss Mississippi Mary Donnelly Haskell. "Thank goodness, or we'd all be worn out!" Considering how hard they've worked to make it to the nationals, most contestants take the killer hours in stride. "It's definitely a tight schedule," says Sophia Symko. "You don't get much sleep and you don't have much free time, but you figure that this is a once-in-a-lifetime experience and it's not going to happen again, so enjoy it."

Sleep may be in short supply during pageant week, but there is certainly no shortage of reporters. More than 300 media representatives cover the event annually, ranging from small town papers to the *New York Times* and *USA Today*, from stately *Newsweek* to sexy *Cosmopolitan*, from local TV news crews to *Entertainment Tonight*. Interviews are tightly scheduled between rehearsals and competitions by appointment. Not surprisingly, eagle-eyed hostesses supervise all interviews as a precaution. Unlike past eras when fatherly reporters asked contestants about their favorite foods and colors, or—shucks—if she had a sweetheart, today's entrants are asked questions presidential candidates would find challenging. It's all part of the job they're applying for. "Media attention goes with the crown," notes television host Deborah Norville, a 1989 Miss America judge. "Because of my profession I am looking for a young woman who is going to be able to take the heat." Press coverage culminates after the crowning of the national titleholder when she is officially introduced to reporters at a midnight press conference.

In addition to the throngs of reporters covering the event, thousands of family members, friends, and supporters are in town to support their candidate. Easy to spot with their contestant photo buttons and matching "Miss State" T-shirts, the crowds of relatives and supporters roam the Boardwalk, try their luck in casinos, shop for souvenirs, browse at the Miss America Trade Show, and party until all hours. Never forgetting what they are there for, the state delegates bombard their contestants with daily reminders of their support: gift baskets, flowers, and inspirational cards. One Miss Virginia received a fifty-nine-foot telegram signed by 1,800 people and a Miss Texas received a sixty-five-foot message signed by 3,000 hometown fans. Once the on-stage

In spite of the hectic schedule of Pageant week, contestants find time for fun by relaxing on the beach, enjoying a stroll down the famous Boardwalk, and tasting a chef's special ice cream creation at the Trump Plaza. (left: Irv Kaar; middle and right: J. M. Frank/C P News)

competitions begin, families, friends, and the state delegates pour into the auditorium to boisterously cheer their candidates, then encourage them during postcompetition "state visitation" in the main ballroom. Such unwavering support is an invaluable confidence booster for contestants. "It was great," recalls Kim Boyce, Miss Florida 1983. "When I came to Atlantic City, Florida was so supportive of me that I thought, 'I really could *be* Miss America here!' It was great and I think everybody should go feeling that way."

Another highlight of the Pageant week experience is the Miss America Parade when as many as 200,000 people cram into town to get a close-up look at the candidates for the crown. Decked out in their glitziest gowns and perched atop convertibles, the contestants ride down the Boardwalk basking in one of the few opportunities when they can simply relax and have fun. No eagle-eyed judges, no life-changing score cards, no stomach-wrenching nerves . . . just a pleasant parade along the Boardwalk to the serenade of ocean breezes, a setting sun, band music, and cheering crowds. "The parade was one of the best experiences of the whole week," says former Miss America Terry Meeuwsen. "You just felt so loved by the time the parade was over. It was an unbelievable high!"

The Competitions Begin

Of course, the major focus of Pageant week is *competition*—the two days of private interviews and three nights of onstage preliminary competitions to determine which ten contestants graduate

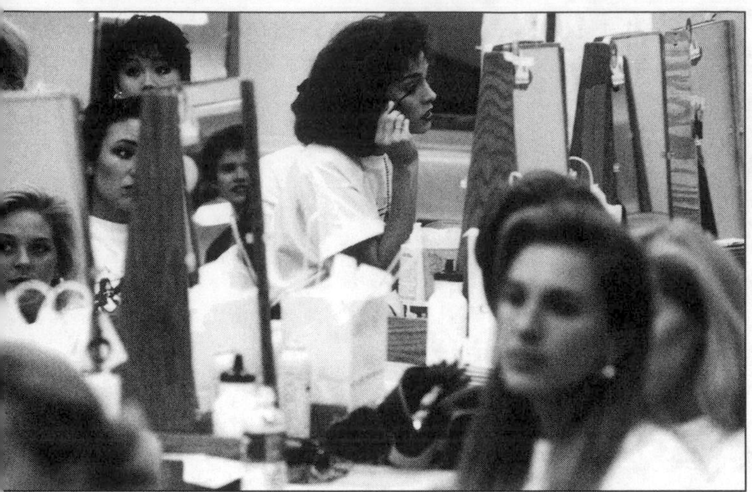

As the competitions begin, the dressing room becomes a blizzard of activity. "It's an organized madhouse," says Jane Kubernus, the recently retired dressing room chairman. (Danny Drake/The Press, Atlantic City)

to the televised finals. But before the judging begins, the judges are introduced to the fifty young women whose lives their scores will change. "In an effort to lessen the tension, the contestants are introduced to the preliminary panel during a rehearsal," explains Horn. "We want to let the contestants know who these people are before they undergo the judges' interviews so they see they are real, caring people," he says, "not ogres." It is an enjoyable, yet meditative, moment for the judges. The contestants, who are dressed down for rehearsals in jeans, T-shirts, and ponytails, look every inch the fresh-faced college kids they actually are, and the realization that their judging will begin—and end—dreams that week is sobering for the panel. "It's a very difficult job," says Marian McKnight Conway, a former Miss America and national judge. "It's very difficult because the judges are very conscientious and you realize that you are going to change somebody's life. I would go to bed at night thinking, 'Should I have given her a six instead of a five?' After the fact, I think it all works out in the end," she observes, "but I'm glad I don't have to do it every day!"

The first competition is the judges' interviews. For the fifty young women seeking the position of Miss America, the private interviews with the judges are a job interview for a prestigious $150,000-$200,000-a-year position. If there was ever a moment on which a young woman's future rested, it is this twelve-minute conversation with strangers. "I knew that if I wanted to be Miss America I had to score well in—if not win—the interview," explains Marjorie Vincent, Miss America 1991. In keeping with the pageant's increasing emphasis on community service, each contestant opens with a two-minute speech about herself and her "platform," a cause she is actively addressing in her community. The remaining ten minutes are open for general questions from the panel. Since judges are asked to probe deeply to find a young woman who exemplifies intelligence, leadership, and "courage of her convictions," interviews are friendly, yet challenging. Judges can ask anything they want, with questions ranging from her personal goals, to controversial issues, to politics. "To walk into that room and sit in front of those judges and express your ideas about the world, your community, your role as a woman, and the

United States' role in the world requires an awful lot of inward evaluation," says former judge Deborah Norville. "That, in and of itself, whether these girls ever make it down the runway, is a positive thing."

Although unseen by the public, the interview process is considered the most important competition, the private "stage" where judges develop crucial impressions of each candidate's qualifications to serve as the national titleholder. "Everyone has their own ideas about who should win," says Judi Ford Nash, a former Miss America and national judge, "but you don't know how the interviews went, or how well they can speak, articulate, and handle themselves. That's the most important thing," she explains, "because that's what Miss America is going to do all year. She's not necessarily going to perform her talent, and she's never going to appear in a swimsuit again. But how well she can handle herself and think on her feet is going to determine how good a Miss America she is. So those interviews are very important."

While the interviews provide a clear indication of who is likely to win, one can never be entirely certain. After all, there remain three evenings of on-stage preliminary competitions. As those competitions begin, the dressing room becomes the contestants' headquarters and the center of a virtual blizzard of activity. To be heard over the commotion, the head hostess shouts instructions over a microphone. "It's an organized madhouse," says Jane Kubernus, the longtime dressing room chairman, recently retired, "but it's definitely under control—because my women *keep* it under control. We can handle any problem that comes up."

At first, contestants are awed by the massive stage, but days of rehearsals diminish some of its mystique—and produce spectacular production numbers like this one in 1992. (J.M. Frank/C P News)

The first event, the swimsuit competition, is the Pageant's original competition and an enduring, although somewhat controversial, tradition. Naturally, it has undergone major changes since flappers paraded along the beachfront in bloomers. Today, the competition is titled "Physical Fitness in Swimsuit" and contestants are judged on "statement of physical fitness and health" and "energy and charisma" rather than mere beauty. The young women compete in conservative swimwear and are scored on their own merits, rather than being compared against others. As always, the swimsuit competition mirrors prevailing ideals about American beauty . . . only today, it's not flappers or cheesecake glamour girls,

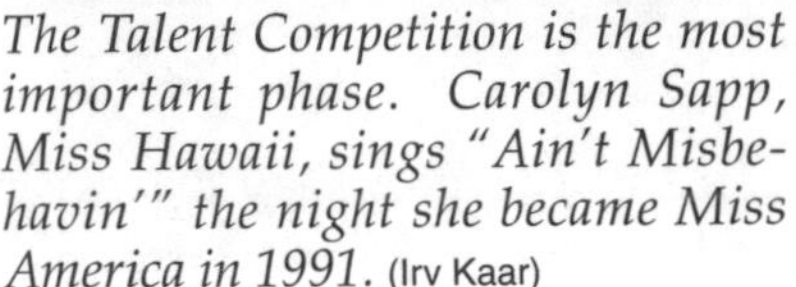

The Talent Competition is the most important phase. Carolyn Sapp, Miss Hawaii, sings "Ain't Misbehavin'" the night she became Miss America in 1991. (Irv Kaar)

The Evening Wear Competition celebrates the beauty of the individual. Tamara Hext, Miss Texas 1984, was a runner-up to Miss America. (Irv Kaar)

In the Physical Fitness in Swimsuit Competition, Stephanie Michels, Miss Georgia 1992, and others are judged on "statement of physical fitness and health." (J.M. Frank/C P News)

but modern women proudly demonstrating feminine athleticism.

The evening wear competition provides an opportunity for each contestant to express the personality and style that make her a unique individual. Traditionally, the event has two portions, an on-stage question and a modeling phase. When an on-stage interview is included, each contestant is asked a question related to the platform issue she would address if chosen as the winner: how she would promote AIDS awareness, how she would diminish violence in schools, and so on. The second phase, when contestants model their gowns, allows the panel to evaluate their confidence, beauty, poise, and carriage. Because of its elegance, the event is a favorite with contestants, who find it a breeze next to the pressures of the interview and talent segments.

Interestingly, the event provides a fascinating pictorial of American fashion trends from decade to decade. In past eras, the evening gown competition has showcased the expensive beaded "walking chandelier" gowns popularized in the 1980s by *Dynasty* and *Dallas*, the elegant tailored styles inspired by Jacqueline Kennedy in the sixties, the lavish ball gowns of the golden fifties, the frugal dresses of the World War II and Depression eras, and the drop-waisted dresses favored by flappers. Today, in keeping with the economic challenges of the decade and the Organization's increasing focus on education and community service, the emphasis is on classic clothing suitable for the career woman of the nineties. Contestants are encouraged to forgo expensive beaded gowns and choose more modestly priced formal wear reflecting understated elegance.

The talent competition has been a perennial favorite with audiences since it was first included in 1935. Today, it is a very important phase of competition, weighted at 40 percent of preliminary judging. The event has produced some of the pageant's most memorable moments. One creative contestant hauled homemade furniture on-stage, another won the talent award after driving a tractor around the stage, and a trampolinist so thrilled the judges that they named her Miss America. There have also been a few close calls. A baton twirler accidentally tossed a fire baton into the judges booth, while another scorched her eyelashes off. Then, after a stage light bulb exploded during a magician's act, her doves escaped and dropped "calling cards" on the audience. Another year, Miss Montana's horse slipped and nearly plunged into the orchestra! Presumably to spare judges and onlookers from accidentally being crushed or ignited, officials barred animal "assistants" and potentially dangerous talents.

The professionalism of talent performances has improved considerably over the years, as evidenced by recent national winners. Gretchen Carlson, Miss America 1989, had studied classical violin for seventeen years and performed with the Minnesota Orchestra; Marjorie Vincent (1991) was a trained classical pianist and semi-finalist in the Stravinsky International Piano Competition; and Leanza Cornett (1993) had starred as Ariel in *The Little Mermaid* at Disney's MGM theme park. However, the most inspiring talent ever presented was the classical ballet performed by Alabama's Heather Whitestone, who has been profoundly deaf since infancy. Although unable to hear her music, Heather performed flawlessly by memorizing and counting beats between the vibrations of high and low pitches. Moved, the audience acknowledged her remarkable achievement with an ovation and the judges awarded her the 1995 Miss America crown. With its fascinating history and impressive caliber of modern-day performances, the talent competition is the event that has distinguished the Miss American Pageant for decades.

At the conclusion of each of the three nights of preliminaries, the winners in talent and swimsuit are publicly announced, although evening wear and interview winners are not revealed to preserve an element of surprise about the probable semi-finalists. With over half of such award winners moving on to the top ten, the preliminaries offer a promising hint of what the Saturday night finals may hold. Then again, there's no sure bet in pageantry. Until the emcee officially bellows the announcement, it's anybody's crown.

It's Pageant Day . . . At Last!

As the weekend arrives, pageant auditors have completed their tabulations and know the identities of the semi-finalists who will compete in Saturday's finals. The second panel of judges for the television finals has arrived and been prepared for the responsibility of determining which young woman is most qualified to serve as Miss America. On Saturday morning, the panel watches tapes of the private interviews, held earlier in the week, to study the women they will judge that night.

Meanwhile, contestants are secluded in the Convention Center to protect them from exposure to unsettling press predictions. Throughout the day they run through television rehearsals for the announcement of the top ten, top five, the final questions, and the crowning. As rehearsals conclude, contestants return to the dressing room to have a light supper and prepare for the broadcast. The mood backstage is markedly different as the moment of truth approaches. "Back in the dressing room there's a lot of tension," says Christi Taunton, Miss Arkansas 1985. "Everyone is wondering, 'Well, is it *me*—or is it *one of them*?' because it can't be *all* of us. Before you go on-stage you want to prepare yourself for whatever the outcome will be," she explains, adding softly, "and that's not the easiest thing in the world to do."

While contestants quietly prepare in the sanctuary of the dressing room, the Convention Center is being transformed into a giant television arena, with 150 specialists engrossed in last-minute preparations for the broadcast. Television cameras must be positioned, equipment tested, lighting adjusted, props positioned, soundtracks organized, and hosts Regis Philbin and Kathie Lee Gifford put through final rehearsals. Every moment viewers will see on-screen must be perfectly timed: production numbers, the competitions, and the crowning of Miss America. Somehow, all the frantic preparations come together by the time fifty-five million people around the country tune in to hear the announcement, *"Live from Atlantic City . . . It's the Miss America Pageant!"*

After the opening production number and introduction of the state titleholders, the emcee is handed the auditor's list revealing the semi-finalists. The fifty women on-stage are instantly rigid with anticipation. This is the moment that determines where their years of hard work have led. "If you haven't been up there, no words can express how you feel," says Phyllis George, Miss America 1971. "But one thing is for sure—you can't wait to hear those names!" And yes, those surprised expressions when they *do* hear their names announced are authentic. "Believe it or not," says Kylene Barker, Miss America 1979, "when all fifty contestants walk out on-stage and you see them on the air, or you're in the audience watching them, no one knows who made the top ten. The girls are kept under wraps and we have no idea, so those surprised faces are real."

For the ten young women who have made the semi-finals, performing on live television is the most exciting experience of their lives. As millions of viewers look on, each young woman pours her heart and soul into convincing the judges she is the one who should wear the crown. "To be competing on that stage in Atlantic City with over 20,000 people watching you there, and 50 to 70 million people across the country watching you on television, is probably the most intense pressure any young woman could put herself through," says Debra Maffett, Miss America 1983.

Indeed, during the telecast the schedule is so brisk and intense that hostesses must carefully guide the semi-finalists through the evening's events. "On Saturday night it all comes to a head and it's a whole different situation in the dressing room," says Marilyn Feehan, chairman of the national hostess committee. "There is some pressure, especially when there are very fast changes between production numbers and competitions and we need to get them out there on time. We assign one hostess to each one of the top ten to take care of her individually." Meanwhile, she says, "the forty sit in the dressing room and have submarine sandwiches and cake and they watch the competition on the monitor and cheer. There is a nice camaraderie among the forty and they're very supportive."

The talent competition can be the most stressful—or sensational—aspect of the evening. "I think of all of the areas of competition, talent is where they really put themselves on the line," says Feehan. "They have butterflies and there is definitely pressure." For entrants who are not professionals, performing before a huge television audience can be unnerving. Marti Phillips, Miss Florida 1979, an amateur musician, remembers how, as she nervously waited to follow a superb vocal performance by the eventual winner, she couldn't shake the memory of a disastrous college audition when she had forgotten how to play her clarinet. "I thought, 'Oh my goodness, how in the world am I going to do this?'" Somehow, when she stepped into the spotlight she summoned the confidence to perform like a pro—and earned a runner-up trophy in the process. "I played the very best I had ever played," Marti says, chuckling. "It was a miracle!" For experienced performers who aspire to entertainment careers, the opportunity to show off their talent before millions of viewers is exhilarating. "I just kept thinking, 'This is *it!* Girls dream of doing this their whole lives, so let's just have a good time and enjoy it,'" says Kim Boyce, a former Miss Florida and recording artist. "It was a wonderful, wonderful experience for me!"

After the talent, swimsuit, and evening wear competitions conclude, the year-long quest for the crown nears its conclusion, as the top contestants narrow down to five and are announced and brought on-stage for interviews with the host. The pressure is enormous, with contestants aware that what they say in these next few minutes could change the judges' final decision. In 1992, Miss Florida, Leanza Cornett, so impressed the panel with her discussion of her AIDS awareness platform that she earned the national title. Two years later, the question segment presented viewers with an inspiring demonstration of victory over adversity. When Regis Philbin turned to interview Heather Whitestone, Miss Alabama, who has been profoundly deaf since infancy, millions of viewers held their breaths. Only once before had a hearing-impaired contestant faced the enormous challenge of understanding and communicating on live television. During the 1989 Miss America Pageant telecast, Jennifer Wall, Miss Washington, who is profoundly deaf, masterfully answered one *question* posed to her by co-host Phyllis George. In contrast, Whitestone would be required to carry on a *conversation.* The picture of serenity, Heather read Regis Philbin's lips, responded to his questions gracefully, and clinched the title.

Following that last crucial competition, the fifty state representatives are ushered back on-stage and the exhilarating evening in the national spotlight begins to wind down. The on-stage competitions have concluded, the judges have handed in their score sheets, the auditors are tabulating the scores—and ten young women are left standing on-stage awaiting the announcement that will change someone's destiny. While every semi-finalist hopes to win and each state delegation ardently supports its contestant, there is the underlying realization that the crown could go to any one of the gifted candidates. "It's very hard," admits Mary Jennings, a former Miss Arkansas and 1988 Miss America judge, "because I would say that any of the top ten could probably be Miss America—and do a beautiful job. That's how close it is."

Suddenly the auditor hands Regis the envelope containing the judges' decision. Walking back to center stage, the host smiles reassuringly at the finalists, then faces the audience and begins announcing the results. One by one, the runners-up step forward. As each accepts a bouquet of roses and is ushered out of view, she smiles almost numbly, realizing she has come so very, very close. . . . Soon there are only two women left at center stage. Their families and state directors are on the edge of their seats, nearly beside themselves with excitement. It is the exhilarating moment every young woman on-stage has yearned for. After a year filled with hard work, excitement, and unparalleled experiences, "the dream of a million girls" is about to become reality for one of these young women. But which one of them will it be? The two contestants struggle to maintain their composure, realizing that in mere seconds, one of them will be named Miss America and receive the most coveted title in the country.

The Miss America Experience

"I remember my father said, 'Do not think of yourself as the queen, because you are really the servant.' "
Sharon Ritchie, Miss America 1956

At last, after a year of competition, the original pool of thousands of contestants has been narrowed to two women—the crowd favorites all week. Both accomplished and deserving, they are outstanding representatives of American young womanhood. They are so similar . . . and yet so different. Miss Virginia, Cullen Johnson, is a vice-admiral's daughter. President Clinton has extended personal wishes for her success to her father, away commanding naval troops. Years of classical piano training and practice have earned her this moment in the spotlight. Winning a swimsuit award has only brought it closer. Miss Alabama, Heather Whitestone, is the daughter of a furniture store manager and a math teacher, now divorced. Her dual victories in the swimsuit and talent competitions make her the odds-on favorite. Her courage makes her the emotional favorite, for Miss Alabama is profoundly deaf. Each woman is deserving—but only one will wear the Miss America crown.

As Heather Whitestone, Miss America 1995, takes her victory walk, the audience realizes that the "handicapped" ballerina who hoped to share the message "Anything is Possible" has just proven it. (K.A. Frank/C P News)

As Regis Philbin opens the envelope that contains the announcement that will change their lives, he turns to face the two candidates. *"And our new Miss America is . . . Heather Whitestone, Miss Alabamaaaaa!"* The crowd roars its approval—but the winner doesn't hear. Miss Virginia points to her with both hands, and silently mouths the words, "It's you, it's you. You've *won*!" As the new Miss America glides down the runway victoriously, she cannot hear the beloved melody, "There She is, Miss America," and the thunderous

Moments after being crowned Miss America 1991, Marjorie Vincent, formerly Miss Illinois, is escorted backstage to meet the national press. (Terry Chenaille)

applause of the crowd is a mere whisper to her damaged ears—but the significance of the moment couldn't be heard more clearly. The beautiful ballerina who hopes to share the message "Anything Is Possible" has just proven it. For the first time in pageant history, a woman with a disability has stepped into the Miss America spotlight. And there isn't a dry eye in the audience.

There seldom is. For more than seven decades that magical moment, with all its beautiful variations, has whisked lucky young women from the obscurity of small town life into the sparkling spotlight of the Miss America runway. While millions of girls have dreamed of experiencing that life-changing moment, only sixty-eight women have achieved the distinction. The stunned reaction of the original Miss America, Margaret Gorman, foreshadowed the sentiments dozens of her successors would later share: "I am afraid I am going to wake up and find this has all been a dream." It's more like a dream come true.

When "the Dream of a Million Girls" Becomes Reality

While the thrill of achieving that dream remains unchanged, each Miss America's road to victory has been as unique as the woman so honored. For some bewildered winners, earning the famous crown has been as unexpected as snowflakes in August. When Mary Ann Mobley was named Miss America 1959, she was a southern belle with no inkling of the drama about to unfold in her life. She won her state title two weeks before the Miss America Pageant and arrived with a hastily thrown together wardrobe and without an orchestration for her talent. By her own account, there couldn't have been a more unlikely candidate to win. Nevertheless, judges realized that whatever Mobley lacked in sophistication she more than made up for in charm. When Bert Parks shouted her name as the winner, she was flabbergasted. "I had no idea!" Mary Ann exclaims, still oblivious to whatever qualities the judges found so appealing. "I was short with a round face that looked like a Moon Pie. When they called my name I was in shock! There weren't just a few tears running down my face—it was these great big sobs! I thought someone was going to come running down the runway and say, 'Little girl, we made a mistake. Come back!'"

As Mary Ann glided down the runway, Deborah Bryant, a little girl from a small Kansas town, was dreaming of taking the same heart-stirring walk. In one of the oddest twists of fate in pageant history, *Post* magazine chronicled her achievement of that dream. When editors chose Kansas to cover for an article on "the road to Miss America" and watched Debbie Bryant, Miss Kansas City, walk off with the state title, they had no idea they were watching the making of Miss America. Debbie was equally unsuspecting as she headed for the national contest. "I can't say I went there expecting to win," she admits. "I felt that I had less than one-fiftieth chance of winning." To her shock, destiny reversed her odds and she found herself gliding down the runway as Miss America 1966. The *Post* staff was delighted, but unnerved, by the crowning coup. "They had no idea that Kansas would ever win," Bryant explains. "They said they were a little bit afraid of accusations—you know, 'How did *you* know what state?'" She smiles. "And *I* certainly didn't know!"

After being named Miss America 1993, a wide-eyed Leanza Cornett gets a hug from Miss Iowa, Catherine Ann Lemkau, the First Runner-Up. (AP/Wide World Photos)

Yet, not every Miss America is astonished to hear that the coveted crown is hers. For some, destiny offered them a thrilling hint of what awaited them at the end of the runway. "I had a premonition that day that I would win," admits Jacquelyn Mayer, Miss America 1963. "I tried to get it out of my mind, although I did tell my aunt, who was with me, that I would be Miss America that night. And of course, she said, 'Oh you silly girl, why would you say that?' But it was a strong enough premonition that I was surprised—yet I wasn't. I think the good Lord kind of showed me what was in store for me."

Sharon Ritchie's father experienced a similar premonition of impending victory after his daughter won the Miss Colorado title. "About a month before I went to Atlantic City, my father had a heart attack and the doctor said he couldn't go," Sharon recalls, "but he said, 'Yes I am going to go because I know that my daughter is going to win.' He felt so strongly about that." Sure enough, weeks later, he watched from the Convention Hall audience as his daughter

It is difficult for a winner to be prepared for her first national press conference. "There's a zillion people, flash bulbs going off, TV cameras, and everybody's yelling," recalls Sharlene Wells, Miss America 1985. "I was overwhelmed!" (Irv Kaar)

was crowned Miss America 1956. "It was as though it was all supposed to happen that way," she says. "It was eerie. I remember so vividly coming back from the walk down the runway with Bert Parks singing "There She Is, Miss America." They had my parents up on-stage and my father had tears in his eyes. He was just short of shaking his head up and down like, 'Yes, I knew that this would happen.' It was emotionally charged for the obvious reasons—but there was, for us, that other dimension."

Sometimes the other dimension isn't supernatural, but slapstick. One of the most famous—and funniest—crownings took place in 1970, during the pageant's fiftieth anniversary when Miss Texas, Phyllis George, was crowned Miss America—and instantly made her mark on the crown. "They put the crown, the scepter, the banner, and the robe on me," Phyllis recalls. "That's a lot of stuff to balance! As I nodded to the judges, my crown wobbled and fell off onto the floor and stones splattered all over the place. Then the robe fell down around my elbows and the banner unpinned. It was quite a sight! I remember going back to my room and just crying, 'This is so embarrassing. My big moment, I've won Miss America, and my crown is in my *hand*!' About three nights later, I went on the Johnny Carson show and when I walked on he said, 'Phyllis, it's good to see you, but where's your crown? Afraid you'd drop it again?' So I started laughing and saying, 'Yeah, funny Johnny, I'm the klutzy one.' From that moment on, the story that I had been so embarrassed about turned out to be a funny human interest story, and I used that all year—'I'm the klutzy one who dropped the crown and had to pick it up and carry it.'"

Whether her rise to royalty has been comical, poignant, expected, or unexpected, every winner's reaction is the same. "To me," Debbie Bryant says in an emotional tone every Miss America can relate to, "that night was everything I ever would have hoped for or imagined."

A Year in the National Spotlight

That's also an apt description of the thrilling experience that lies ahead, for the stint in the national spotlight is more exciting, glamorous, life-changing, and exhausting than a young woman can ever conceive. "It's something no one can be totally prepared for," says Debra Maffett, Miss America 1983. From the moment she glides off the runway, the winner is whisked away by pageant officials and a police escort to face a gauntlet of functions that will have her up until the wee hours of the morning. "We give her a moment to regain her composure because they're pretty much in shock," says Marilyn Feehan, chairman of the national hostess committee and a past pageant president. "We needed smelling salts for Kaye Lani! Then we brief her on what the rest of the evening will hold. She has her first live press conference, an official photo shoot, and she attends state visitation where she says a few words, then we whisk her over to the Trump Plaza for the sponsors' reception. I stay close to her and brief her as we're moving along, giving it to her a little at a time so she can get *through* the evening."

For the new Miss America, the whirlwind evening is both unnerving and exhilarating. "My mind was just swirling!" says Kaye Lani Rae Rafko, Miss America 1988. "You can't possibly imagine the different emotions that you feel. Of course, you're elated that all the hard work has paid off and you're thinking, 'Oh, what an exciting year!' but you're also nervous and sad because you know that you'll be away from your family. And you're very frightened because all these people you've never met before are suddenly *tugging* at you and guarding you from the world. I was a nervous wreck."

The single most important post-coronation function is Miss America's midnight press conference. What she says to this standing-room-only crowd of national press will make headlines, establish her public identity, and set the tone for her year. There is simply no way to prepare for the crucial introduction. "I remember thinking, 'Oh, this'll take about five minutes', because nobody wanted to interview me before, why would they want to interview me now?" recalls Sharlene Wells, Miss America 1985, now an ESPN sportscaster. "Then they opened up the door and there's a zillion people, and flash bulbs going off, and TV cameras, and everybody yelling. I was overwhelmed. I remember thinking, 'Okay, the things that have always mattered to me will continue to matter to me now, those are the things that I'm going to draw from and hold on to—my family and my belief in Jesus Christ.' As we walked in I felt scared for just a moment and then a favorite scripture came to mind: *Don't fear what man can do, for I am with you*. It's amazing how much courage and confidence you can gain from a strong faith. Otherwise," she says, "I would have been blown away."

The days to come bring a mind-boggling barrage of national publicity, nonstop activity, and challenging new responsibilities that put most titleholders through a period of adjustment. "It was really overwhelming," says Marian McKnight, Miss

America 1957, "and it wasn't until a few days later that it sort of sunk in because after you're crowned, you're whisked away to New York and you're having press conferences and TV news and radio interviews and it's just one, two, three. And it really takes a couple of days to sort of settle down and realize that it's a big responsibility and there's a hard year ahead with a lot of work and a lot of traveling—and of course, a lot of wonderful experiences. But you really have to experience it to know how it feels because words can't describe it."

When the new Miss America arrives in New York, she is welcomed in grand style as a VIP guest of the famed Plaza Hotel. The first round of events includes meeting with the Organization's CEO Leonard C. Horn to discuss her schedule and platform, holding her New York press conference, selecting her designer wardrobe, and meeting about 20 million Americans via the national talk show circuit: from *The Today Show*, *Regis and Kathie Lee*, and *Larry King Live*, to *The Late Show with David Letterman*, or *The Tonight Show*. Then she settles into "The Schedule"—the 360 days of speeches, performances, autograph sessions, photo shoots, media interviews, and nonstop travel, hotel-hopping, packing, and unpacking. By the time her year concludes, the average titleholder has seen the country from coast to coast and clocked more than 200,000 miles of air travel alone. In fact, travel is such an integral part of that year that Rebecca King, Miss America 1974, told reporters, "It's a *job*. I go to work every day. I just go to work on an *airplane*!"

What few people realize is that the "job" comes without an entourage. Miss America does her own hair, nails, packing, and laundry. "That's another shock," Judi Ford, Miss America 1969, admits with a smile. "I didn't bother to investigate this stuff because I never thought that *I* was going to win. So when I won I asked, 'Who's going to be doing my hair this year?' and they said, 'You are.'" Judi gasped, "You mean, I don't have someone to do my hair and my makeup and pack for me?" No such luck. "I thought I was going to get waited on hand and foot and have an entourage of people traveling with me, so that was kind of eye-opening!" Somehow she managed to survive—and even laugh about—her "glamorous" year. "It was one of those things where we were up until two in the morning, we had to get up at five, and my chaperon would come in singing "There She Is, Miss America" as I'm standing in the bathroom with my hair in curlers, washing my underwear out in the sink," she recalls, chuckling. "But that's life on the road! It takes a while to get used to, and it's not quite the glamorous life, but it was a job for which I was well paid and I got to see almost all the United States."

In addition to extensive first class travel, Miss Americas experience an array of personal appearances beyond the wildest dreams of other college girls: privately visiting with the President, appearing on talk shows such as *Oprah!*, *The 700 Club*, and *The Home Show*, and being interviewed by Barbara Walters on *20/20*, performing during half-time of the Super Bowl or on a Bob Hope special, appearing on sitcoms like *Home Improvement* and *The Love Boat*, riding in the Macy's Day Parade, singing at the Cotton Bowl, co-hosting the Rose Bowl Parade or the NAACP Image Awards, addressing Congressional and Senatorial subcommittees and state legislatures, speaking at a private reception for the First Lady, attending a "rattlesnake roundup," being officially "knighted," appearing on magazine covers, doing a *Vogue* layout, being a VIP guest at the presidential inauguration, dining with senators, prime ministers, and ambassadors, hobnobbing with stars like Bill Cosby, Billy Joel, and Kevin Costner, playing racquetball with Olympic athletes, and being invited to perform with Lionel Hampton and Michael Bolton. "You *do* feel like Cinderella," admits Kylene Barker, Miss America 1979. "Sure you have your times when you're exhausted and you're like, 'What am I doing here?' But most of the time it is a Cinderella story. It really is."

Miss Americas experience an array of personal appearances beyond the wildest dreams of other college women. Gretchen Carlson (1989) dines with Betty Ford, recipient of the Miss America Woman of Achievement Award. (Irv Kaar)

Realizing that life has handed them a unique opportunity leaves winners feeling a deep sense of honor and awe. "I was very conscious of it being extremely humbling," says Debra Maffett, Miss America 1983. "I had a big responsibility to the other girls onstage, to the pageant, and to young women who look up to the Miss America Pageant." On a more personal level, she says, "It was so hard to *get* there that I loved even the hard parts. As demanding as that year became—with the red eyes and hurting feet, living out of suitcases, and long hours—I never disliked it, even once. I was paid more money than I could ever have imagined and I was so grateful to have won and to have such a wonderful opportunity that I felt a deep sense of obligation and duty. I approached the year as this wonderful gift I had been given, and I was determined to do the best job that I could humanly do."

But, even with all the appreciation for the honor that has been bestowed upon them, Miss Americas are real people who get headaches, catch colds, and get bone-numbingly *tired*. There are days when even Cinderella wants to ditch the glass slippers, put her feet up, and schlep around the house. "It's very demanding meeting people and traveling day after day after day," says Shirley Cothran, Miss America 1975. "There are some days when you just want to get up and stick your tongue out at everyone, but you can't do that when you're Miss America. You have to be nice, congenial, and enthusiastic. What makes that difficult is that you have to be nice, congenial, and enthusiastic 365 days in a row! That's the real catch—*in a row*. You can't have a day off," she says, adding with a sigh, "You get so *tired*, but my faith helped me to persevere and that made the year more bearable and gave it purpose."

The Power of the Crown

Purpose. It's the quality that puts the spring back in Miss America's step and adds sparkle to her crown. Keenly aware of their visibility as role models, titleholders use their year in the national spotlight to positively affect lives around them. "There's a power to the crown," says former Miss America Marilyn Van Derbur, now a spokesperson for survivors of incest and abuse. "I found that Miss America has a wonderful opportunity that year to reach out and touch people and make a difference. I'd get letters from people telling me that I impacted their lives and *how*. I found that you could make such a contribution. You begin to understand the opportunity you have with this position to positively affect a person's life."

That sense of purpose was epitomized by Kaye Lani Rae Rafko, a registered nurse specializing in oncology-hematology who had worked with the terminally ill and dreamed of opening hospices. Her untiring efforts visiting hospitals, raising money for medical charities, and promoting hospice care and the nursing profession earned her such public recognition that she was invited to speak around the world and before a congressional subcommittee. "People would not listen to my views on nursing as 'Kaye Lani Rae Rafko, RN,'" she asserts, "but the minute you say 'Miss America 1988,' there's some power to it. People *listen*! The recognition and visibility are phenomenal, and you have the opportunity to do so much."

That increasing appreciation of the opportunities the title provides to positively affect society has radically changed Miss America's role. Today, each titleholder has an official "platform" to allow her to dedicate her year to a meaningful cause. National winners address congressional subcommittees and state legislatures, visit hospitals, women's prisons, crisis shelters, schools—everywhere and anywhere they can help make a difference. Recent Miss Americas have spoken out on domestic violence, motivating youth to excellence, education, AIDS awareness and prevention, the homeless crisis, youth motivation, and "Anything Is Possible." As Leanza Cornett, Miss America 1993, whose effort to promote AIDS awareness helped raise a million dollars for AIDS causes, wrote at the conclusion of her year of service:

When I stood on the steps of the Capitol with congresswoman Nancy Pelosi this year, I thought that presenting the first AIDS legislation had to be the most powerful thing that I'd ever done—or ever will do. . . . But I am certain of one thing: This has been a very powerful year. I've changed from a person with mere dreams of being formidable to one who actually wields the credibility to create change. Thanks to the Miss America Organization, I have the ears of Congress, the financial support of American industry, and the heartfelt support of the American people, everywhere I go.

"I think that they are all fully aware of the role model status they play," says Leonard C. Horn, the Organization's CEO. "They are women who have something to *say*. That is why we have adopted the platform—to give them an opportunity to make a difference. Miss America is an intelligent, accomplished woman of the nineties, and an articulate spokesperson to relevant social issues."

Miss America Meets the Public

But the public expects Miss America to represent more than her platform. Many winners are shocked to discover that the public also expects them to exemplify *perfection*. "I found the most difficult part of that year was living up to the public's image of Miss America," says Terry Meeuwsen, Miss America 1973. "I think they had very unrealistic expectations. They expected me to look like I had just walked off a runway every time I arrived in town. You know—the same dress and a dozen roses that hadn't wilted. Everybody had a special event for which they were paying their top dollar and they expected the max from you. It was extremely exhausting." She remembers one day when her plane arrived late at night after she had appeared in two cities and been up since before dawn. "I was so tired," she says. "I felt like my makeup was on my ankles, my hair was just hanging, my face felt oily, and my feet felt like they were swollen over the sides of my high heels. I just wanted to go to bed." Instead, she faced a VIP welcome, complete with a band, television crews, and dignitaries. "I thought, 'Oh no! You must be kidding!' But that's the kind of pressure you're under. They're really paying you to be Cinderella everywhere you go."

Of course, dealing with such lofty public expectations can make Miss America's year an ego-*buster*. Usually the culprit is a member of the opposite sex. Rebecca King, Miss America 1974, once overheard a little boy complain, "Gee Mommy, she's not very pretty." During her reign in 1962, Maria Fletcher faced a tyke who refused to believe she was Miss America. Amused, she flashed her official photo. "Gee," the boy said, aghast, "when you first sat down, I thought you were just an ordinary old lady!" She was nineteen at the time. And Judi Ford, Miss America 1969, remembers having a teenage boy look her over and snort, "Ahhhh, my *sister's* better looking!"

Despite—or perhaps because of—such moments, Miss Americas quickly learn to take people's reactions in stride. "Maybe you *don't* measure up the way they want you to," says former Miss America Evelyn Ay Sempier, "but you have to be confident that for the majority, you are all right." She smiles. "It's an interesting phenomenon being Miss America."

It's especially interesting when things don't go quite according to plan. Miss Americas' public appearances present a host of opportunities for the unexpected, often with comical results. During an appearance in her home state of Texas, Shirley Cothran was performing a flute medley with a forty-piece orchestra. "Well, someone had forgotten to tighten the stand microphone, and as I was playing I noticed that it was slipping down," she recalls. "Of course, when one is playing the flute one's hands are busy, so I couldn't adjust it." The mike slipped farther and farther down, until by the end of her performance, Miss America was playing on her *knees*. "The audience was laughing uproariously," she says. "So after the piece was over, I turned around and this forty-piece orchestra was playing the accompaniment on their knees! It was quite a sight to behold."

Since so many appearances of the year are a sight to behold, Miss Americas quickly learn to employ a sense of humor. Lee Meriwether, Miss America 1955, recalls that Philco, a television company, booked her to appear at appliance stores. "Well, they didn't know what to *do* with me, so they dressed me up in my royal attire and put me in store windows next to a television set. I would stand there smiling and waving. Well, I got so bored that I thought, 'Gee, if I just hold still they'll think I'm a mannequin.' People would stare at me and I could hear them talking to each other trying to decide if I was real—then I'd move and *scare* them!" she admits, laughing.

The moment when a Miss America passes the title on to her successor brings a flood of emotions: gratitude for having been afforded an experience millions can only dream about and excitement for the woman who will follow in her footsteps. Suzette Charles takes her final walk as Miss America 1984. (Irv Kaar)

The worst are the unexpected—and painfully public—falls. Like the time Marilyn Van Derbur literally tumbled into the public spotlight at her Colorado Homecoming gala. The grand finale majestically presented their new Miss America at the top of a flight of stairs bathed in a spotlight. Unable to decide upon a suitable escort for state royalty, organizers had asked Marilyn to descend alone. One problem: there was no railing. "I was standing at the top of the stairs, carrying roses, and wearing my crown and this big red cape, and tall, spiky heels," she says. "The choir started singing "There She Is, Miss America," there's a spotlight on my face, and—I *fell down the stairs*!" Marilyn admits, guffawing at the recollection. "Everyone, everyone I ever knew was there, and I just humiliated myself!"

Seeing the humorous side of being famous helps titleholders to cope with the demands—and surprises—the year can dish out. "You've got to have a sense of humor to get through that year!" former Miss America Evelyn Ay Sempier admits with a laugh. "Because if you start taking yourself too seriously, you couldn't get up in the morning."

The VIP Treatment

Thankfully, there are many moments that more than compensate for the occasional humbling fiasco. Miss America's state "homecoming," when the small-town girl who made good returns, is unquestionably *the* highlight of any winner's year. Thrilled at having their hometown girl become Miss America, proud communities have honored their celebrity resident with billboards and named streets and buildings after her. Monroe, Michigan, has Kaye Lani Avenue; Galax, Virginia, a Kylene Barker museum exhibit; and Elk City, Oklahoma, the Susan Powell Performing Arts Center.

Like so many winners, Jane Jayroe was born and raised in a small town—Laverne, Oklahoma, population 1,200. The daughter of a teacher and basketball coach, she knew everybody in town. When she won, pandemonium reigned. "Everyone was so excited that they left their houses and drove downtown with their lights on and horns going," Jane says, adding with a smile, "People like to say it was the first and last traffic jam that Laverne ever had. Since they didn't have a landing strip for planes, they built one after I won. When I returned, they held a parade and renamed Main Street Jane Jayroe Boulevard and erected a huge sign over the stop light—and it's still there." For the small towns that produce a Miss America, the impact of her victory lingers long after her year of service. Says Jayroe, "It just had an incredibly long-lasting impact on the community and its identity."

Another highlight of Miss America's year is meeting the President of the United States. Sharlene Wells (1985) had the honor of being a VIP guest at Ronald Reagan's presidential inauguration where she visited with Muhammad Ali and the U.S. Olympic team. When Cheryl Prewitt (1980) chatted with President Jimmy Carter, known for his religious faith, he was curious about the childhood car accident that had crushed Cheryl's leg and how it had been divinely healed. "I understand that you had a miracle and your leg grew an inch and a half," he said. "How do people react when you say that to them?" Cheryl's answer, "I just tell 'em, 'Well, take a look yourself!'" elicited laughter from the President. "And I bet they *do!*" he quipped. When Debbie Bryant (1966) was ushered into the Oval Office for a private chat with Lyndon Johnson, the President shocked his visitor speechless by pulling up his shirt to show off his surgical scars. "I was so appalled," says Bryant, "because he had just had appendectomy surgery or something and he *showed* me his scar! I was going, 'What in the world!' I couldn't believe it. He was really outgoing," she says, laughing. "Not embarrassed by anything!"

Indeed, from hometown homecoming galas to the White House, one thing every Miss America can expect wherever she goes is VIP treatment. Sharlene Wells Hawkes cites an example of the special treatment that typifies the year. "I had one speaking engagement at Disneyland for a big convention," she says. "We flew in at 10:00 in the morning. I spoke at 10:30, and my flight was at 3:00." When the Disney staff offered to give her a tour of Disneyland, she reluctantly declined, citing her tight flight schedule. "Well then," they responded enthusiastically, "we'll just take you VIP to the head of the line on everything!" "So I put on my jeans and for two hours I ran through Disneyland doing everything I wanted to," she says. "And that was classic of the whole year. Miss America's year is like Disneyland: you're running, your feet hurt, everything hurts, and you've gotta grab a flight—but you're having a great time trying to squeeze in as much fun as you can wherever you are!"

The Tradition Continues

Then, as quickly as the whirlwind year in the national spotlight began, it concludes, and Miss America returns to the runway that changed her life so dramatically. The moment when she passes on the coveted crown to her successor brings a flood of emotions: gratitude for having been afforded a once-in-a-lifetime experience millions can only dream about, and sincere happiness for the young woman who will follow in her footsteps. "As I looked at Marilyn Van Derbur, whom I crowned, I knew that she was going to have the same experiences that I had, and I was thrilled for her," says Marian McKnight Conway. "It was really almost a relief to pass on the crown—although I sobbed. It's a very emotional experience because it's a major part of a young woman's life at that stage of the game. It's exciting, but after all the excitement of who was going to win, who my successor would be, I woke up the next morning very happy," she says, adding with a smile, "and excited to go back *home.*"

As the famous crown changes hands, the cycle begins anew, with another awed young woman embarking on the experience of a lifetime. As the latest winner in this special sorority of Miss Americas glides toward center stage to begin her year of service, she realizes that her victory has irrevocably altered the course of her life. "It just thrills my heart that out of all the young women across the nation who would love to step into Miss America's shoes, I was the one for that year," says Laurel Schaefer. "There's a feeling that what you have attained for yourself—although only short-lived for a year—is a lifetime venture." She pauses, wonder still evident in her voice. "It's a feeling of *destiny.*"

The Real Winners

"Even if you don't win, the opportunities are phenomenal!"
Kaye Lani Rae Rafko, Miss America 1988

A new Miss America has been crowned. Her life is instantly and dramatically changed. For the lucky young woman singled out to wear the most coveted crown in the country, life will never be quite the same. But as the winner takes her thrilling victory walk down the runway into the national spotlight, the forty-nine women who were almost Miss America look on wistfully. "It's a very mixed feeling," says Michele Passarelli, a former Miss Rhode Island, "a feeling that a part of you is there with her because you were a part of that year. She will forever be your Miss America and she sort of becomes the embodiment of your dreams. But," she adds softly, "you also realize that it is only her and not you. You feel a part of it—yet so far away at the same time."

The real winners are all the aspiring contestants nationwide, in both local and state contests. Nancy Humphries is crowned Miss South Carolina 1987. (Irv Kaar)

Other contestants have had more comical reactions to that moment of truth. Delta Burke, who competed as Miss Florida in the 1974 Miss America Pageant, once quipped that as she watched her fellow contestant, Texas's Shirley Cothran, being crowned Miss America 1975, the thought crossed her mind, "I'll bet if I run down there and tear that crown off her head, I'll get on the Johnny Carson Show!"

Despite the inevitable disappointment that their paths have not led to the throne, national contestants appreciate that the exhilarating weeks in Atlantic City have provided them with cherished memories millions of other girls have only dreamed of experiencing. As

Carrie Folks, Miss Tennessee 1988, put it, "Now that I've been here, I realize that regardless of how I did, I have been in the Miss America Pageant and nothing is going to take that away. I've been in the *Miss America Pageant!* Not many people have been," she says, "and it's all been worth it!"

Although every state titleholder hopes to become Miss America, each realizes that, while only one can wear the national crown, every young woman who pursued that respected symbol is a winner. After the national pageant concludes, each state representative continues what the Pageant calls her "year of service," serving as a role model for youth in her state and as a spokesperson for her platform. The year is not only emotionally fulfilling, it is financially rewarding—particularly in the South where Miss America is a popular tradition. Miss South Carolina, for instance, makes over 500 appearances during her year and can earn $85,000 in addition to the $10,000–$25,000 she has accumulated in local, state, and national scholarships. "Once they get over that initial disappointment in Atlantic City, they realize that they have a wonderful year ahead of them in their states," says Marilyn Feehan, a past president of the Miss America Pageant. "In many states, they have a real full-time job ahead of them with bookings and representing the program. Although some states aren't as active as others, there's something there for all of them."

Winners from Coast to Coast

Yet a contestant needn't win a state title to gain significantly from participating. The pageant, from the local to national levels, is intended to provide contestants with the financial help and opportunities to pursue their educational and professional goals. "The crown is a by-product of competition," states Robert Arnhym, president/CEO of the Miss California program. "The real rewards of competition are the tremendous opportunities for personal development."

Those opportunities, which are rarely available to females elsewhere, can transform their lives. Each year 50,000 to 80,000 young women from coast to coast enter the Miss America program, competing in roughly 2,000 local preliminary pageants sponsored by their communities. There they mingle with community leaders, have an opportunity to win thousands of dollars in scholarships, gain publicity and career exposure, and benefit from a nurturing environment in which to develop their talents and public speaking/interviewing skills. Whether or not they ever win a state title or compete in the national pageant, they benefit significantly from the opportunities available through the program. "Most of our contestants are ambitious, goal-oriented young women who view the Miss America system as a vehicle for attaining their goals," observes Karen Aarons, the Organization's executive vice president. "Right now there are still limited opportunities for women and we try to provide a pathway for those women who choose to use the Miss America Program as their stepping-stone. We stress that the benefits are derived, not just by that one girl at the end of the year who wins Miss America, but by

Former Miss Americas gathered for the Pageant's 70th anniversary top, from left: *Phyllis George (1971), Laurel Schaefer (1972), Tawny Godin (1976), Dorothy Benham (1977), Susan Perkins (1978), Cheryl Prewitt (1980), Susan Powell (1981), Sharlene Wells (1985), Kellye Cash (1987),* bottom, from left: *Marilyn Meseke (1938), Yolande Betbeze (1951), Evelyn Ay (1954), and Maria Fletcher (1962).* (Irv Kaar)

everyone who participates. It is an incredible base for thousands of women."

Because the pageant provides such a positive environment and effective base for improving women's lives, it attracts young people who are achievement oriented. "The Miss America program is relevant because it stresses positive qualities," says the Organization's CEO, Leonard C. Horn. "It gives young people goals to strive for. It stresses courage, ambition, and education. The young woman who comes before us in this competition is articulate, poised, intelligent, courageous enough to put herself on the line for a specific goal, and ambitious enough to want to do something with her life that many people would like to do, but don't have the courage to do."

Largest Source of Women's Scholarships

In today's society, reaching one's potential as a woman requires a quality education. Therefore, since 1945, when the Miss America Pageant awarded its first scholarship, the very cornerstone of the program has been its efforts to help young women achieve their dreams through financial assistance for higher education. Today, Miss America is the world's largest private scholarship program for women, making available more than $24 million in scholarship opportunities annually. "The Miss America Organization offers scholarships to continue your education and career opportunities," says Karen Aarons. "One of our main goals is to encourage our participants to continue

In 1946, the Miss America Pageant Scholarship Foundation had expanded to $25,000, which was shared by fifteen finalists and Miss America. State and local pageants soon developed scholarship programs and contributed more than $50,000 in awards. Today, Miss America makes more than $24 million in scholarship opportunities available annually. (Central Studios)

their educations, at the very least to obtain their undergraduate degree. And we are very proud that our contestants are continuing their educations."

Since the vast majority of entrants participate on the local and state levels, that is where the bulk of scholarship opportunities are found. For instance, according to Marie Finnell, president of the Miss Florida Pageant, their state pageant offers more than $600,000 in awards. "Our cash scholarships totaled $49,450, and our tuition scholarships were $503,100 from schools such as Stetson, Rollins, Jacksonville University, and the University of Tampa. At our local level, we awarded $94,558 in cash scholarships and had $40,806 in tuition scholarships." The Miss Tennessee Pageant awards $114,000 in cash scholarships, the Miss California Pageant provides nearly $100,000 in cash scholarships alone, and the Miss South Carolina program offers over $55,000 in cash scholarships and over $2 million in tuition grants to specific colleges and universities. Volunteers work year-round to build those cash scholarship funds and encourage local colleges and universities to provide tuition grants for contestants. "Education is extremely important to us," affirms Robert Arnhym. "That's what we all work so hard for, to raise those scholarship dollars. We are here to open doors for her and to make those opportunities available."

That financial assistance can make a major impact on young women's lives. "My scholarships covered everything," says Michele Passarelli, who now runs a local pageant. "It paid for my entire college education, all my books, every little pencil—all four years! It made a major difference in my life—major! I'd say that the Miss America Pageant changed my life more than anything I've done since. It changed my life for the better and I am a strong supporter of the program."

Miss America Pageant Scholarships (1994)

Miss America	$35,000
First Runner-Up	20,000
Second Runner-Up	14,000
Third Runner-Up	11,000
Fourth Runner-Up	8,000
Semi-finalists (5)	6,000
40 national contestants	2,500
Talent winners (3)	1,500
Swimsuit winners (3)	500
Non-finalist talent winners (8)	1,000
Non-finalist interview winner	1,000
Fruit of the Loom Quality of Life Awards	10,000, 2,000, 1,000
Rembrandt Mentorship Award	5,000
Waterford Crystal Business Scholarship	2,500
Bernie Wayne Memorial Performing Arts Award	2,500
Albert Marks Memorial Fund Award	2,500
Allman Medical Scholarships	Vary

Miss Florida Scholarships (1994)

Miss Florida	$16,000
First Runner-Up	7,000
Second Runner-Up	4,000
Third Runner-Up	3,000
Fourth Runner-Up	2,000
Semi-finalists (5)	1,000
Swimsuit winners (3)	600
Talent winners (3)	600
Non-finalist talent award	500
Community service award	3,500

Career Opportunities

In addition to the lucrative scholarships available, the pageant is also an effective career stepping-stone, providing invaluable public exposure and professional contacts. Whether their aspirations have been in the entertainment industry or the demanding fields of law, medicine, politics, or business, past contestants have gone on to succeed in an impressive array of professions. "Over the years," says Horn, "hundreds of young women who have competed in this program have used their scholarship money for higher education and then developed successful professional careers—the kinds of things you don't always hear about."

Indeed, the list of Miss America "graduates" includes: Academy and Emmy award winners, state judges, medical doctors, attorneys, executives, professors, principals, military officers, Wall Street stock brokers, drug abuse counselors, government officials, a White House staff member, psychiatrist, mayor, dentist, historical romance novelist, investigative journalist, tanker navigator, flight simulator technician, aerospace engineer, and state senator. "These women are not fluff," says Laurel Schaefer, a past Miss America and founder and CEO of the Women's Leadership Foundation. "They are women of substance who have proven themselves."

Furthermore, the exposure offered through the pageant can be invaluable for those entering the entertainment field. On several occasions, contestants who competed in televised state or national pageants have been spotted by talent agents, modeling agency heads, and producers and offered entertainment contracts. In fact, several familiar faces from television and films took their first steps toward fame and fortune on local runways: Sharon Stone (Miss Crawford County), Loni Anderson (Miss Roseville), Shirley Jones (Miss Pittsburgh), Barbara Eden (Miss San Francisco), and Betty Buckley (Miss Fort Worth).

Indeed, the impressive track record of former local and state titleholders demonstrates the pageant's value as a career launch pad. As Mary Ann Mobley puts it, "The association with the Miss America Pageant never stops working to help a young lady's career."

Who's Who of Former Contestants

Delta Burke, Miss Florida 1974—Emmy-nominated actress, *Designing Women*

Debra Cleveland, Miss South Dakota 1984—Aerospace engineer

Mary Hart, Miss South Dakota 1970—*Entertainment Tonight*

Dr. Barbara Jennings, O.D., Miss Maryland 1976—Vascular clinic director

Dr. Carla Huston Bell, Miss Montana 1955—Doctorate from Columbia University

Nancy Stafford, Miss Florida 1976—Actress, *St. Elsewhere, The Doctors, Matlock*

Mabel Bendikson Pina, Miss Massachusetts 1965—Harvard M.P.A.

Susan Anton, Miss California 1969—Recording artist and actress, *Golden Girl*

Angela Baldi Bartel, Miss Wisconsin 1964—Wisconsin Supreme Court judge

Dr. Charmaine Kowalski, Miss Pennsylvania 1978—Psychiatrist, Penn State/Harvard degrees

Cynthia Sikes, Miss Kansas 1972—Actress, *St. Elsewhere, L.A. Law, Arthur 2: On the Rocks*

Dr. Katherine Karlsrud, Miss New York 1970—Medical doctor

Cloris Leachman, Miss Chicago 1946—Academy and Emmy award winner, *The Last Picture Show*

Dr. Sandra Adamson Fryhofer, Miss Georgia 1976—Medical doctor, first woman diplomat on American Board of Medicine

Rebecca Graham, Miss Indiana 1972—Past director of Illinois and Florida lotteries

A Platform for Community Service

As effective as it is in promoting education and career development for women, the Miss America program also promotes inner development—character, if you will—through its emphasis on community service. The pageant's "platform" program requires entrants to submit a written essay on a meaningful cause they are volunteering with in their community and then use their year as a titleholder to promote that cause. While national titleholders have addressed education, domestic violence, AIDS, and homelessness, local and state participants also volunteer their efforts on behalf of important causes:

- Miss Wisconsin 1992, Stephanie Klett, helped raise $120,000 for AIDS, and shared her message "Attitude on AIDS" with 60,000 students and on *Good Morning America*.
- Dana Stephenson, Miss North Carolina 1994, launched CRUSADE to educate youth about the dangers of drugs and alcohol. Today, her program has nationwide participation.
- After surviving cancer, Suzanne Lawrence, Miss Texas 1990, founded a support program, "Smiles Against Cancer," gave countless media interviews, and launched a support network in London. Fruit of the Loom awarded her its $10,000 National Quality of Life Award.
- After a personal brush with breast cancer, DuSharme Carter, Miss Oklahoma 1992, promoted "Breast Cancer Funding" nationwide and addressed the House and Senate.
- In 1994, the Miss Florida Pageant's Community Service Program involved 1,181 projects by contestants, donated 23,798 volunteer hours, and raised $1,249,300 for worthy causes.

By encouraging young people to explore the critical issues of their day and involve themselves in meaningful causes—and their solutions—the pageant helps them to learn more about themselves and their communities, and to help bring positive change to our world. In essence, the platform program is a character-builder, teaching young people not only to benefit from programs like Miss America—but to give back that others may also benefit.

When Jane Jayroe was named Miss America 1967, her home town of Laverne, Oklahoma, renamed Main Street Jane Jayroe Boulevard. For a small town that produces a Miss America, it has "an incredibly long-lasting impact on the community and its identity," said Jane. (The Miss America Organization)

The "Real" Miss Americas

Although casual viewers may not realize it, the Miss America Pageant is about far more than one lucky young woman's teary-eyed walk down the runway. "Miss America" is a life-changing experience. By providing millions of dollars in scholarships and encouraging women's academic achievements, personal and career development, and civic volunteerism, the time-honored program bestows upon its participants invaluable financial, professional, and personal rewards that last a lifetime.

The famous coronation song, "There She Is, Miss America," puts it best: "The dream of a million girls who are more than pretty may come true in Atlantic City." But those dreams also come true in places like Elk City, Oklahoma, Miami, Florida, and Powdersville, South Carolina, where today's contestants are using local and state Miss America runways to navigate their way into executive offices, judges' chambers, operating rooms, and Congress. "It's so important for these women to understand what the competition is about," advises Mary Donnelly Haskell, a former Miss Mississippi. "If a young woman approaches the competition with a healthy attitude, her participation will offer many invaluable benefits—whether or not she wins the crown. The Miss America Pageant wants young women to build themselves up," she stresses. "While only one woman can win the crown, anyone who participates with a spirit of positive competition and a desire to better herself will always be a winner."

Providing opportunities for young women to empower themselves through personal, educational, and professional achievement is the essence of today's Miss America program. Whether or not a contestant ever achieves her goal of becoming Miss America, the self-discipline, commitment, and competence she demonstrates while pursuing that goal distinguish her as a leader, role model, and real "winner in life."

Miss Americas In Review

For seventy-five years Miss Americas have comprised an exclusive sorority of American achievers. Their exemplary personal qualities—beauty, personality, intelligence, talent, achievement, faith, and character—have made them role models for millions.

Each winner has brought to the crown qualitites for which she alone will be remembered—from the original Miss America, Margaret Gorman, whose cherubic innocence established a standard of wholesomeness for future winners, to the indomitable individualism Yolande Betbeze symbolized as the mid-century queen who refused to model swimsuits, to the inspiring courage epitomized by Heather Whitestone, the first woman with a physical disability to earn the national title. Individually and collectively, they have endowed the historic crown with personal excellence.

An asterisk (*) after a Miss America's name indicates that she is deceased.

1921 MARGARET GORMAN
Washington, D.C.

The original Miss America, Margaret was selected from 1,500 local photo entries and represented Washington, D.C. at the first national beauty tournament. She married Victor Cahill, a real estate investor, and is now widowed.

*1922–1923 MARY CATHERINE CAMPBELL**
Columbus, Ohio

The only woman to win the crown twice, Campbell turned down movie contracts to care for her invalid mother. She later married Frederick Townley, a DuPont executive.

*1924 RUTH MALCOMSON**
Philadelphia, Pennsylvania

Ruth eventually married Major Carl Schaubel, a printing company president, and had one son. Her niece and grand-niece competed as Miss Pennsylvania 1956 and Miss Delaware 1981.

*1925 FAY LANPHIER**
California

The first Miss America from the west coast, Fay later appeared in a Laurel and Hardy movie and in *The American Venus*. She married Winfield Daniels, an engineer/store owner, and reared two daughters.

*1926 NORMA SMALLWOOD**
Tulsa, Oklahoma

Norma endured a scandalous divorce from an oilman and then married a wealthy petroleum executive, George Bruce. She had two children, one of whom was named Des Cygnes l'Amour (of the swans of love).

*1927 LOIS DELANDER**
Illinois

Lois won the crown on her parents' anniversary and became the last winner before the Pageant was discontinued. She married Ralph Lang, a stockbroker, and reared three daughters.

1933 MARIAN BERGERON
Connecticut

Chosen Miss America when the Pageant was briefly revived, Marian reigned for two years, then married an executive and reared three children. Twice widowed, she is married to Fred Setzer and enjoys her twelve grandchildren and volunteering.

*1935 HENRIETTA LEAVER**
Pittsburgh, Pennsylvania

A sales clerk, Leaver was dubbed "the million-dollar baby from the five-and-ten-cent store." She eloped during her reign after a flap about a "nude" sculpture she had actually posed for in a bathing suit. She divorced twice, remarried, and reared two daughters.

1936 ROSE COYLE
Philadelphia, Pennsylvania

Rose appeared with Abbott and Costello and married a top Warner Brothers executive with whom she had a daughter. Widowed, she married Robert Dingler, an executive.

1937 BETTE COOPER
Bertrand Island, New Jersey

Bette, the Miss America who disappeared with her handsome chaperon because she didn't want to leave school to tour the country, later married William Moore, an engineer, and reared two children.

1938 MARILYN MESEKE
Ohio

The first Miss America to win when talent was mandatory, Marilyn was a gifted dancer who opened a dance school. Now twice widowed, Marilyn was first married to pilot Major Stanley Hume, with whom she had a son, and then to pilot Benjamin Rogers.

1939 PATRICIA DONNELLY
Michigan

Patricia performed on Broadway and in the movie *Cover Girl* before marrying publicist Robin Harris and rearing two children. She won the crown singing and plucking a bass fiddle.

1940 FRANCES BURKE
Philadelphia, Pennsylvania

A renowned East Coast fashion model, Frances later married Lawrence Kenney, a funeral supply firm owner, with whom she had four children.

*1941 ROSEMARY LAPLANCHE**
California

After finishing as First Runner-Up in 1940, Rosemary became Miss America the next year. She signed with RKO Pictures, appeared in eighty-four films, married TV producer Harry Koplan, reared two children, and became a renowned oil painter.

1942 JO-CARROLL DENNISON
Texas

Jo-Carroll signed with 20th Century Fox, then married and divorced comedian Phil Silvers. She later married a CBS executive and has two sons. Today she lives in California where she is an advocate of hospice care.

1943 JEAN BARTEL
California

A UCLA student, Jean inspired Lenora Slaughter to develop the Pageant's scholarship program. She starred on Broadway, had a TV show, produced documentaries, and reportedly did intelligence work in Lebanon. Jean is married to William Hogue.

1944 VENUS RAMEY
Washington, D.C.

Noted for her unusual name and red hair, Venus won the crown as a secretary in the nation's capital, although she was actually from Kentucky. She later ran for state office in Kentucky, married and divorced an automobile dealer, and reared two sons.

1945 BESS MYERSON
New York City

One of the most famous Miss Americas, Bess was the first scholarship recipient and later served as co-host for Miss America telecasts. She was appointed New York City's commissioner of consumer affairs and ran unsuccessfully for the U.S. Senate.

1946 MARILYN BUFERD
California

After her reign, Marilyn studied at Berlitz in Rome, signed with MGM Studios, appeared in fifteen Italian films, and had a romance with Roberto Rossellini before marrying businessman Milton Stevens. Now widowed, she has one son.

1947 BARBARA JO WALKER
Memphis, Tennessee

The only winner to officially and publicly marry during her reign, Barbara Jo wed Dr. John Hummel during a widely publicized ceremony attended by her judges. She hosted a TV show, reared three children, and is active in church work.

1948 BEBE SHOPP
Minnesota

The first winner to travel overseas, BeBe graduated from Manhattan School of Music, married Bayard Waring, a business executive, and reared four daughters. She is a licensed lay minister and conducts motivational shows for children.

*1949 JACQUE MERCER**
Arizona

Jacque eloped during her reign, quickly divorced, and asked officials to bar future winners from marrying during their year. She later married Richard Curran, an all-American football player and advertising executive, and had two children.

1951 YOLANDE BETBEZE
Alabama

Yolande's refusal to wear swimsuits after her crowning prompted sponsor Catalina to start the Miss Universe Pageant. A superb classical singer, she married movie tycoon Matthew Fox and bore a daughter. Now widowed, she is a prominent socialite.

1952 COLLEEN KAY HUTCHINS
Utah

One of the tallest winners at 5'10", Colleen won her title with a portrayal of Queen Elizabeth I. She married Dr. Ernest Vandeweghe, a prominent doctor and former New York Knick, with whom she has four children, one of whom played in the NBA.

1953 NEVA JANE LANGLEY
Georgia

Neva, a Floridian, won Miss America while attending Georgia's Wesleyan Conservatory. She married investor William Fickling, reared four children, was awarded an honorary doctorate and the "Lady Bird Johnson Award," and remains a superb classical pianist.

1954 EVELYN AY
Pennsylvania

The last pre-television queen and a favorite with the public, Evelyn won the crown after reciting a poem she had never spoken aloud. She later married Navy Lieutenant Carl Sempier, an IBM executive, now retired, and has two grown daughters.

1955 LEE MERIWETHER
California

The first winner crowned on live television, Lee studied with Lee Strasberg, achieved fame as an actress in TV programs including *Barnaby Jones* and *The Munsters Today*, and was nominated for an Emmy. Married to Marshall Borden, Lee has two daughters.

1956 SHARON KAY RITCHIE
Colorado

The first winner to whom Bert Parks sang "There She Is, Miss America," Sharon later married famed performer Don Cherry and had two sons. An actress and corporate spokesperson, Sharon is now happily remarried to Terry Mullin.

1957 MARIAN MCKNIGHT
South Carolina

Marian won the crown with a charming impression of Marilyn Monroe. Later a "Clairol Girl," she married actor Gary Conway, and has a son and daughter. A devoted marathon runner, she carried the Olympic torch in 1984.

1958 MARILYN VAN DERBUR
Colorado

Marilyn became a public speaker and film producer, and married attorney Larry Atler, with whom she has one daughter. Her honors include "Outstanding Woman Speaker of America." Today, Marilyn is a respected advocate for survivors of incest and abuse.

1959 MARY ANN MOBLEY
Mississippi

Mary Ann, famous for her mock striptease talent, later starred in movies and in *Different Strokes* and *Falcon Crest*. She married Gary Collins, who became the Pageant's emcee. Diagnosed with Crohn's Disease, she is an inspiring role model for others.

1960 LYNDA LEE MEAD
Mississippi

The second of Mississippi's famous back-to-back Miss Americas, Lynda later married Dr. John Shea, a surgeon, with whom she has grown children. She resides in Memphis where she is prominently involved in community affairs.

1961 NANCY FLEMING
Michigan

The last high school student to win the crown, Nancy earned her college degree and hosted TV's *A Whole New You*, *A.M. San Francisco*, *Heartbeat of the City*, and *Sewing Today*. Now married to Jim Lange, she has two children from a previous marriage.

1962 MARIA BEALE FLETCHER
North Carolina

A Radio City Music Hall Rockette, Maria danced her way to the crown. She later graduated from Vanderbilt, married, and reared two children. Today, Maria enjoys being a writer and performer, and is committed to animal rights and the environment.

1963 JACQUELYN MAYER
Ohio

After a massive stroke at age 28 left her partially paralyzed and unable to speak, Jackie battled her way to health and is a spokesperson for the Stroke Association, which awarded her its "Hope and Courage Award." She and husband John have two children.

1964 DONNA AXUM
Arkansas

Donna, who holds a master's degree and is a Distinguished Alumnus of the University of Arkansas, is a noted speaker and TV spokesperson. The mother of a son and daughter, she is married to Bryan Whitworth, a petroleum executive.

1965 VONDA KAY VAN DYKE
Arizona

Vonda is the only ventriloquist to earn the crown and the only winner to be voted Miss Congeniality by her fellow contestants. A well-known Christian speaker and author, she is married to David Scoates, a minister, and has one daughter.

1966 DEBORAH BRYANT
Kansas

A Phi Beta Kappa graduate and past TV commentator for Miss America broadcasts, Debbie married Phoenix auto dealer Brent Berge and has five children. *Post* magazine chronicled her rise from Miss Kansas City to Miss America.

1967 JANE JAYROE
Oklahoma

Noted for conducting the pageant orchestra for her talent, Jane earned a master's degree, became a TV news anchor, and was named "Outstanding News Personality." She is married to Gerald Gamble, has one son, and is pursuing her PhD.

1968 DEBRA DENE BARNES
Kansas

Debra and her husband, Mitchell Miles, are the pastors of Full Faith Church of Carthage, Missouri. She is active in Christian ministries, Teen Challenge, MADD, and the Multiple Sclerosis Society. Debra has two grown daughters.

1969 JUDITH FORD
Illinois

The only trampolinist to win the crown, Judi is also the blonde who ended a decade of brunette winners. Now a P.E. teacher and corporate spokesperson, Judy is married to attorney James Nash, and the mother of two sons by a previous marriage.

1970 PAMELA ELDRED
Michigan

Pamela, who won the crown with a ballet to *Romeo and Juliet*, later lived in Korea with her former husband, a military surgeon. She has one daughter, owns a cosmetics business in Michigan, and is a fashion and beauty columnist.

1971 PHYLLIS GEORGE
Texas

Phyllis became the first successful female sportscaster, co-hosted scores of TV programs, and married John Y. Brown, governor of Kentucky. They have two children. Phyllis is chairman of "Chicken By George," and author of several books.

1972 LAUREL SCHAEFER
Ohio

An actress-singer, Laurel has appeared on *L.A. Law*, *Stranger at Jefferson High*, *Get Christy Love*, *Falcon Crest*, and *Quantum Leap*, and in numerous musicals. A motivational speaker, Laurel is founder of the Women's Leadership Foundation.

1973 TERRY MEEUWSEN
Wisconsin

Remembered for her moving rendition of "He Touched Me," Terry later recorded a gospel album, *Meet Terry*, co-wrote a book, *Terry*, and hosted television shows. Now co-host of *The 700 Club*, she and husband Andy Friedrich have four children.

1974 REBECCA KING
Colorado

One of the most accomplished of the winners, Becky used her scholarship to earn her law degree and is a partner in a Denver law firm. She married George Dreman, a banker, and is the mother of two daughters.

1975 SHIRLEY COTHRAN
Texas

Shirley earned her PhD. in educational counseling. She returned home to Denton and married her longtime beau, Richard Barret, with whom she has four children. Today, she is a respected educator and Christian writer and speaker.

1976 TAWNY GODIN
New York

The bicentennial queen, Tawny became a television anchor-producer for KABC *Eyewitness News, A.M. L.A.,* and *The Love Report,* and was nominated for an Emmy. She is married to Tom Corsini and has two sons.

1977 DOROTHY BENHAM
Minnesota

Noted for her glorious voice, Dorothy has performed on television and Broadway, including Jerome Robbins' *Broadway.* Now married to Michael McGowan, a Minnesota businessman, she is the mother of six children.

1978 SUSAN PERKINS
Ohio

Remembered as an especially articulate winner, Susan became a television host, spokesperson for DuPont and Gillette, and emcee for more than seventy-five pageants. She married Alan Botsford, an executive, and has two children.

1979 KYLENE BARKER
Virginia

Kylene opened a ladies' clothing boutique in Palm Beach. She is the author of *Southern Beauty* and a fitness album, *Stamina with Style,* and has been a fashion commentator for *The Today Show.* Today she runs a Polo Ralph Lauren business in Toronto, Canada.

1980 CHERYL PREWITT
Mississippi

Famous for the divine healing of her crushed leg, Cheryl has recorded several gospel albums, written five books, and owns C.P. Annie Productions, a pageant swimwear firm. She is now married to Harry Salem and has three children.

1981 SUSAN POWELL
Oklahoma

Susan, a classical singer remembered for her hilarious rendition of "The Telephone," has performed in major productions with the New York City Opera and others. Now host of the Discovery Channel's *Home Matters*, she is married to David Parsons.

1982 ELIZABETH WARD
Arkansas

Elizabeth, who now goes by the stage name Elizabeth Ward Gracen, has been a guest performer for the Miss America Pageant and appeared in *Matlock, The Flash, Pass the Ammo,* and *Marked for Death.* She is married to actor-writer Brenden Hughes.

1983 DEBRA MAFFETT
California

Debra enjoys a multifaceted career that has included recording an album, *Die Trying;* composing country music; an Emmy nomination as host of *PM Magazine;* and hosting numerous television programs including *Hot, Hip and Country.* She is married to Buster Wilson.

1984 VANESSA WILLIAMS
New York

The first black woman to become Miss America, Vanessa is a best-selling recording artist and music video star, Grammy nominee, television and film actress, and Broadway leading lady. Married to publicist Ramon Hervey, she has three children.

1984 SUZETTE CHARLES
New Jersey

Suzette assumed Vanessa's duties after her resignation and has achieved success as an actress, singer, and entertainer who has performed with Liza Minnelli, Bill Cosby, and Stevie Wonder. She married Dr. Leonard Bley, a plastic surgeon.

1985 SHARLENE WELLS
Utah

Sharlene, who grew up as a missionary's kid in South America, is now a sportscaster for ESPN where she hosts *Scholastic Sports America*. She enjoys Christian motivational speaking, is married to Robert Hawkes, a physical therapist, and has two daughters.

1986 SUSAN AKIN
Mississippi

Susan's successful career has included television appearances with Bob Hope. She is the spokesperson for the National Down's Syndrome Association in honor of her late sister who was a Down's child. Now married to Jet Taylor, they have one child.

1987 KELLYE CASH
Tennessee

Kellye, the grand-niece of country star Johnny Cash, served as a spokesperson for the Governor's Alliance for a Drug Free Tennessee, performs as a gospel singer, and is recording an album. Married to Todd Sheppard, she has two children.

1988 KAYE LANI RAE RAFKO
Michigan

The first nurse to win, Kaye Lani's visibility addressing medical issues led to the development of the Pageant's "platform" program. She is a spokesperson for nursing and hospice. She married her sweetheart, Chuck Wilson, with whom she has a son.

1989 GRETCHEN CARLSON
Minnesota

Gretchen, a student at Stanford, was the first classical violinist to win. She used her year to promote fine arts education, returned to Stanford to complete her degree, and became a television reporter and anchor.

1990 DEBBYE TURNER
Missouri

This marimba-playing Miss America used her pageant scholarships to complete her doctorate in veterinary medicine. She also continues to work in Christian youth ministry, sharing her inspiring message, "Motivating Youth To Excellence."

1991 MARJORIE VINCENT
Illinois

A first generation American and the daughter of Haitian immigrants, Marjorie used her year of service as an advocate for ending violence against women. Today, she works in television broadcasting and is the mother of an infant son.

1992 CAROLYN SAPP
Hawaii

Carolyn became an inspiration to victims of domestic violence after she left an abusive relationship. After starring in a movie about her experiences, she founded "Safe Places" to provide shelter for abused women. She travels the globe as a speaker and entertainer.

1993 LEANZA CORNETT
Florida

Leanza became a respected spokesperson for AIDS education, helping to raise over $1 million for related causes. Now a co-host on *Entertainment Tonight*, she has emceed Miss America preliminaries.

1994 KIMBERLY AIKEN
South Carolina

Kimberly, who underwent brain surgery in childhood for an aneurysm, dedicated her year to ending homelessness and worked with HUD and Habitat for Humanity. She plans to earn her degree in accounting and continue performing.

1995 HEATHER WHITESTONE
Alabama

Profoundly deaf since infancy, Heather won the talent competition after performing a classical ballet to music she was unable to hear. The first woman with a disability to become Miss America, she is proof of her platform, "Anything is Possible."

Recipes

Recipes contributed by Miss Americas are indicated by a crown.

Appetizers & Beverages

Salmon Balls

1 16-ounce can salmon (freshly caught and cooked is better)
1 8-ounce package cream cheese, softened to room temperature
2 teaspoons lemon juice
3 teaspoons grated onion
1 teaspoon prepared horseradish
¼ teaspoon liquid smoke
¼ teaspoon salt
Chopped nuts (pecans or walnuts)

Drain and clean the salmon. Combine all of the ingredients in a bowl. Mix carefully to a smooth consistency and form into balls. Roll balls in the finely chopped nuts and chill for several hours before serving. These balls can be frozen. Yields 12 to 16 servings.

Keri Baumgardner Schroeder, Miss Alaska 1992

Crab and Avocado Quesadilla

½ pound crab meat, cooked
1 ripe avocado, diced
2 tablespoons sour cream
1 small can green chilies, diced
Salt and pepper to taste
1 tablespoon diced green onion
4 tablespoons vegetable oil
4 medium flour tortillas
½ cup Monterey Jack cheese, grated

Place the crab, avocado, sour cream, green chilies, salt, pepper, and onion in a medium bowl and mix with a fork. Heat the oil in a skillet over medium heat until hot. Fry each tortilla in the pan for 10 seconds on each side. Spread ¼ of the crab mixture on half of each tortilla and fold it over. Place the filled, folded tortillas on a baking sheet. Sprinkle cheese on top and broil quesadillas until the cheese is melted. Cut the quesadillas into bite-size wedges and serve immediately. Great before dinner with wine! Yields 4 to 6 servings.

Karen Jan Maciolek Salb, Miss New Mexico 1968

Pommerey Shrimp

16 large shrimp
1 tablespoon olive oil
¼ cup Pommerey mustard
1½ cups heavy cream
2 tablespoons Italian parsley, chopped

. . . .

Peel and devein the shrimp, leaving the tail section intact. Butterfly the shrimp. Heat the oil in a large sauté pan. Sauté the shrimp, flat side down, for 1 to 2 minutes then turn them over and add the mustard and cream. Cook for 3 to 5 minutes on medium heat until the sauce has reduced by half. Place 4 shrimp per person and some of the sauce on a cocktail plate. Garnish with parsley. Yields 4 servings.

Deanna Fogarty Hardwick, Miss California 1979

Hot Crab Canapés

3 cups grated Swiss cheese
10 to 12 ounces imitation crab sticks, chopped
⅓ cup chopped green olives with pimiento
Mayonnaise
White bread rounds (2 rounds from 1 slice of bread)

. . . .

Preheat oven to 400°. Combine the Swiss cheese, chopped crab sticks, and green olives in a bowl. Add just enough mayonnaise to moisten the cheese and crab mixture. Spread the mixture on top of each bread round and arrange the rounds on a cookie sheet. Bake for 10 to 12 minutes or until the cheese is hot and bubbly and the bread is crisp or toasted. Yields 8 to 10 servings.

Note: May be frozen before baking.

Gretchen Carlson, Miss America 1989

Crabbies

1 stick butter or margarine, softened to room temperature
1 jar Kraft cheese spread, softened to room temperature
1½ teaspoons mayonnaise
½ teaspoon garlic salt
1 7-ounce can crab meat (or 1 6-ounce package frozen crab meat)
6 to 8 English muffins, split

. . . .

Combine the butter and cheese with the mayonnaise. Add the garlic salt and crab meat. Spread the mixture on the muffin halves. With a sharp knife, cut the muffins into quarters. If using immediately, freeze the muffins for 10 minutes, then broil until bubbly and crisp. If not, wrap crabbies in plastic wrap and freeze in bags until needed. No need to thaw before broiling. Great to have on hand for drop-in guests! Yields 12 to 16 servings.

Laura Ludwig Moss, Miss Delaware 1988

Lomi Lomi Salmon

This dish is a traditional part of any Hawaiian Luau. It is easy to prepare and a refreshing raw fish favorite.

1 pound fresh raw red salmon
2 medium tomatoes, diced
1 medium sweet Maui onion, diced
½ cup green onions, thinly sliced
1 teaspoon salt (Hawaiian rock salt preferred)

. . . .

Pull off the skin and debone the salmon. Cut the salmon into small chunks. Combine all the ingredients in a large bowl. Toss lightly and chill. Yields 4 servings.

Desiree Moana Cruz, Miss Hawaii 1988

Pinwheels

1 8-ounce package cream cheese
1 4-ounce can chopped black olives
1 small can chopped green chilies
1 onion, minced
Garlic salt to taste
Picante sauce to taste
Flour tortillas

. . . .

Combine all of the ingredients except for the tortillas. Spread the mixture on the flour tortillas, roll the tortillas into logs, and slice into rounds. Yields about 60 pinwheels.

Kimberly Kay Christiansen, Miss Colorado 1980

Mushrooms au Chaurice

16 large or 24 small mushrooms
1 green bell pepper, finely chopped
1 large onion, chopped
1 stick butter
1 pound bulk hot pork sausage
1½ cups bread crumbs
Dash of Tabasco sauce
Dash of salt
Dash of pepper
½ cup sour cream

. . . .

Preheat oven to 400°. Remove the stems from the mushrooms and chop. Sauté the onion and pepper in butter. Add the chopped stems and sauté for 2 to 3 minutes. Brown the sausage and drain; reserve the drippings. Stir the sautéed vegetables into the sausage. Add the remaining ingredients, including the sausage drippings. Stuff each mushroom cap with the sausage mixture and arrange on an ungreased baking sheet. Bake for 20 to 30 minutes or until the tops are browned. Yields 12 to 16 servings.

Laurel Schaefer, Miss America 1972

Stuffed Mushrooms

1 to 2 dozen medium mushrooms
¼ cup chopped onion
½ stick butter
¼ cup crumbled bleu cheese
⅓ cup bread crumbs
Salt and pepper to taste

. . . .

Preheat oven to 350°. Remove the mushroom stems. Chop and sauté with onions in butter until tender. Add the cheese and bread crumbs; season with salt and pepper. Stir to blend; remove from heat. Fill the mushroom caps with the cheese mixture and arrange them on a baking sheet. Bake for 12 minutes. Yields 12 servings.

Note: Prepare ahead if you wish.

Evelyn Ay Sempier, Miss America 1954

Strombolis

2 cans crescent rolls
½ pound boiled ham, sliced
½ pound Provolone cheese, sliced
¼ pound Genoa salami, sliced
Pepper salad (sweet peppers in oil)

. . . .

Preheat oven to 350°. Pinch the rolls together to make 8 rectangles. Place 2 ham slices, 2 cheese slices, and 4 salami slices on each rectangle. Chop and drain the peppers and arrange them on top of the meat and cheese. Roll the rectangles up jelly-roll style and bake on an ungreased cookie sheet for 15 minutes. Slice and serve. Yields 4 servings.

Cathy Lawton Reilly, Miss Delaware 1972

Bourbon Franks

1 14-ounce bottle ketchup
1 cup firmly packed brown sugar
1 cup bourbon
4 8-ounce packages miniature cocktail franks

. . . .

Combine the first 3 ingredients in a large saucepan. Heat to boiling. Cover, reduce heat to low, and simmer for at least 2 hours, stirring occasionally. At this point, the sauce may be chilled for 24 hours if desired. Add the franks to the simmering sauce and cook 5 minutes longer. Place in a chafing dish. Serve with toothpicks. Yields 64 servings.

Dottye Nuckols Lindsey, Miss Kentucky 1951

Party Beef Balls

2 pounds ground beef
1 cup Italian bread crumbs
1 small onion, minced
½ cup evaporated milk
2 eggs, beaten
1 teaspoon salt
¼ teaspoon pepper
1 stick butter

Sauce

⅔ cup firmly packed brown sugar
¼ cup chili sauce
3 tablespoons soy sauce
3 tablespoons white vinegar
2 tablespoons ketchup
½ teaspoon ginger
½ teaspoon Worcestershire sauce
1½ cups water

. . . .

Combine the first 7 ingredients and form into tiny balls. Brown the balls in butter. Combine the sauce ingredients in a saucepan and heat until boiling. Add the meatballs and simmer for 10 minutes. Serve on a warming tray or over low flame. Yields 10 dozen meatballs.

Wendy Lynn Wagner, Miss Wisconsin 1983

Sauerkraut Balls

½ pound bulk pork sausage
¼ cup minced onion
1 1-pound can sauerkraut, rinsed, drained, and snipped into fine shreds
2 tablespoons fine dry bread crumbs
1 3-ounce package cream cheese, softened to room temperature
1 teaspoon prepared mustard
¼ teaspoon garlic salt
⅛ teaspoon pepper
¼ cup all-purpose flour
2 eggs
¼ cup milk
¾ cup fine dry bread crumbs
Vegetable oil

. . . .

Crumble and cook the sausage and onion in a large skillet until lightly browned. Drain the excess fat. Mix in the next 6 ingredients and refrigerate until cool (overnight is better). Shape the mixture into small balls and coat them with flour. Combine the eggs and milk. Dip the floured balls in the egg mixture, then in the remaining bread crumbs. Deep fry in about 1½ inches of 375° oil for 2 to 3 minutes, or until golden brown. Serve hot. Keep warm in a chafing dish. Yields 12 to 16 servings.

Beverly Cheryl Cooke, Miss Virginia 1982

1920s—The Roaring Twenties Birth a National Tradition

When a new Miss America is crowned each September, millions of people tune in for the enduring American tradition. Although a star today, Miss America was conceived inauspiciously during the Roaring Twenties, an era of new ideas and colliding social values. World War I was a fading memory, the airplane had given mankind a new global perspective, bootleggers battled over Prohibition, women had won the right to vote, Coco Chanel's fashions had freed women from corsets, and women could finally expose their ankles without being dragged off to jail. For females, it was an intoxicating era of newfound freedoms.

The first Miss America, in 1921, was 16-year-old Margaret Gorman, an "amateur beauty" from Washington, D.C.

In 1921, the spirited era gave birth to the grande dame of pageants, Miss America. Her birthplace, Atlantic City, New Jersey, was a seaside vacation mecca. Determined to entice tourists to prolong their vacations past Labor Day, which ended the season, business leaders decided to stage an autumn beach festival. Their fall "pageant" would include a brilliant gimmick—a contest to select "the most beautiful bathing beauty in America." Herb Test, a local reporter, added the crowning touch: "And let's call her 'Miss America!' " Eight eastern newspapers ran mail-in photo contests to send contestants.

When the contestants arrived in town that September, the era's colliding ideas about beauty quickly colored the proceedings. At the time, "nice" girls wouldn't dream of touching cosmetics and cherished the long ringlets popularized by America's Sweetheart, matinee idol Mary Pickford. Daring flappers preferred the controversial short "bobbed" hairstyle and plenty of makeup. Worried that the public would be incensed if school girls were compared against tawdry showgirls, organizers separated the entrants into two categories: "amateur beauties" and "professional beauties" (stage actresses, "professional mermaids," and models). Spectators flocked to town to watch the beauties parade down the beach in swimsuits—baggy dresses draped over bloomers and knee socks. "Beach censors," who policed public attire, were instructed to overlook breaches of clothing etiquette that week, and could only gape in shock as the more daring entrants rolled down their stockings to expose bare knees!

A panel of renowned male artists judged the girls on beauty, awarding points for various body parts. The experts had the daunting task of deciding whether "Miss America" would be the seductive or strait-laced, virtuous or vampish. Virtue won. Convinced that America's "queen of beauty" should represent modest womanhood, the judges awarded the first crown to Margaret Gorman, a sixteen-year-old "amateur beauty" with tame measurements to match: 30-25-32. Nevertheless smitten, one elderly gent gushed, "She represents the type of womanhood America needs: strong, red-blooded, able to shoulder the responsibilities of homemaking and motherhood." It didn't hurt that tiny Margaret, with her cherubic face and blonde ringlets, was a dead ringer for Mary Pickford, thus establishing from day one that Miss Americas reflect wholesome beauty standards of the day. Her successor, Mary Campbell, was so innocent that when she heard she'd won because of her figure, she inquired, "Mother, what's a figure?" Appalled, Mrs. Campbell snapped, "None of your business, Mary!"

Although innocence won the male vote, even entering such a contest was a not-so-subtle act of feminist rebellion. At the time, females were defined by two words: matrimony and motherhood. After all, experts warned, academic pursuits could strain the female mind and lead to health problems, from headaches to insanity. Thus, most law, medical, and graduate programs were reserved for males, whose minds presumably could survive the strain. Sidestepping the confines of women's roles, Atlantic City's pageant offered females a rare opportunity: like males, they could now be competitors. It was one baby step down a road of liberation that would revolutionize women's lives.

The early pageants were an enormous success, drawing an estimated 100,000 tourists, generating incalculable publicity for the resort, and drawing entrants from as far away as Canada. Despite such successes, the pageant was also stung by several scandals. The runner-up to Mary Campbell was found to be married to a baseball player, a "Miss" Boston showed up with her husband and baby, and one Miss Alaska turned out to be married and a resident of New York City! Harried officials quickly added a no-marriage clause, but, alas, in 1928, after such revelations tarnished the pageant's image and public support evaporated, the contest was discontinued. A year later, the stock market crashed, plunging the nation into the Great Depression.

In 1921, when contestants competed for the title of "The Most Beautiful Bathing Beauty in America," spectators gasped at the display of feminine charms. Margaret Gorman, Miss America 1921, is third from the left. (The Miss America Organization)

Unbelievably Easy Sweet-n-Sour Meatballs

1 18-ounce jar grape jelly
1 20-ounce bottle ketchup
2 teaspoons lemon juice, divided
2 tablespoons onion powder, divided
Garlic powder to taste
1 pound ground turkey or beef
½ cup seasoned bread crumbs
1 egg
Salt and pepper to taste

. . . .

Combine the jelly, ketchup, 1 teaspoon of the lemon juice, 1 tablespoon of onion powder, and garlic powder in a saucepan. Cook over medium-low heat for 10 minutes. Set aside. Preheat oven to 350°. Combine the meat, bread crumbs, egg, salt, pepper, remaining lemon juice and onion powder, and more garlic powder if desired. Form into small meatballs. Bake for about 20 minutes, or until browned. Pour the sauce over the meatballs; stir and enjoy. Yields 6 to 8 servings.

Lisa Desroches, Miss Massachusetts 1992

Spicy Buffalo Wings

1 5-pound bag fryer chicken wings
½ stick margarine
1 bottle Louisiana Hot Sauce
1 jar bleu cheese salad dressing (I like Marie's best)

. . . .

Deep fry the chicken wings until golden brown. Drain the wings on a paper towel to remove any excess grease. Melt the margarine in a saucepan then remove from heat and allow to stand for a few minutes. Add the Louisiana Hot Sauce to the melted margarine. Pour the sauce over the chicken wings and stir until completely coated. Serve immediately with bleu cheese dressing and celery sticks. Yields 20 to 24 servings.

Terri Kettunen Muschott, Miss Arizona 1986

Babes of the Boardwalk

In 1923, an *Atlantic City Press* reporter described the Miss America contestants:

"They were piquant jazz babies who shook the meanest kinds of shoulders, pink-skinned beauties of all types. Tanned athletic girls, shapely of figure and wearing togs gracefully, olive-hued and bejeweled favorites of the harem, stately colonial dames in hoop skirts, mandarin ladies with black eyes peeping coyly from behind waving fans." Liked 'em, huh?

Ham Balls

1½ pounds freshly cooked ham
1 pound smoked ham
2 cups milk
2 eggs
½ cup tapioca
½ teaspoon salt
¼ teaspoon pepper
¾ cup firmly packed brown sugar
½ cup water
½ cup vinegar
1 teaspoon dry mustard

. . . .

Grind the hams and combine. Mix the milk, eggs, tapioca, salt, and pepper with the ground ham. Roll into small balls about ½-inch in size and arrange them in a shallow pan. Preheat oven to 350°. In a separate bowl, combine the brown sugar, water, vinegar, and mustard and pour this mixture over the ham balls. Bake for 1 hour. Baste and turn the balls while cooking. Yields about 48 ham balls.

Debbie Bryant Berge, Miss America 1966

Senate Cheese Sticks

1 pound grated sharp Cheddar cheese
1¾ cups all-purpose flour
1 teaspoon salt
½ teaspoon cayenne pepper
1 stick butter, softened to room temperature

. . . .

Preheat oven to 425°. Combine all of the ingredients. Add a small amount of water if the mixture is too stiff. Roll out and cut into thin strips. Twist the strips and bake on an ungreased cookie sheet until brown. Yields 24 to 36 sticks.

Patricia Donnelly Harris, Miss America 1939

Party Mold

2 8-ounce packages cream cheese
8 ounces sharp Cheddar cheese, shredded
1 3-ounce package Roquefort cheese
1 teaspoon garlic salt
½ teaspoon curry powder
2 tablespoons Worcestershire sauce
1 teaspoon paprika
1 tablespoon mayonnaise
1 tablespoon lemon juice
1 6½-ounce can crab meat, drained
Chopped parsley (optional)

. . . .

All of the ingredients should be at room temperature. Combine the cheeses, garlic salt, curry powder, Worcestershire sauce, paprika, mayonnaise, lemon juice, and crab meat in a mixing bowl. Mix thoroughly with an electric mixer. Turn the mixture into a greased 1-quart mold and chill for several hours or overnight. Unmold and garnish with chopped parsley, if desired. Serve with crackers. Yields 16 servings.

Marian McKnight Conway, Miss America 1957

Baked Cheese Puffs

1 3-ounce package cream cheese, softened to room temperature
1 stick butter
¼ pound Cheddar cheese, grated
¼ teaspoon dry mustard
Salt and pepper to taste
2 egg whites, stiffly beaten
1 1-pound loaf white unsliced bread, crust removed and cut into 1-inch cubes

In a double boiler, combine the cream cheese, butter, Cheddar cheese, mustard, salt, and pepper. Melt the ingredients over low heat, stirring until smooth. Transfer the mixture to a bowl and fold in the egg whites. Dip the bread cubes into the mixture. Place on waxed paper and refrigerate until ready to bake. Bake at 400° for 8 to 10 minutes or until golden brown.

Note: These can be frozen before baking.

S. Jill Wymer, Miss Oregon 1983

Cheese Spread

1 8-ounce package sharp Cheddar cold pack cheese, softened to room temperature
1 8-ounce package cream cheese, softened to room temperature
2 tablespoons margarine
2 teaspoons chopped onion
2 teaspoons chopped green bell pepper (optional)
2 teaspoons chopped pimiento
1 teaspoon Worcestershire sauce
½ teaspoon lemon juice

Combine the cheeses and margarine. Blend in remaining ingredients until well mixed. Yields 2 cups.

Debbie Weuve Rohrer, Miss Iowa 1975

Cheese Roll Pizazz

1 pound American cheese
3 3-ounce packages cream cheese, softened to room temperature
1 2-ounce jar pimientos, mashed
¼ teaspoon hot red pepper
1 small clove garlic, mashed
Chili powder
Paprika

Combine all of the ingredients except the chili powder and paprika. Roll into 3 separate balls. Roll the balls in equal portions of chili powder and paprika. Chill and serve with crackers.

Julie Phillips, Miss Missouri 1982

Charity Cheese Balls

½ pound bleu cheese, softened
2 8-ounce packages cream cheese, softened
1 10-ounce package Wispride cold pack cheese, softened
2 tablespoons minced onion
¼ cup parsley flakes
½ cup finely chopped pecans
1 teaspoon Worcestershire sauce
¾ to 1 cup finely chopped pecans
¼ cup parsley flakes

Mix the first 7 ingredients with an electric mixer. Divide the mixture into two large or four small balls. Chill for easy handling. Combine the pecans and parsley flakes in a separate bowl. Roll the balls in the pecan and parsley mixture until well coated. Wrap in plastic wrap until ready to serve. Cheese balls will keep nicely for two weeks. They can also be frozen for later use. Yields 2 to 4 cheese balls.

Marilyn Feehan, National Hostess Committee Chairman

Salsa Colorado

1 15-ounce can whole tomatoes
¼ to ½ medium onion, diced
¼ hot jalapeño pepper (more or less according to taste), diced
2 dashes of oregano
2 dashes of salt
2 dashes of garlic salt
1 teaspoon chili pequin (more or less according to taste)

Place all of the ingredients in a blender; blend on chop mode for three seconds. Store the salsa in a pint jar in the refrigerator (it will keep for 5 to 7 days). Serve with chips, over eggs, or on tacos; many uses. Yields 2 cups.

Kay Anne Goforth Gatz-Wilhelm, Miss Kansas 1952

Lito de Cuevas Salsa

2 quarts water
3 tomatoes
1 onion
3 or 4 green or red toasted chili peppers
2 cloves of garlic, peeled
1 bunch of green onions
1 bunch of cilantro

Bring 2 quarts of water to a boil. Add tomatoes and boil until mushy; remove from heat. Add onion and toasted chilies. Stir in garlic and green onions (you can leave the tops on). Add cilantro; place all ingredients in a blender. Blend well. Add salt and pepper to taste. Serve chilled or hot. Can be stored for 3 or 4 weeks in refrigerator. Yields 2½ quarts.

Debra Maffett, Miss America 1983

Spinach Dip

1 cup plain nonfat yogurt
½ teaspoon dill weed
Garlic powder to taste
½ cup nonfat sour cream
½ teaspoon seasoned salt
½ of a 10-ounce package chopped spinach, thawed and drained

Combine all of the ingredients. Chill for at least 2 hours before serving. Serve with cut-up raw vegetables. Yields 2 cups.

Tara Erickson, Miss South Dakota 1982

Fruit Dip

This recipe is not only tasty... but the fruit is good for you, too! The traveling companion for Miss Western New York gave this recipe to me. She first served it at a homecoming party for one of New York's local contestants. Now I serve it at my parties and it is always a staple for any "Pageant" function because so many people are trying to watch their weight and eat healthy!

1 8-ounce package lite cream cheese, softened to room temperature
1 8- to 10-ounce jar marshmallow fluff
1 grated orange peel (whole orange rind)
Fresh fruit, cut into bite-size pieces (apples, strawberries, kiwi, grapes, bananas, etc. Use your imagination!)

Combine the cream cheese, marshmallow, and grated orange peel. Mix well and refrigerate. Arrange the fruit on a platter. Place the dip in a bowl in the center of the platter. Serve and enjoy! Yields 20 to 30 servings.

Kelli Krull Russell, Miss New York 1979

Green Mountain Salad Dressing or Veggie Dip

1 4-ounce package pressed tofu
5 whole scallions
2 tablespoons vinegar
2 tablespoons lemon juice
¼ teaspoon black pepper

Blend all of the ingredients until smooth. Serve cold over salad or as a dip with vegetables. Yields 4 servings.

Wendy Masino Stebbins, Miss Vermont 1960

Hawaiian Stuffed Bread Dip

1 10-ounce package frozen chopped spinach, thawed, drained, and squeezed
1 8-ounce can water chestnuts, drained and chopped
1 package dry vegetable soup mix
1 cup sour cream
1 cup mayonnaise
½ cup chopped green onion
1 loaf Hawaiian Bread

Combine the spinach, water chestnuts, vegetable soup mix, sour cream, mayonnaise, and green onions. Scoop or cut out the middle section of the bread so it forms a bowl. Cube the extra bread to dip. Pour the dip into the bread shell. You can also serve fresh cut raw vegetables with this. Yields 3½ cups.

Joni McMechan Checchia, Miss Indiana 1988

King Neptune, the official monarch of the National Beauty Tournament, crowns Miss America 1926, Norma Smallwood, formerly Miss Tulsa. (Atlantic City Foto Service)

Guacamole

8 fresh avocados, peeled
1 Serrano pepper, seeds removed and minced
1 ounce fresh lemon juice
2 tablespoons chopped cilantro
¼ cup diced white onion
Salt to taste
White pepper to taste

Combine all of the ingredients and mash thoroughly. Serve immediately. Yields approximately 2 cups.

Deanna Fogarty Hardwick, Miss California 1979

Jack's Hot Crab Dip

½ to ¾ pounds fresh crab meat, cleaned and picked over
1 16-ounce package cream cheese, softened to room temperature
2 tablespoons minced dry onion
2 tablespoons milk
Garlic powder to taste
Parsley flakes
Bell pepper strips

Mix the crab meat and cream cheese together in a bowl. Mix dry onions and milk together; let stand for two minutes. Add all of the remaining ingredients, except the parsley flakes and pepper strips, and mix well. Warm the mixture in a conventional or microwave oven. Remove dip from oven and garnish with parsley flakes and bell pepper strips. Serve with crackers or potato chips. Yields 8 to 10 servings.

Jack W. Francis, Miss Washington Pageant

Hot Crab Dip

1 6-ounce can crab meat, rinsed and drained
1 8-ounce package cream cheese, softened to room temperature
½ cup mayonnaise
¼ cup grated Parmesan cheese
1 tablespoon dry minced onion
Dill weed
Paprika
1 box Triscuit crackers

Preheat oven to 350°. Combine the crabmeat, cream cheese, mayonnaise, Parmesan, and dry minced onion in an oven-proof serving dish. Sprinkle with dill weed and paprika. Bake for 15 to 20 minutes, or until hot and bubbly. Serve as a dip with Triscuits. Yields 2 cups.

Mignon Merchant Ball, Miss Oklahoma 1986

Taco Dip

1 12-ounce carton sour cream
1 8-ounce package cream cheese, softened to room temperature
3 tablespoons taco sauce
1 envelope taco seasoning
Shredded lettuce
Chopped tomatoes
Shredded cheese
Sliced black olives

Combine the first 4 ingredients and spread on the bottom of a platter. Cover with shredded lettuce, tomatoes, cheese, and decorate with black olives. Serve with corn or tortilla chips. Yields 2 cups.

Phyllis Hankey, Miss North Dakota 1983

Alaskan King Crab Dip

2 8-ounce packages cream cheese, softened to room temperature
3 tablespoons horseradish
3 tablespoons salad dressing
½ cup finely chopped onion
Salt and pepper to taste
Dash of lemon juice
1 cup shredded king crab
Paprika, optional

. . . .

Preheat oven to 350°. Combine all of the ingredients, except the crab, in a blender until smooth. Fold the crab into the mixture and spoon into an ovenproof dish. Bake until the mixture bubbles and browns on top. Sprinkle paprika on top before serving. The dip may be reheated or frozen for your next party. Yields about 3 cups.

Note: If the dip is too thick, thin with up to ¼ cup milk.

Kay Linton, Miss Alaska Queens Hostess Club

Garlic Dip

1 head fresh garlic
2 8-ounce packages Neufchâtel cheese, softened to room temperature
½ cup mayonnaise
2½ tablespoons dried onion flakes

. . . .

Crush the garlic cloves in a garlic press. (Remember to remove the paper skins from the garlic cloves.) Combine all of the ingredients and mix well. Cover with plastic wrap and refrigerate until ready to serve with crackers or vegetables. Yields 2½ cups.

Marie McLaughlin Cascone, Miss Pennsylvania 1976

Artichoke Dip

1 8-ounce package cream cheese, softened to room temperature
½ cup mayonnaise
½ cup sour cream
1 cup Parmesan cheese
Minced garlic to taste
1 7-ounce can artichoke hearts, drained

. . . .

Preheat oven to 325°. Combine the cream cheese, mayonnaise, sour cream, Parmesan cheese, and garlic. Cut up the artichoke hearts and add them to the cream cheese mixture. Place in an ovenproof dish and bake for 45 minutes. Yields 4 cups.

Debbie Bryant Berge, Miss America 1966

Hot Pecan Dip

½ cup chopped pecans
2 tablespoons butter
½ teaspoon salt
1 8-ounce package cream cheese, softened to room temperature
2 teaspoons milk
½ cup sour cream
1 package chipped beef, cut or torn into small pieces
¼ green bell pepper, chopped
1 small onion, grated
½ teaspoon garlic salt
¼ teaspoon black pepper

. . . .

Preheat oven to 350°. Sauté the pecans in the butter and salt. Combine the remaining ingredients and spread the mixture in a pie plate. Sprinkle the pecans over top and bake for 20 minutes. Yields 4 to 6 servings.

Dorothy Benham McGowan, Miss America 1977

There She Is . . .

The original Miss America, Margaret Gorman, was crowned "the most beautiful bathing beauty in America."

Avocado Layer Dip—California Style

1 16-ounce can refried beans
1 pint sour cream
2 avocados, peeled, chopped, and mashed
1 8-ounce jar salsa
1 large tomato, chopped
2 cups grated Cheddar cheese
Black olives, sliced

. . . .

Line the bottom of a baking dish with the refried beans. Layer the next 5 ingredients over the beans in order. Decorate with sliced black olives. Yields 8 to 10 servings.

Jean Bartel, Miss America 1943

Crab Dip

1 cup mayonnaise
1 tablespoon parsley flakes
1 6½-ounce can crab meat
1 teaspoon lemon juice
½ cup sour cream
Salt and pepper to taste

. . . .

Combine all of the ingredients and chill. Serve with crackers and/or raw vegetables. Yields about 12 servings.

Jill Shaffer Swanson, Miss Pennsylvania 1981

Hot Beef Dip

1 8-ounce package cream cheese, softened to room temperature
2 tablespoons milk
2 tablespoons instant onion
1 2-ounce jar chipped beef
2 tablespoons chopped green bell pepper
½ cup sour cream

. . . .

Preheat oven to 350°. Blend the cheese and milk together using an electric mixer. Add the remaining ingredients. Bake for 15 minutes. Yields 2 cups.

Note: Great when kept hot in a fondue pot or chafing dish.

Dean Herman Maguire, Miss Florida 1981

Sooner Spread

1 pound ground beef
1 pound bulk hot pork sausage
1 pound Velveeta cheese, diced
1 tablespoon Worcestershire sauce
1 tablespoon oregano
½ tablespoon garlic salt
½ tablespoon pepper
2 loaves party rye bread

. . . .

Brown the meats and drain. Add the diced cheese and stir until melted. Add the Worcestershire sauce, oregano, garlic salt, and pepper. Spread on the rye bread. Place on a cookie sheet and freeze until firm. Store frozen in plastic bags. When ready to use, broil until cheese bubbles. Yields about 80 servings.

Tiffany Craig, Miss Oklahoma 1994

Clam Dip

½ teaspoon garlic salt
1 8-ounce package cream cheese, softened to room temperature
1 teaspoon Worcestershire sauce
1 teaspoon lemon juice
1 tablespoon mayonnaise
½ teaspoon grated onion
1 6½-ounce can minced clams, drained, reserving 1 to 2 tablespoons juice

. . . .

Combine the garlic salt, cream cheese, Worcestershire sauce, lemon juice, mayonnaise, and grated onion in a mixing bowl. Blend together well. Add the minced clams and reserved juice and mix well. Yields 8 servings.

Patti VanHorne Smith, Miss Nebraska 1966

Cheese Pinwheels

Throughout the history of the Miss Nevada Pageant Jessie Acrea worked in many jobs. This was a recipe she served over the years, never sharing the recipe until just prior to her death in 1989. "Easy & Delicious" is what she wrote on the card. Kids love it as well, which is a bonus.

1 loaf fresh sandwich bread
1 can small sliced olives
2 jars sharp Old English Cheddar cheese
Garlic salt to taste
Chili powder to taste
Melted butter

. . . .

Cut the crusts from the bread. Roll the bread with a rolling pin until it is flattened and thin. Combine the olives, cheese, garlic salt, and chili powder and allow the mixture to stand for a few hours to enhance the flavor. Spread cheese mixture on the bread. Roll up the bread jelly-roll style. With a sharp knife cut each roll into four pieces. Place the pinwheels seam-side down on a cookie sheet. Brush with melted butter. Broil until toasted. Yields 8 to 10 appetizers.

Note: Can be made ahead and frozen, but do not cut if you freeze; let stand at room temperature for one hour, then cut, brush with butter, and broil.

Ellen Roseman, Miss Nevada 1964

Notorious Norma

Miss America 1926, Norma Smallwood, had a spat with pageant officials and refused to return to Atlantic City to crown her successor unless the pageant agreed to pay her the $600 fee she demanded. They didn't pay. Miss A didn't show. But she did appear in headlines not long after, when she married a wealthy oilman, had a baby named Des Cygnes l'Amour (of the swans of love), followed by an affair and widely publicized divorce.

Maryland Crab Spread

2 8-ounce packages cream cheese, softened to room temperature
1 teaspoon Old Bay seafood seasoning
1 teaspoon chopped parsley (or parsley flakes)
⅛ teaspoon black pepper
½ red bell pepper, finely chopped
1 pound fresh lump Maryland crab meat, cleaned and picked over

. . . .

Combine all of the ingredients except the crab meat. Gently stir in crab meat. Cover and refrigerate until about 15 minutes before serving. Serve in a clear glass bowl with assorted mildly seasoned crackers. Yields 16 servings.

Carol Jennette Shook, Miss Maryland 1955

Chili Con Queso

2 pounds Velveeta cheese, cubed
1 10-ounce can Ro-Tel tomatoes and chilies (if not available: 1 can tomatoes, undrained and 1 can green chilies, drained and chopped)
1 pound bulk sausage (optional)

Melt the cheese in a double boiler. Mash the tomatoes and chilies with a fork and add them to the cheese. Brown the sausage and add it to the cheese mixture. Stir constantly for about 3 minutes. Serve warm in a fondue pot, chafing dish, or crock pot with tortilla chips or crackers. Freezes well. Yields 25 to 50 servings.

Note: This is also an excellent topping for hamburgers or use it in place of cheese sauce over asparagus and other vegetables.

Susan Spartz, Miss New Mexico 1979

Chili Appetizer

1 stick margarine
10 eggs
½ cup all-purpose flour
1 teaspoon baking powder
¼ teaspoon salt
1 8-ounce can diced green chilies
1 pint cottage cheese
1 pound Cheddar cheese, cubed

Preheat oven to 350°. Melt the margarine in a 13 x 9-inch baking dish. In a separate bowl, beat the eggs. Using a hand beater, add the flour, baking powder, and salt to the eggs. Add the chilies (juice and all), cottage cheese, and Cheddar cheese to the mixture. Pour into the baking dish and stir in the melted margarine (it will float to the top). Bake for about 1 hour or until a knife inserted in the center comes out clean. Cut into small squares and serve hot. Yields 12 servings.

Note: Can be frozen ahead.

Debbie Bryant Berge, Miss America 1966

Spinach-Mushroom Quiche

1 pie crust recipe
1 10-ounce package frozen chopped spinach, thawed and drained well
2 tablespoons butter or margarine
¼ cup thinly sliced onions
¼ pound fresh mushrooms, sliced
½ pound natural Swiss cheese, grated
4 eggs
1 cup heavy cream
½ cup whole milk
¾ teaspoon salt
⅛ teaspoon nutmeg
⅛ teaspoon pepper

Preheat oven to 425°. Roll the pastry to form a 12-inch circle. Line a quiche pan with the pastry. Prick the bottom and sides with a fork. Bake for 15 minutes or until the pastry begins to brown. Cool. Place the spinach in a colander or sieve and press out as much water as possible. Set aside. In a medium skillet on medium heat, melt the butter or margarine and sauté the onions. Remove the onions, then sauté the mushrooms. Set each aside. Reduce oven temperature to 375°. Sprinkle the bottom of the pastry with half of the grated cheese. Layer the onion, then the spinach, then the mushrooms. Sprinkle with the remaining cheese. In a medium bowl, whisk the eggs, cream, milk, and remaining ingredients until combined. Pour the egg mixture into the quiche pan. Bake for 40 minutes or until the quiche is puffy and golden brown. Yields 4 to 6 servings.

Beth Guthmiller Hughes, Miss South Dakota 1976

Bacon Wrapped Water Chestnuts

This recipe is from my aunt, Joy Robbins.

1 5-ounce can whole water chestnuts, drained
¼ cup soy sauce
6 slices bacon, cut in half

Cut each water chestnut in half and marinate in soy sauce for 30 minutes. Meanwhile, arrange the bacon on a plate lined with paper towels. Cover the plate with a paper towel and cook the bacon in a microwave on high for 2½ minutes or until partially cooked. Wrap each water chestnut with a bacon slice and secure with a toothpick. Arrange the wrapped chestnuts on another plate lined with paper towels and cook uncovered for 2 to 3 minutes more, or until the bacon is the desired crispness. Yields 4 servings.

Note: To make ahead, marinate the water chestnuts, partially cook the bacon, and wrap it around chestnuts. Cover and refrigerate. If desired, use pineapple chunks instead of water chestnuts.

Joni McMechan Checchia, Miss Indiana 1988

Green Pepper Jelly

¾ cup green bell pepper, firmly packed (4 to 5 peppers)
¼ cup hot green pepper, seeded (about 4 ounces)
1½ cups apple cider vinegar
6 cups sugar
4 ounces Certo
4 drops green food coloring

Wash and seed the peppers. Run them through a grinder or blender; drain well. Combine with the vinegar and sugar in a saucepan. Bring to a rolling boil, stirring occasionally, over medium heat. Remove from heat at once. Add the Certo. Bring to a rolling boil again. Remove from heat immediately. Add the green food coloring and stir well. Pour into sterilized glass jars and seal with paraffin. Serve over a block of cream cheese and spread on your favorite snack cracker. Yields 4 to 5 jars.

Note: Recipe can be doubled.

Carole Johnson Weeks, Miss West Virginia 1961

Marinated Artichokes and Mushrooms

This is a winner! Men love it!
It's easy and leftovers keep in the refrigerator!

Marinade
1 cup white vinegar
½ cup vegetable oil
1 clove garlic, crushed
1½ tablespoons salt
½ tablespoon pepper
½ teaspoon thyme
½ teaspoon oregano
1 tablespoon dried parsley
1 tablespoon sugar
1 onion, sliced into rings

2 pounds fresh mushrooms
2 7-ounce cans artichoke hearts
Spinach

Combine all of the ingredients for the marinade. Pour over the mushrooms and artichoke hearts. Marinate overnight. Drain and serve on a platter lined with spinach. Yields 16 to 20 servings.

Note: For 60 to 70 people use 4 pounds of mushrooms, 5 cans of artichokes, and 3 times the marinade.

Evelyn Ay Sempier, Miss America 1954

A Case of the Royal Jitters

Poor Miss America. When Miss California, Fay Lanphier, won the crown in 1925, the attention that went with her newfound celebrity was too much for even royalty to bear. A *New York Times* reporter tattled that Miss America "suffered a nervous breakdown" during Pageant week, missed some events, "and frequently burst into tears." She recovered sufficiently to reign over the glamorous American Beauty Ball, however. Hey, it's a tough job, but somebody's got to do it!

Apple-Tizer

I have never seen this recipe in writing.
You may need to adjust quantities depending
upon the size of your platter and
the number of guests you plan to serve.
It always gets rave reviews.

4 large apples, cored and thinly sliced (leave the peel on for color)
Lemon juice
1 8-ounce package cream cheese, softened to room temperature
½ to ¾ cup caramel sauce

. . . .

Sprinkle the apple slices with lemon juice. Spread cream cheese over the center of a large, flat plate or platter to within about 2 inches of the edge, building up a little rim around the edge of the cream cheese circle. Spread the caramel sauce over the cream cheese. Arrange the apple slices, slightly overlapping, around the edge of the platter. Cover and keep refrigerated until ready to serve. Then, scoop up a little cream cheese and caramel with an apple wedge and enjoy. Yields 16 to 20 servings.

Terri Bartlett Osborne, Miss Virginia 1977

Laurel's Christmas Nog

12 eggs, separated
1 cup sugar
4 ounces cognac
14 ounces bourbon
6 ounces Myers dark rum (no other dark rum works)
2 quarts milk
1 quart half and half
1 pint unwhipped whipping cream
Nutmeg

. . . .

Separate eggs. Whip yellows to batter consistency, then add sugar slowly. Continue to beat while slowly adding cognac, bourbon, and rum. Whip egg whites to stiff peaks. Fold into yellows. Add milk, half and half, and cream. Chill for at least 24 hours, stirring occasionally. Shake or stir well and serve. Garnish with a pinch of nutmeg. Yields 1 gallon.

Laurel Schaefer, Miss America 1972

Banana Punch

8 cups water
4 cups sugar
2 quarts unsweetened pineapple juice
4 to 6 cans frozen orange juice diluted with 12 cans water
½ cup lemon juice
5 large firm bananas, puréed in blender
2 quarts ginger ale

. . . .

Combine the water and sugar, boil 15 minutes and cool. Stir in all of the remaining ingredients except for the ginger ale. Freeze. Remove from the freezer 3 to 4 hours before serving. Add the ginger ale at serving time. Ice is unnecessary. Yields 50 servings.

Carol Ruth Olson Larsen, Miss North Dakota 1960

Christmas Punch

3 quarts apple cider or juice
1 quart cranberry juice
1 cup crushed hard peppermint candy
½ cup red hots

Heat the juices in a large pan over medium heat. Add the crushed peppermints and red hots. Stir until dissolved. Yields 1 gallon.

Kellye Cash, Miss America 1987

Fruit Drink

2 bananas
2 cups pineapple juice
2 carrots (or more), cut into chunks
6 ice cubes

Combine all of the ingredients in a blender and blend well. Store in the refrigerator. Before serving, blend for an additional 20 seconds. Yields 2 to 4 servings.

Susan Eby, Miss Idaho Pageant

Hot Spiced Punch

9 cups unsweetened pineapple juice
9 cups cranberry juice cocktail
4¼ cups water
1 cup firmly packed brown sugar
4½ teaspoons whole cloves
4 cinnamon sticks, broken
¼ teaspoon salt

Combine the juices and water with the brown sugar in a 30-cup percolator. Place the cloves, cinnamon, and salt in the filter basket. Perk. Yields 24 servings.

Note: Looks beautiful served in a glass warmer over a candle. Wine may be added to taste.

Bob Wheeler, Miss Arkansas Pageant

Judicial Nightmare

Judging is always a tough job, but the 1924 contest was the most grueling of all, described as "an intense drama that had the entire city in suspense." With a crowd of 15,000 people awaiting its verdict, the panel was deadlocked. Calling the contestants forward time and time again, the judges resorted to personally tape-measuring their figures, down to finger size and instep shape. Finally, after five hours of deliberations, the announcement came that Ruth Malcomson had beaten the returning champion, Miss America 1923, to wear the crown. The frenzied crowd pushed aside police to swarm the winner, while the exhausted judges slumped in their chairs, "looking worried and nervous after a five-hour ordeal."

Hot Spiced Tea

1 cup powdered orange drink
1 cup instant tea (with lemon is ok)
1 cup sugar (omit if tea is pre-sweetened)
1 teaspoon cinnamon
1 teaspoon allspice
¼ teaspoon ground cloves

Combine all of the ingredients and store the mixture in a jar. Use 2 to 3 teaspoons of tea mix to one cup of hot water. Yields 3 cups of tea mix.

Kellye Cash, Miss America 1987

Greek Coffee

1 heaping teaspoon Greek or Turkish Coffee
1 level teaspoon sugar
½ cup water, cold

. . . .

Traditionally, this coffee is made in a brass pot called a *briki,* but a small saucepan may be used. Mix all ingredients in briki and place over low heat. Stir constantly until coffee comes to a rolling boil. Pour immediately into a demitasse cup making sure that the *kaimaki* (froth) is floating on top. Ouzo liqueur may be added, if desired. Yields 1 serving.

Rena Michaelides, Miss New York State Pageant

Coffee Liqueur

4 cups sugar
4 cups water
4 tablespoons instant coffee
2 tablespoons water
1 quart 100-proof vodka
1 vanilla bean

. . . .

Cook the sugar and water in a saucepan for about 40 minutes over medium heat. The liquid should reduce to about one quart. Combine the coffee with the remaining 2 tablespoons of water, then add it to the saucepan. Add the vodka. Split the vanilla bean lengthwise and put one piece in each of two 1-quart bottles. Fill the bottles with the coffee mixture and age for 21 days. Yields approximately 2 quarts.

Gail Bullock Odom, Miss Georgia 1973

Kentucky Mint Julep

The first Saturday in May is time for the annual running of the Kentucky Derby, an event of magnitude not only for racing fans but also for mint julep makers. Great food, fast horses, and beautiful people are ingredients that are hard to match and they spell success for Derby Parties all over the world. Many of these parties have become traditions in themselves, with recipes as carefully handed down as the pedigree of a fine Thoroughbred.

2 cups sugar
2 cups water
Fresh mint leaves
Crushed ice
Bourbon (2 ounces per serving)

. . . .

Combine the sugar and water in a saucepan; heat to boiling. Boil for 5 minutes without stirring. Let cool. Place the fresh mint in a 2-quart jar; pour the cooled syrup over the mint. Cover; chill for at least 24 hours. Remove the mint leaves and use as needed. For each serving, fill an 8-ounce glass with crushed ice; add 1 tablespoon of the mint syrup and 2 ounces of bourbon. Garnish with a fresh sprig of mint. Yields 32 servings.

Ann Shirley Gillock Brooks, Miss Kentucky 1955

Soups & Salads

Gazpacho

I could live on this in the summer time. It's healthy, tasty, light, and very low in fat. Just make a batch and keep it in the refrigerator.

1 large cucumber, peeled, seeded, and diced
½ green bell pepper, seeded and diced
4 spring onions
2 tablespoons fresh basil
1 large garlic clove, minced
2 ribs celery, chopped
1 14-ounce can tomatoes
1 tablespoon olive oil
1 tablespoon Worcestershire sauce
1 tablespoon red wine vinegar
1 tablespoon sugar
Dash of ground cumin
Salt and freshly ground pepper to taste
Red food coloring

Simply throw everything into a blender and blend. Add the red food coloring for a pretty, healthy red color. Garnish with cucumber slices, croutons, and sour cream. Yields 4 servings.

Note: Best if refrigerated overnight.

Kylene Barker, Miss America 1979

Gazpacho from Spain

This is different from the gazpacho that is generally known and probably was eaten in early California when the Spaniards were here. It uses ingredients that are all produced in California. It is very refreshing. Also healthy and low calorie!

3 tomatoes, diced
1 cucumber, diced
1 green bell pepper, diced
¼ melon, diced (any melon except watermelon)
1 cup seedless grapes
¼ cup olive oil
½ cup vinegar
1 8-ounce can tomato juice
1 clove garlic, pressed (or garlic powder)
Salt to taste

Combine all of the ingredients and serve cold. Yields 4 servings.

Marquerite Skliris Alvarez, Miss California 1939

Mushroom Soup

2 scallions, chopped with the tops
½ stick butter
1 clove garlic
4 tablespoons all-purpose flour
3 cups hot chicken stock
2 cups sliced mushrooms
1 cup light cream
1 tablespoon chopped dill

. . . .

Sauté the scallions in the butter. Add the garlic and flour. Gradually stir in the hot chicken broth. Cook until the liquid comes to a boil. Remove the garlic. Pour some of the soup into a blender, add some of the mushrooms, and blend. Repeat with the remaining soup and mushrooms. Add the cream and blend. Serve with dill sprinkled on top.

Frances Burke Kenney, Miss America 1940

Fresh Mushroom Soup

1 pound fresh mushrooms
¾ stick butter (6 tablespoons)
2 cups chopped onion
½ teaspoon sugar
¼ cup all-purpose flour
1¼ cups water
2 cups chicken broth
½ cup dry vermouth
1 teaspoon salt
¼ teaspoon pepper

. . . .

Slice ⅓ of the mushrooms and finely chop the rest. Melt the butter in a large saucepan. Add the onions and sugar. Sauté over medium heat, stirring for about 15 minutes or until golden. Add the mushrooms and sauté for 5 minutes. Stir in the flour until smooth. Cook for 2 minutes, stirring constantly. Pour in the water and stir until smooth. Add the rest of ingredients and heat to boil, stirring constantly. Reduce the heat and simmer for 10 minutes. Yields 6 servings.

Kent and Deb Goyen, Miss Kansas Pageant

YOC French White Onion Soup

In 1965 I was in Japan while I was Miss Nevada. This delicious French onion soup, which was not the traditional "red" version, was a favorite at the Yokota Air Base Officers' Club. The recipe was given to me after a trip to the kitchen to visit the chef. It is particularly popular on cold winter days. My teenage daughters and their friends jokingly refer to this as "yuck" onion soup, but still devour it.

2 cups thinly sliced sweet onions
1 stick butter
¼ cup all-purpose flour
2 teaspoons salt
¼ teaspoon pepper
4 cups milk
4 to 6 slices French bread
4 to 6 slices Swiss cheese
Grated Parmesan cheese

. . . .

Sauté the onions in butter over low heat until tender, about 5 to 10 minutes. Blend in the flour and seasonings. Cook over medium heat until bubbly, stirring constantly. Add the milk slowly, stirring while the mixture thickens. When ready to serve, place a slice of French bread in a bowl and pour in the soup. Top with Swiss and Parmesan cheeses. Broil for a couple of minutes, or until the cheese is bubbly. Yields 4 to 6 servings.

Ellen Roseman, Miss Nevada 1964

New England Clam Chowder

Clams can be dug or raked from the sandy bottoms of coastal areas of Connecticut or bought in seafood markets.

1 quart fresh clams
1 onion, sliced
1 ½-inch cube fat salt pork, finely chopped
4 tablespoons butter
2 tablespoons all-purpose flour
4 cups potatoes, cut in ¾-inch cubes
1 tablespoon salt
⅛ teaspoon pepper
4 cups scalded milk
8 crackers, crushed

Finely chop the large parts of the clams that have been cut off. Sauté them with the sliced onion and salt pork for 10 minutes. Add the rest of the clam parts. Melt the butter and add the flour. Add this to the first mixture. Set aside. Put the potatoes and just enough water to cover them in a large pot, add salt and pepper and parboil for 5 minutes. Add the potatoes to the first mixture. Add the milk and crackers. Yields 8 servings.

Carol Norval Kelley, Miss Connecticut 1969

Crab Meat Soup

4 tablespoons butter
1 cup finely chopped celery
1 large onion, finely chopped
8 ounces fresh mushrooms, chopped
2 10¾-ounce cans cream of mushroom soup
2 soup cans milk
Dash of mace
1 teaspoon Worcestershire sauce
Dry or fresh parsley
Cayenne pepper to taste
1 pound crab meat, well picked over

Melt the butter and sauté the chopped celery, onion, and mushrooms in a soup pot. Add the soup and milk and stir over low heat until smooth. Add the dash of mace, Worcestershire sauce, parsley, and cayenne pepper. Simmer for about 15 minutes and add the crab meat, heating throughout but never letting the mixture come to a boil. Yields 6 to 8 servings.

Phoebe Stone, Miss Alabama 1981

Dandy's Fish Chowder

This recipe comes from a friend who grew up on the Maine coast, cooking for her dad and brothers who were lobstermen and liked hearty meals.

1½-inch cube salt pork, diced (3 slices of bacon can be used but it changes the flavor)
1 small onion, diced
2 cups cubed potatoes
1 cup water
1 pound fillet of haddock, halibut, or any white fish
2 cups milk (for rich, creamy chowder use 1 cup cream and 1 cup whole milk; for lighter chowder use 1 cup 2% milk and 1 cup water)
3 tablespoons butter
Salt and pepper to taste

Dice the salt pork and fry it in a large soup pot for 2 to 3 minutes. Add the onion and fry an additional 5 minutes. Remove the pieces of salt pork from the pot. Add the potatoes to the drippings before adding the water. Be generous with water if you feel you need a touch more. Cook for 5 minutes. Add the fish, cover, and simmer for 10 minutes. Add the milk and simmer for 10 minutes. Then add the butter, salt, and pepper. Heat through, stirring to blend. Yields 4 to 5 servings.

Georgia Taggart Brackett, Miss New Hampshire 1963

Gourmet Lobster Bisque au Rhum

A brilliant soup that tastes like you've spent hours preparing it. Shrimp or crab may be substituted for the lobster. Ideal as an elegant starter for a special dinner party.

1 10¾-ounce can condensed tomato soup
1 10¾-ounce can condensed split pea soup
1 cup sweet cream or evaporated milk
½ to 1 pound fresh or frozen lobster, thawed
1½ ounces light rum

. . . .

Combine the soups in a double boiler. Add the sweet cream and blend. Add the lobster and bring to a boil, stirring slowly. Add the rum and stir well. Serve immediately. Yields 4 servings.

Linda Phillips, Miss Wyoming 1959

Mom's Minestrone

2 tablespoons olive oil
6 to 8 ounces Kielbasa sausage, diced
2 garlic cloves, minced
1 medium onion, diced
1 large celery stalk, diced
1 carrot, diced
½ teaspoon oregano
1 14-ounce can tomato juice
½ bunch broccoli, cut into pieces
1 28-ounce can tomatoes
1 can chickpeas (garbanzo beans), rinsed and drained
½ cup uncooked rotini
1 teaspoon dried basil
Grated Parmesan cheese for garnish

. . . .

Heat the oil, Kielbasa, garlic, onion, celery, carrot, and oregano in a deep pan over high heat for approximately 5 minutes, stirring several times. Add the tomato juice, broccoli, tomatoes, and chickpeas. Cook for 20 minutes, bringing the mixture to a boil; then turn the heat down to medium. Stir occasionally. Add the rotini and basil. Cook for 15 minutes, stirring occasionally. Ladle the soup into bowls and sprinkle with Parmesan. Serve hot. Yields 8 servings.

Joni McMechan Checchia, Miss Indiana 1988

Beef and Vegetable Soup

1 soup bone
1 pound stew beef, cubed
2 tablespoons vegetable oil
3 quarts water
1 12-ounce can tomatoes, crushed and drained
1 6-ounce can tomato paste
½ small head cabbage, cut in small pieces
1 pound potatoes, cubed
4 small carrots, chopped
2 stalks celery, diced
½ green bell pepper
1 16-ounce package small lima beans
1 17-ounce can whole kernel corn
3 tablespoons salt
1 tablespoon sugar
12 peppercorns
¼ cup barley

. . . .

Brown the soup bone and the beef cubes in the vegetable oil. Add the water. Stir in all the remaining ingredients except the barley. Let the soup simmer, covered, for about 4 hours. Add the barley and cook for another hour. Add more water if necessary. Yields about 4 quarts.

Barbara Walker Hummel, Miss America 1947

The 1930s—The Great Depression and The Influence of Hollywood

The 1930s were an era of gloom and glitter. The nation was in the grip of the Great Depression, unemployment was epidemic, and gangsters Al Capone and Bonnie and Clyde rampaged. On the bright side, it was the heyday of Hollywood and the screen performances of stars Clark Gable, Ginger Rogers, and Shirley Temple offered a reprieve from the nation's troubles.

With entertainment always welcomed, Atlantic City revived the beauty tournament—with farcical results. The contest was delayed when a judge overslept, three contestants were disqualified, officials discovered that Miss Arkansas was married, Miss New York State collapsed on-stage from an abscessed tooth, and Miss Oklahoma was rushed to the hospital for an appendectomy. Marian Bergeron, a curvaceous blonde who resembled screen sex symbol Jean Harlow, won the crown—and nearly had to give it back when officials learned she was only fifteen. When the judges stood their ground, the sexy schoolgirl kept her crown and earned the nickname "Baby Vamp." She lost the crown anyway. "Someone stole it out of my hotel room the night I was crowned," Marian recalls. "It just vanished." So did the pageant. A public relations failure, Miss America was promptly put back in mothballs.

In 1933, when the defunct beauty tournament was revived, Marian Bergeron, a lookalike for screen sex symbol Jean Harlow, won the crown—and nearly had to give it back when officials discovered she was only fifteen. (Atlantic Foto Service)

Then, in 1935, the city made the fateful decision to bring back Miss America in style, renaming the event "The Showman's Variety Jubilee" and hiring Lenora Slaughter, a special events director, to run the event. Star-struck organizers dreamed of finding a winner to become the pageant's first Hollywood star. In an era dominated by glamorous leading ladies, when the average woman had little but domesticity and unemployment to look forward to, ambitious girls viewed Hollywood as their key to the American Dream. An informal poll of entrants of the era revealed that the hopefuls would gladly ditch their hopes for marriage for screen stardom. Reflecting the nation's infatuation with Hollywood musicals, a talent segment was introduced—with mixed reviews. "At least half of the girls would get out there and sing or dance or do something—badly!" Slaughter admits, "and they still picked the pretty girls."

And anywhere pretty girls were to be found, Hollywood agents were right on their high-heels. With movie moguls like Howard Hughes sending agents to sign promising new talent, and winners awarded Hollywood screen tests, aspiring starlets viewed Miss America as a runway to Hollywood. Soon, the Pageant achieved its goal of seeing a winner make it to the Silver Screen. Fay Lanphier, Miss America 1925, appeared in a Laurel and Hardy movie and in *The American Venus*, Patricia Donnelly (1939) appeared in the movie *Cover Girl*, Miss Dallas 1926 became movie star Joan Blondell, and Miss New Orleans 1935, Dorothy Lamour, swung to stardom in *The Jungle Princess*.

In 1937, the newly-crowned Miss America, Bette Cooper, ran off with her handsome chaperon only hours after her coronation. As officials and police frantically searched for the missing winner, photographers recorded the unprecedented scene. (The Miss America Organization)

In 1937, the Pageant made headlines again when the new Miss America, Bette Cooper, vanished after her crowning. When her disappearance was discovered the next morning, a statewide police search ensued. Soon, shocking rumors surfaced that Miss America had eloped with her pageant chaperon, Lou Off, a handsome, wealthy bachelor. With King Edward having abdicated the British throne months earlier to marry American divorcee Wallis Simpson, radio announcers conjectured that America's Queen had abdicated her throne for true love. The truth was less glamorous. Shocked to have won and unwilling to leave school to tour vaudeville, the reluctant queen and her parents conspired with her bachelor chaperon, who slipped her out of the hotel at 2 A.M. and stashed her on his cabin cruiser until he could quietly return her home the next day.

By the close of the 1930s, the nation was recovering from the Depression and movie newsreels enabled more than one hundred million people to watch the crowning of a Miss America for the first time. Despite some stumbles along the runway, the contest had survived the darkest decade of the century, hinting at the enduring popularity the event would achieve in the years to come.

Chilly Night Cheddar Cheese Soup

1 whole onion, chopped
1 green bell pepper, chopped
1 carrot, grated
1 stick butter
¼ cup all-purpose flour
4 cups low-fat, reduced-sodium chicken broth
3 cups grated low-fat Cheddar cheese
2 cups skim milk
Salt to taste
Freshly ground black pepper to taste
Fresh parsley, chopped

Cook the onion, pepper, and carrot in butter until limp. Stir in the flour. Add the broth and simmer for 5 minutes. Add the cheese, stirring until it all melts. Add the milk and seasonings. Heat through. Pour the soup into serving bowls and garnish with parsley. Yields 6 servings.

Note: Great served with a tossed salad and hot crusty rolls or bread sticks.

Cathy Burnham, Miss New Hampshire 1975

Beer-Cheese Soup

1 stick butter
1 cup all-purpose flour
2 14½-ounce cans chicken broth
1½ cups half and half
2 16-ounce jars Cheez Whiz
¾ cup warm beer
1 tablespoon Worcestershire sauce
½ cup minced chives
Popcorn for garnish

Melt the butter in a soup pot and add the flour. Heat for 4 minutes, stirring well. In a separate pan, heat the broth and slowly add the flour mixture. Stir until smooth. Slowly add the half and half. Add the Cheez Whiz, stirring well until smooth. Add the beer, Worcestershire sauce, and chives. Simmer and stir. Garnish with popcorn and serve immediately. Yields 10 servings.

Suzanne Bunker Jordheim, Miss Oregon 1977

A Crowning Comedy of Errors

When Marian Bergeron entered the 1933 Miss America Pageant as a fifteen-year-old, she was thrilled to make the final three. The pageant director rushed them backstage, where the winner was to change out of her swimsuit into a special gown and robe. One problem was that no one had informed Marian—nor told her she was the winner. When a male official ordered, "Take off your bathing suit. Hurry!" Marian gasped, crossed her arms over her chest, and scolded, "Absolutely not!" Noticing her fright, a hostess rushed to her side. "We're running out of time and she won't take her suit off," the official fumed, "and she's IT!" "That was how I learned I was Miss America," says Marian, chuckling. Some hostesses formed a human curtain and Bergeron dropped the swimsuit and slipped on the winner's gown and robe, "a magnificent red velvet robe the women of Atlantic City had hand-embroidered with sequins, stones, and fourteen-carat gold lace," she says. "I think Princess Di could have been married in it. They had four little pages carrying this huge train and when we got to the end of the runway the poor little fellas were like a bunch of puppies tripping over each other trying to turn it. It was hysterical! Then they put this gorgeous crown on me that was so large it slid down over my eyebrows. It looked like the littlest angel with the crown rakishly angled. It was a comedy of errors," she remembers, smiling, "but so beautiful."

The Last Contestant Left Standing Wins

In 1936, the pageant's dawn-to-midnight schedule was such a killer that contestants were dropping from exhaustion. During a bicycle parade on the Boardwalk, Miss Illinois fell off her bike and hurt her ankle, Miss Wilmington toppled into the crowd, and Miss Cincinnati was treated at the hospital after an exhausted contestant stomped on her foot and infected it. Poor Miss Kentucky simply laid her bike down and sobbed. "I know you're worn out, honey," consoled a chaperon. "I know it's hard, but you've got to learn to take it. It's part of the contest." "Oh, I can't," she cried. "I'm so tired of smiling." Reporters tattled that the schedule was so bad that one of the hostesses, a prominent judge's wife, "suffered a severe migraine from the strain" and her husband "sheepishly took over her duties." Fed up, the overworked beauties and their chaperons threatened to go on strike.

Curried Butternut Squash Soup

This soup is a good starter for a poultry meal, but we usually just serve it solo with a tossed green salad and crusty bread.

1 large or 2 small butternut squash, cut in half and seeded (about 3 pounds)
2 medium yellow onions, thinly sliced
2 tablespoons curry powder (or to taste)
2 tablespoons olive oil
1 49½-ounce can chicken broth
½ broth can water
Salt to taste

. . . .

Preheat oven to 450°. Place the squash, cut side down, on a foil-lined baking pan, add 1 inch of water and roast until tender, about 45 minutes. In the meantime, sauté the onions and curry powder in olive oil over very low heat in a large, heavyweight saucepan until the onion is soft and has absorbed the curry. Set aside. When the squash is tender, scrape off the skin, cut it into pieces, and add it to the onions along with any pan juices from roasting. Add the chicken broth, water, and salt. Simmer for 30 minutes to blend the flavors. Run the mixture through a food processor, purée with a blender, or mash with a potato masher, depending on the texture you prefer.

Note: You can add 1 cup half and half or yogurt if you prefer a creamier soup, but we like the low-fat version. Yields 6 to 8 servings.

Nancy Fleming, Miss America 1961

Chili

2 pounds ground beef
8½ cups water
¾ of an 8-ounce can Contadina tomato paste
1 15-ounce can dark red kidney beans (undrained)
1 tablespoon cocoa powder
1 tablespoon vinegar
1 tablespoon chili powder (more or omit to taste)
3 tablespoons cinnamon
3 tablespoons oregano
2 teaspoons allspice
1 teaspoon nutmeg
3 large stalks celery, diced
5 large onions, diced
1 whole head garlic, each clove diced
1 tablespoon sugar
1 tablespoon salt and 1 teaspoon freshly ground pepper, or to taste
5 large bay leaves

. . . .

Brown the ground beef in a large skillet with ½ cup of water, mashing with a fork so there are no clumps. Transfer the browned meat, including the water it was cooked in, to a heavy-

N. Rokos/C P News

Arrival. The "dream of a million girls" will become a reality for one of the fifty state titleholders who are all smiles as they arrive in Atlantic City.

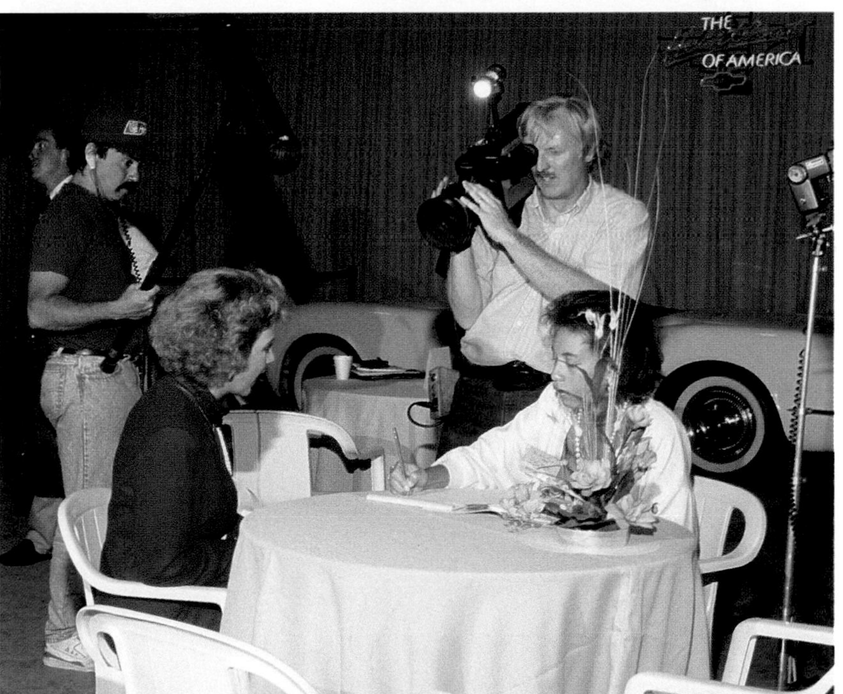

K. A. Frank/C P News

Meeting the Media. Behind the scenes at the Miss America Press Center, interviews with the national media are squeezed into the contestants' hectic schedules.

J.M. Frank/C P News

J.M. Frank/C P News

Words of Wisdom. New Jersey Governor Christie Whitman addresses the contestants during a rehearsal, noting, "You are true role models."

J.M. Frank/C P News

Rehearsals. Contestants soon discover that the Miss America Pageant is not all glamour. Tiring dawn-to-dusk rehearsals are a major part of the Pageant week experience.

Frank/C P News

Rehearsals. Days of tiring rehearsals eventually evolve into glamorous stage production numbers.

J. M. Frank/C P News

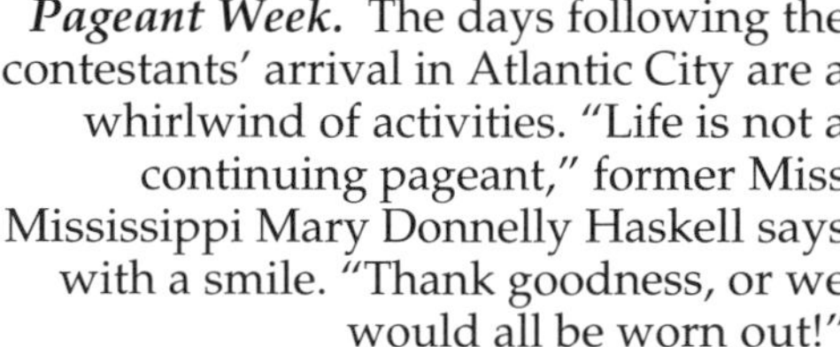

Pageant Week. The days following the contestants' arrival in Atlantic City are a whirlwind of activities. "Life is not a continuing pageant," former Miss Mississippi Mary Donnelly Haskell says with a smile. "Thank goodness, or we would all be worn out!"

J. M. Frank/C P News

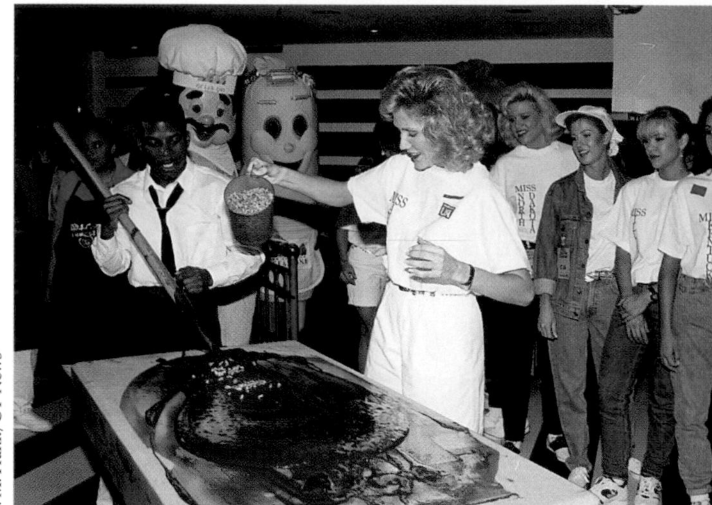

J. M. Frank/C P News

C P News

Irv Kaar

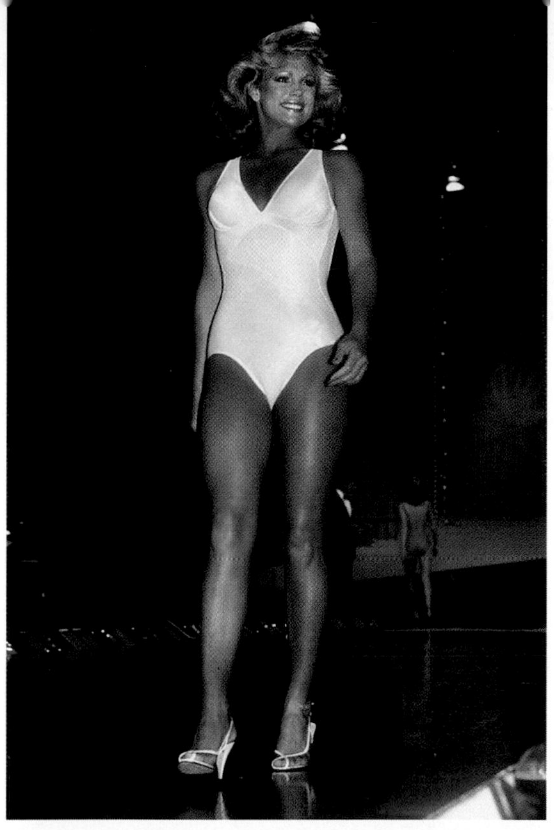

The Competitions Begin. The "Physical Fitness in Swimsuit" competition celebrates today's physically fit woman, as demonstrated by Mississippi's Susan Akin, who won both the swimsuit competition and the Miss America title.

J.M. Frank/C P News

The Judges. As competitions begin, the judges face the daunting task of awarding two hundred scores during interview, talent, evening wear, and swimsuit competitions. "You realize you are going to change somebody's life," says Marian McKnight Conway, a former Miss America and judge.

N. Rokos/C P News

Talent Competition. Talent is the most important competition, worth forty percent of the scoring. Leanza Cornett, Miss Florida, turns a winning vocal performance into the 1993 Miss America title. Soon after, she also received a contract with *Entertainment Tonight.*

N. Rokos/C P News

Swimsuit Competition. Contestants go Hawaiian during a 1992 swimsuit production number.

N. Rokos/C P News

Remarkable Achievement. Profoundly deaf since infancy, Heather Whitestone, Miss Alabama, performs a classical ballet to music she is unable to hear. She won the talent trophy and the 1995 Miss America title.

J.M. Frank/C P News

The Preliminaries End. The winners in talent and swimsuit competitions are announced at the conclusion of each night of preliminary competition. Miss America 1992, Carolyn Sapp, presents an evening's winners to the audience.

bottom pot along with the remaining ingredients. Cook for 1½ to 2 hours on medium heat. The chili should thicken by this time. Skim the grease off, if desired. Serve over spaghetti with grated Colby or Cheddar cheese and finely diced onions on top. Yields 6 to 8 servings.

Note: For the full effect of a "5-way," serve as follows: place the chili on a bed of spaghetti. Add diced onions, followed by a mound of grated cheese. Top off with Tabasco sauce.

Doris King Olson, Miss Illinois 1951

The "Real" Miss America?

In 1938, beautiful Miss California, Claire James, was passed over for the Miss America title because she wore too much eye makeup. Incensed at being named first runner-up, James quit the Pageant in protest, crying that the judges had "insulted" her. Her theatrical manager, Earl Carroll, denounced the judges as "incompetents" and took Claire to New York City the next day where he crowned her "The *Real* Miss America—The People's Choice." She toured the country thereafter as a "former Miss America," to the chagrin of pageant officials.

Miss Michigan's Homemade Chili

Good the first day, better the second day.

2 pounds ground beef
2 medium onions, chopped (about 1 cup)
1 cup chopped green bell pepper
1 cup diced celery
1 28-ounce can tomatoes
1 8-ounce can tomato sauce
1 46-ounce can tomato juice
2 teaspoons chili powder
1 teaspoon salt
¼ teaspoon cayenne pepper
¼ teaspoon paprika
1 15-ounce can kidney beans, drained

Cook the ground beef, onion, green pepper, and celery in a Dutch oven or large kettle until the meat is browned and the onion is tender. Drain off the fat and stir in the remaining ingredients except for the kidney beans. Heat to boiling. Reduce heat, cover, and simmer for 2 hours, stirring occasionally (or cook uncovered for 45 minutes). Stir in the beans, heat through. Yields 8 servings.

Denise Gehman, Miss Michigan 1983

Nebraska "Big Red" Chili

When someone thinks of Nebraska, farming and football usually come to mind. My husband was a Cornhusker football player as well as an NFL player. This recipe has been a huge success at many a football party.

2 pounds ground beef or turkey
4 tablespoons chili powder
4 tablespoons all-purpose flour
2 tablespoons sugar
4 teaspoons onion salt
2 16-ounce cans tomato sauce
1 cup ketchup
1 cup water
1 16-ounce can chili beans

Brown the meat and drain. Combine the chili powder, flour, sugar, and salt together and add to the meat. Add the tomato sauce, ketchup, water, and beans. Bring to a slow boil and simmer for 2 hours. Great served with cheese and cheese taco chips. Yields 10 to 15 servings.

Alison Lenee Boyd Traynowicz, Miss Nebraska 1984

A Model Scandal

During the heyday of Hollywood, pretty sales clerk Henrietta Leaver was crowned Miss America 1935. Assuming she would become the Pageant's first film star, reporters dubbed her "the million dollar baby from the five-and-ten cent store." She made headlines all right. A week later a sculptor unveiled a nude statue she had posed for earlier, neglecting to mention that she had worn a modest swimsuit and had her granny chaperoning. Nevertheless tainted by scandal and her hopes for screen stardom dashed, Miss America eloped with her boyfriend.

Chicken Corn Soup

1 3- to 4-pound chicken
3 quarts cold water
2 teaspoons salt
2 cups uncooked noodles
1 20-ounce can white shoepeg corn, undrained
2 tablespoons chopped parsley
⅛ teaspoon pepper
2 hard-boiled eggs, chopped

. . . .

Cook the chicken slowly in the water and salt until tender. Remove the chicken; reserve the broth. Remove the meat from the bones and chop fine. Add the noodles to the simmering broth and cook until soft. Add the corn, chicken, and parsley. Season with pepper and additional salt to taste. Simmer for several minutes. Add the chopped eggs before serving. Soup can be refrigerated and reheated. Yields 8 to 10 servings.

Lynne Grote Tully, Miss Pennsylvania 1977

King's Arms Tavern Cream of Peanut Soup

1 medium onion, chopped
2 ribs celery, chopped
½ stick butter
1 tablespoon all-purpose flour
2 quarts chicken stock (or canned chicken broth)
1 cup smooth peanut butter
2 cups light cream
Chopped peanuts

. . . .

Sauté the onion and celery in butter until soft, but not brown. Stir in the flour until well blended. Add the chicken stock, stir constantly, and bring to a boil. Remove from heat and rub through a sieve. Add the peanut butter and cream, stirring to blend. Return to low heat. Heat through; do not boil. Yields 10 to 12 servings.

Nancy Glisson, Miss Virginia 1993

Pumpkin Soup

Although I've lived in California for fifteen years, I still feel nostalgic each autumn, as I remember crunchy leaves under my feet and a nip in the air—this recipe celebrates that glorious time of year I love so dearly—autumn! This delicious autumn soup can be served in a hollowed-out pumpkin.

2 pumpkins, 1 large and 1 medium
2 medium onions, chopped
2 tablespoons butter
1 tablespoon all-purpose flour
3 cups chicken broth
½ teaspoon nutmeg
½ teaspoon ginger
1 cup heavy cream
Freshly ground pepper to taste
Nutmeg to taste

. . . .

Set aside the large pumpkin...it will be your serving bowl! Cut the medium pumpkin in half and throw away the seeds and strings. Cut the pumpkin in pieces. Steam until tender. Let the pieces cool then scrape the pumpkin away from its shell. Set aside 3 cups of the mashed pumpkin. In a large saucepan, sauté the onions in butter until tender. Sprinkle in the flour and cook for 2 to 3 minutes. Gradually stir in the chicken broth, add the 3 cups of mashed pumpkin, and cook on low for 15 minutes. Add the spices and let cool. In batches, purée the soup in a blender or food processor until smooth. Return the mixture to the saucepan and add the cream. Heat but do not boil. Refrigerate until ready to serve. When ready, cut off the top of the large pumpkin and scrape out the insides. Pour the reheated soup into the pumpkin; sprinkle with pepper and nutmeg, before serving. Yields 8 servings.

Jean Ahern Lubin, Miss Illinois 1974

Potato-Sausage Soup

1 pound sausage
1 tablespoon sausage drippings
1 cup chopped onion
½ cup chopped celery
4 cups diced potatoes
1 tablespoon garlic powder or 1 clove fresh garlic
1 teaspoon sage
1 10½-ounce can chicken broth
2 cups water
1 cup milk
1 small can green beans

. . . .

Brown the sausage in a large skillet. Drain and reserve 1 tablespoon of the drippings. Remove the sausage from the skillet and set aside. In the same skillet, return the drippings and add the onions, celery, potatoes, garlic powder, and sage. Cook until the onions are lightly browned. Transfer the contents of the skillet to a soup pot. Add the chicken broth and water. Boil until the potatoes are done. Remove 2 cups of the potatoes and mash them, then return them to the pot. Add the milk, green beans, sausage, salt, and pepper. Heat through, then serve. Yields 4 servings.

Holly Jan Mayer, Miss Massachusetts 1983

Homestead Potato Soup

This recipe is a spirited version of the soup I ate as a child about once a week on my grandfather's Mohler, Idaho, homestead. Its only ingredients were potatoes, onion, butter, and milk, which, of course, were produced on the farm. The town of Mohler has disappeared, but nearby is Nezperce, a town named for famous Native Americans.

1 10¾-ounce can cream of tomato soup
1 10¾-ounce can Cheddar cheese soup
1 10¾-ounce can cream of celery soup
1 4-ounce can mushroom pieces
3 to 5 soup cans water (reconstituted nonfat dry milk may be used)
1 medium onion, chopped
5 or 6 medium new potatoes, chopped with skins on
Chopped celery to taste
Salt and pepper to taste
Parsley (or other herbs) to taste

. . . .

Combine all of the ingredients in a large pot and simmer until the potatoes and celery are soft. Serve with crusty bread and a green salad for a "homey" meal. Yields 8 servings.

Phyllis Ralstin Goecke, Miss Idaho 1951

Black Bean Soup

2 cups uncooked black beans
1 ham hock or cube of salt pork
6 slices bacon, chopped
1 large onion, chopped
2 bay leaves
Salt and pepper to taste
1 large onion, chopped
1 large green bell pepper, chopped
1 clove garlic
½ cup olive oil
Dry Sack sherry
Hot cooked rice
Chopped onion

. . . .

Place the first 6 ingredients in a large soup pot. Cover with water and cook until tender, about 2 hours. Sauté the second onion, the green pepper, and the garlic in the olive oil. When tender, add them to the beans along with 2 teaspoons of Dry Sack sherry per person. Serve over rice. Top with chopped onion. Yields 6 to 8 servings.

Faye Myers, Miss North Carolina Pageant

Pageant Week Soup

2 cups Great Northern beans
1 cup black beans
6 cups water
2 pounds smoked ham hocks
2 large carrots, grated
¼ teaspoon onion powder
½ teaspoon pepper
1 large onion, chopped
1 teaspoon garlic powder
¼ teaspoon marjoram
½ teaspoon thyme
1 8-ounce can tomato sauce or ½ cup ketchup
10 or 12 mushrooms, sliced

. . . .

Soak the beans overnight in water. Drain the beans and add 5 cups of water. Cook on high in a Crock Pot® for 8 hours. After the first hour, add the remaining ingredients. Yields 6 to 8 servings.

Jeanne Peterson, Miss Oregon Pageant and Miss California Pageant

Sherried Cream of Carrot Soup

2 cups chicken broth
1 cup peeled, sliced carrots
½ cup diced onion
½ cup diced celery
6 tablespoons cooked rice
Salt to taste
Freshly ground pepper to taste
Few grains of cayenne pepper
1 cup heavy cream
4 tablespoons pale dry sherry
1 cup sliced cooked carrots
Parsley sprigs for garnish

. . . .

Combine the broth, carrots, onion, and celery in a medium saucepan. Bring to boil over high heat. Reduce heat, cover, and simmer for 15 to 20 minutes, or until the vegetables are tender. Transfer the broth to a blender, add the rice, salt, pepper, and cayenne. Pulse until blended. Add the cream and pulse again until the mixture is smooth. Stir in the sherry and cooked carrot slices. Garnish each serving with a small sprig of parsley. Serve hot. Yields 8 servings.

Victoria Longley, Miss New York Pageant

Spinach Soup

4 tablespoons butter or margarine
½ cup chopped onion
½ cup thinly sliced celery
3 tablespoons unsifted all-purpose flour
1½ tablespoons salt
½ teaspoon pepper
1 quart skim milk
1 cup chopped spinach, cooked and drained

Melt the butter in a large saucepan. Sauté the onion and celery until tender. Blend in the flour, salt, and pepper; cook until bubbly. Remove the pan from the heat. Gradually stir in the skim milk. Return to the heat. Cook, stirring constantly, until the mixture comes to a boil. Add the spinach; simmer for 2 to 3 minutes longer. Yields 4 servings.

Judith Ford Nash, Miss America 1969

Wild Rice Soup

The state of Minnesota has always been well known for its flavorful wild rice. The Indians raised and harvested it for many years and it is still loved and enjoyed by all Minnesotans. When I was living in California this soup recipe was given to me by good friends who had come out to visit. They were native Minnesotans and thought perhaps I would like a taste of home. They were right—I did!

½ cup wild rice
1½ cups water
¾ cup chopped celery
1 cup chopped onion
⅓ cup chopped green bell pepper
3 tablespoons bacon drippings
2 14½-ounce cans low-sodium chicken broth
½ cup fresh mushrooms, lightly sautéed
3 10¾-ounce cans cream of mushroom soup
1 pound bacon, fried and chopped

Wash the wild rice, then boil it for 15 minutes. Drain and set aside. Sauté the celery, onion, and pepper in the drippings until the onions are clear. Pour into a large kettle, then add the rice, broth, mushrooms, soup, and bacon. Cook on low heat for 1 to 1½ hours. Stir occasionally to prevent burning. No additional seasoning is required. Yields 8 to 10 servings.

Juliana G. Gabor, Miss Minnesota 1970

Cold Cherry Soup

Michigan is noted for being the largest grower of sour cherries in the USA.

2 cans sour cherries, puréed in a blender
Juice from the cherries plus water to make 1 quart
1 stick cinnamon
½ teaspoon salt
¼ cup all-purpose flour
½ cup cold water
1 cup sour cream
¼ cup sherry (optional)

Bring the first 4 ingredients to a boil and simmer 10 to 15 minutes. Remove the cinnamon. Combine the flour with the cold water. Slowly add the flour to the cherry mixture, stirring constantly until thickened slightly. Simmer 5 more minutes. Chill. Whisk in the sour cream and sherry just before serving. Yields 6 servings.

Victoria Fair, Miss Michigan 1990

Excellent Cold Salad

3 bunches broccoli florets
1 medium red onion
1 cup sour cream
1 cup mayonnaise
¼ cup sugar

. . . .

Cut the broccoli florets into small pieces. Next, thinly slice the red onion and then chop it. Combine the sour cream, mayonnaise, and sugar. Toss the broccoli pieces and chopped onion with the sour cream mixture. Yields 8 to 10 servings.

BeBe Shopp Waring, Miss America 1948

Italiano Rotini Salad

½ of a 1-pound package rotini pasta
1 cup sliced fresh mushrooms
1 cup thinly sliced pepperoni
½ cup julienned Cheddar cheese strips
½ cup sliced olives (green or black)
3 large green onions, sliced
½ cup extra virgin olive oil
⅓ cup red wine vinegar
1 teaspoon Italian seasoning
½ teaspoon garlic powder
½ teaspoon salt
¼ teaspoon pepper

. . . .

Prepare the rotini pasta according to package directions, drain. Combine the rotini and the next 5 ingredients. Blend the olive oil, vinegar, Italian seasoning, garlic powder, salt, and pepper. Toss the dressing with the salad mixture. Garnish as desired. Serve immediately or cover and chill. Refrigerate leftovers. Yields 6 to 8 side dish servings or 3 to 4 main dish servings.

Joni McMechan Checchia, Miss Indiana 1988

Seven Layer Salad

A few years ago, my husband Bruce and I decided to publish a family cookbook. Included in the book was a family history section, a family tree, and a wonderful collection of recipes from every family member. As the years pass, it is fun to try Grandma's recipe or cousin Joe's and to have this book to refer to. This recipe came from that book, the salad being a favorite with my children and stepson. Family and all the things that keep us together are most important to me.

1 head lettuce, shredded
½ cup celery, chopped
½ green bell pepper, chopped
½ cup chopped onion
1 10-ounce package frozen peas, cooked and drained
2 cups mayonnaise (can substitute Miracle Whip Lite)
2 tablespoons sugar
1 cup Cheddar cheese, shredded
¼ cup bacon bits or crumbled bacon

. . . .

Layer the first 5 ingredients in a bowl in the order listed. Combine the mayonnaise and sugar and spread them over top. Sprinkle the shredded cheese and bacon bits over the mayonnaise mixture. Cover with plastic wrap and refrigerate 24 hours. (This can be refrigerated for less time if necessary.) Yields 8 to 10 servings.

Jeannette Ardell Dammeyer, Miss Georgia 1958

Pasta Salad with Peanuts

I make this recipe often to take on picnics (no mayo!) and it's good at room temperature!

2 cups bow-tie pasta (or substitute any shape)
½ head Chinese cabbage, chopped
1 small red bell pepper, diced
4 green onions, sliced
½ cup peanut butter

¼ cup rice wine vinegar
3 tablespoons soy sauce
2 tablespoons honey
1 tablespoon sesame oil
Cayenne pepper to taste
¾ cup dry roasted, unsalted peanuts

Cook the pasta. Drain and rinse with cold water. Combine the pasta, cabbage, red pepper, and green onions. Toss well. In a separate bowl, combine the peanut butter, vinegar, soy sauce, honey, and sesame oil, and mix until smooth. Add cayenne pepper, if desired. Pour the dressing over the salad, add the peanuts, and toss well. Yields 4 servings.

Meredith Auld Brokaw, Miss South Dakota 1959

Oriental Cabbage Salad

1 small head cabbage, diced (about 1 pound)
1 can mandarin oranges, drained
1 package Ramen noodles, broken (no seasoning)
1 package slivered almonds, toasted
2 tablespoons sesame seeds

Dressing
½ cup vegetable oil
¼ cup rice vinegar
⅓ cup sugar

Combine the cabbage and oranges. Combine the dressing ingredients and pour over the cabbage. Just before serving, toss with the noodles, almonds, and sesame seeds. Yields 8 to 10 servings.

Stephanie Fisher, Miss North Dakota 1992

King Neptune and the 1938 contestants congratulate the new Miss America, Marilyn Meseke, an Ohio dance instructor whose grand prize was a "deluxe Hollywood screen test." (The Miss America Organization)

Bean and Cilantro Salad

2 16-ounce cans black beans
1 16-ounce can pinto beans
1 16-ounce can white beans
1 16-ounce can corn
1 sweet onion, chopped
½ bunch cilantro, chopped
½ carton cherry tomatoes, halved
1 small bottle of fat-free honey Dijon dressing

Drain and rinse the beans and corn. Add the onion, cilantro, and tomatoes. Toss with the dressing and refrigerate for several hours. Yields 10 to 12 servings.

Cheryl Couch Biegert, Miss Idaho 1966

Bacon-Broccoli Salad

1 to 2 heads broccoli with stalks
2 tablespoons chopped onion
⅔ cup raisins
1 pound bacon, fried crisp and crumbled

Dressing
1 cup mayonnaise
½ cup sugar
3 tablespoons vinegar

. . . .

Shave the stalks of the broccoli until only the tender part is left. Slice the stalks and cut the head into bite-size pieces. Mix in the onion, raisins, and bacon. Combine the dressing ingredients and pour them over the salad ingredients. Mix well. Yields 6 to 8 servings.

Keri Baumgardner Schroeder, Miss Alaska 1992

Hot or Cold Seafood Salad

1 8-ounce can water chestnuts, sliced
1 6-ounce can crab meat, drained and rinsed
1 4-ounce can sliced mushrooms
1 4-ounce package sliced almonds
2 cups diced celery
4 hard-boiled eggs, sliced
1 medium onion, chopped
1 teaspoon salt
1 teaspoon paprika
1 pint Hellman's mayonnaise

. . . .

Combine all of the ingredients in a mixing bowl. Place in the refrigerator overnight. Bring salad to room temperature for 2 hours before baking. Preheat oven to 350°. Bake for 30 minutes or serve chilled (unbaked). Yields 8 to 10 servings.

Nancy Volkert, Miss New York State Pageant

Potato Bacon Salad

3 pounds Idaho red potatoes, cut into ¼-inch slices with the skins, boiled until firm-tender, and cooled
1 1-pound package lean bacon, cut into 1-inch pieces and fried until crisp
1 pound fresh green beans, cooked until firm-tender

Dressing
½ cup olive oil
¼ cup tarragon-flavored vinegar
½ cup chopped green onions
¼ cup fresh chopped parsley
1 garlic clove, crushed or chopped
1 teaspoon salt
½ teaspoon dry mustard
½ teaspoon sweet basil
½ teaspoon tarragon
Pepper to taste

. . . .

Toss the potatoes, bacon, and green beans in a large bowl. Combine the dressing ingredients and shake well. Pour the dressing over room temperature salad ingredients and serve. Do not refrigerate before serving. Yields 8 to 10 servings.

Karen Herd Talbot, Miss Idaho 1971

Chef's Old World Recipe for Cole Slaw

1 medium-large head cabbage
Salt (optional)
2 carrots
1 large green bell pepper (optional)
½ cup water
½ cup vinegar
½ cup sugar

. . . .

Grate the cabbage and place it on a kitchen towel. Sprinkle with a little salt, if desired, and roll the towel up tight. Place the towel on a dish and refrigerate. Next morning, wring out the towel, then place the cabbage in a bowl. Grate in the carrots and green pepper. Bring the water, vinegar, and sugar to a boil. Pour the dressing over the slaw. Spoon the slaw into a large jar, cap it, and turn it over once or twice, then refrigerate. Yields 4 to 6 servings.

Mona Crawford-Shick, Miss Delaware 1943

Mushroom Salad

3 pounds mushrooms
1 cup water
Juice of 1 lemon
1 teaspoon salt
1 large onion, chopped
2 celery stalks, chopped
1 tablespoon chopped parsley
½ teaspoon garlic powder
¼ teaspoon oregano
¼ teaspoon pepper
1 4-ounce jar green olives with pimiento, sliced
1 8-ounce bottle Zesty Italian dressing

. . . .

Wash and slice the mushrooms. Cover them with the water, lemon juice, and the salt. Bring to a boil, then drain immediately. Add the next 7 ingredients and mix well. Cover with Italian dressing. Marinate overnight. Yields 8 servings.

Cathy Lawton Reilly, Miss Delaware 1972

Summer Cantaloupe Chicken Salad

1 whole chicken, boiled and cut into bite-size pieces
2 small cantaloupes, cubed
1 cup chopped celery
⅓ cup slivered almonds
½ cup mayonnaise
2 cans mandarin oranges, drained, juice reserved
2 tablespoons finely chopped crystallized ginger

. . . .

Combine the cubed chicken, cantaloupe, celery, and almonds in a bowl. Combine the mayonnaise with the reserved mandarin juice and ginger. Toss the dressing with the chicken mixture. Chill. Serve in a hollowed-out cantaloupe or on a bed of lettuce leaves. Yields 4 servings.

Dawn Wells, Miss Nevada 1959

Carrot Salad

1 16-ounce package carrots
1 onion
1 small green bell pepper
1 cup sugar
¼ cup vegetable oil
1 10¾-ounce can tomato soup, undiluted
½ cup vinegar

. . . .

Slice the carrots like pennies and cook until tender. Dice the onion and pepper. Combine with the remaining ingredients and pour over the carrots. Chill overnight. Yields 8 servings.

Debra Barnes Miles, Miss America 1968

During the 1930s, elasticized fabrics revolutionized swimwear and baggy bathing dresses were abandoned for the figure-hugging design, modeled by Marilyn Meseke, Miss America 1938. The runner-up from California that year was so insulted at losing, she left for New York City where a promoter crowned her "The Real Miss America—the People's Choice." (The Miss America Organization)

Taboule Salad

This recipe is for a healthful, low-calorie appetizer/salad, which is a favorite of our customers at Charmaine's French Bakery Café in State College, Pennsylvania.

1 cup bulgur wheat, cracked or whole grain
2 cups boiling water
2 tomatoes, cut into 1/4-inch cubes and strained of juice
6 to 8 scallions, chopped
1 cup chopped fresh parsley
3 tablespoons chopped fresh mint (or 2 tablespoons dried tarragon)
¼ cup chopped carrots

Dressing

¼ cup fresh lemon juice
2 tablespoons olive oil
½ teaspoon salt
¼ teaspoon fresh ground black pepper (or ¼ teaspoon char-broiled seasoning)
¼ teaspoon cumin
¼ teaspoon oregano

Garnish (optional)

10 to 12 black olives
1 cucumber, chopped
1 tomato, chopped

Soak the bulgur in boiling water for approximately 1 hour, or until the water is absorbed. Place the bulgur into a strainer and press out the excess water. Return to the bowl. Add the remaining salad ingredients and mix well. Combine all of the dressing ingredients in a separate bowl. Add the dressing mixture to the bulgur and toss thoroughly. Garnish with black olives, cucumber, and tomatoes. Serve chilled. Yields 6 to 8 servings.

Note: For best results, combine the bulgur and dressing no less than 1 hour before serving.

Charmaine Kowalski Rapaport, Miss Pennsylvania 1978

Oriental Chicken Salad

4 chicken breast halves, cooked and cubed
1 head lettuce, broken into bite-size pieces
4 tablespoons thinly sliced green onions
1 3-ounce package Chinese noodles
1 4-ounce package slivered almonds
1 teaspoon toasted sesame seeds

Dressing

4 tablespoons sugar
1 teaspoon salt
½ teaspoon pepper
4 tablespoons white vinegar
½ cup vegetable oil

Combine the chicken with lettuce, onions, noodles, almonds, and sesame seeds in a serving bowl. To make the dressing, combine the sugar, salt, pepper, and white vinegar. Gradually whisk in the oil until the mixture is well blended. Pour the dressing over the salad just before serving. Yields 6 servings.

Penny Tichenor Anthony, Miss Indiana 1974

Spinach and Bacon Salad

2 pounds spinach
1 head iceberg lettuce
½ pound bacon, fried and drained
1½ cups large-curd cottage cheese

Dressing

¼ cup sugar
1 teaspoon salt
1 teaspoon dry mustard
1 tablespoon onion juice
⅓ cup cider vinegar
1 cup vegetable oil
1 tablespoon poppy seeds

Wash, drain, and tear the spinach and lettuce into bite-sized pieces. Combine the two in a large bowl. Crumble the bacon and add to greens. Combine the dressing ingredients and mix well. Toss ½ of the dressing into the greens. Mix the cottage cheese into the remaining dressing and add it to the greens. Yields 6 to 8 servings.

Evelyn Ay Sempier, Miss America 1954

Golden Crown Tangy Yellow Squash Salad

5 medium yellow squash, julienned
½ cup finely chopped celery
½ cup finely chopped green bell pepper
½ cup finely chopped green onions
½ teaspoon salt
½ teaspoon pepper
2 tablespoons wine vinegar
⅔ cup cider vinegar
⅓ cup extra light pure olive oil
½ cup sugar
1 clove garlic, crushed

Combine all of the ingredients and let marinate in the refrigerator for 12 hours before serving. Drain. Form a crown on a bed of lettuce, decorate with parsley.

Note: Be sure to have many copies of this recipe on hand, as every guest will demand a copy. Yields 8 servings.

Dorothy M. Erinakes, Miss Rhode Island 1937

Szechuan Chicken Pasta Salad

This has been a hit wherever I have served it.
It has an "Asian-West Coast" taste,
and is especially healthy when made with
nonfat mayonnaise.

2 whole chicken breasts
1 pound thin mein Chinese noodles or spaghetti
¾ cup soy sauce, divided
¼ cup peanut oil
1½ cups nonfat mayonnaise
1 tablespoon Dijon-style mustard
¼ cup oriental-style sesame oil
2 tablespoons Szechuan chili oil (or to taste)
6 green onions, thinly sliced
2 carrots, peeled and coarsely chopped
1 red bell pepper, coarsely chopped
1 8-ounce can sliced bamboo shoots, drained
1 6-ounce jar miniature corn on the cob, drained and thickly sliced
½ cup chopped fresh cilantro
½ pound fresh snow peas, trimmed, julienned, and blanched until crisp-tender, then cooled in ice water and drained
Fresh coriander (cilantro) sprigs
Lightly toasted sesame seeds

. . . .

Skin, bone, and halve the chicken breasts. Poach and cool. Cut into bite-size pieces and reserve. Cook the noodles in 4 quarts of boiling water until very *al dente*. Drain and toss in a large bowl with ½ cup soy sauce, then the peanut oil. Cool to room temperature, occasionally stirring the noodles to coat thoroughly. Combine the mayonnaise with the mustard, sesame oil, the remaining ¼ cup soy sauce, and chili oil to taste. Refrigerate until ready to use. Add the chicken, green onions, carrots, red pepper, bamboo shoots, miniature corn, and chopped cilantro to the noodles. Mix gently, but thoroughly with hands. Add the reserved mayonnaise mixture and blend well. Cover and refrigerate until ready to serve, preferably overnight. About 30 minutes before serving time, remove the noodle mixture from the refrigerator and toss in the julienned snow peas, adding a little extra soy sauce and peanut oil or mayonnaise if the noodles seem dry. Garnish with cilantro sprigs and sesame seeds. To toast the sesame seeds, place them in a small heavy frying pan over moderate heat. Stir until the seeds are golden. Remove from heat and pour onto a plate to cool. Pass additional soy sauce and chili oil at the table. Yields 6 main course servings or 10 to 12 salad servings.

Note: The flavor of the dish improves from an overnight chilling, but wait until the last minute to add the crunchy snow peas. Please be very generous with the chili oil; cold noodles can take a lot of heat.

Kris Coleman, Miss New York 1974

Marinated Vegetable Salad

1 cup canned or frozen artichoke hearts, cooked and cut into large bite-size pieces
1 16-ounce can diced carrots, drained
1 16-ounce can LeSueur peas, drained
1 16-ounce can sliced green beans, drained
1½ cups cooked cauliflower, cut into large bite-size pieces
½ cup diced onion
½ cup diced celery

Dressing

¾ cup low-fat mayonnaise
¼ cup chili sauce
1 teaspoon salt
1 tablespoon lemon juice
2 teaspoons dried dill weed

. . . .

Drain the artichoke hearts and add to the other vegetables. Combine the dressing ingredients and pour over the vegetables. Yields 12 to 15 servings.

Georgia Taggart Brackett, Miss New Hampshire 1963

Tasty Green Salad

1 small head lettuce, shredded
1 16-ounce bag frozen green peas, thawed
1 medium red onion, chopped
1 cup shredded Swiss cheese
1 cup crumbled bacon
1 cup mayonnaise
½ teaspoon sugar
½ teaspoon curry powder

Layer all of the ingredients in a bowl in the order listed. Marinate in the refrigerator overnight. Serve with garlic bread. Yields 8 to 10 servings.

Note: To make garlic bread put pats of butter onto diced French or Italian bread. Sprinkle with garlic powder, garlic salt, oregano, and Romano cheese. Bake at 400° until golden.

Kylene Barker, Miss America 1979

Garden Rice Salad

1 6-ounce package long grain and wild rice mix
½ cup mayonnaise
¼ cup plain yogurt
1 cup sliced celery
1 cup cubed tomato
½ cup diced cucumber
2 tablespoons chopped parsley
⅛ teaspoon salt
⅛ teaspoon pepper
¼ cup sunflower seeds

Prepare the rice as directed but omit any butter or margarine. Cool. Toss lightly with the next 8 ingredients. Cover and chill. Garnish with sunflower seeds. Yields 3 or 4 servings (4½ cups).

Terry Meeuwsen Friedrich, Miss America 1973

The Definitive Caesar

This recipe can be made at the table for a festive gourmet treat. The original recipe came from a famous restaurant in Columbus, Ohio—The Kahiki—which was my favorite place to go when celebrating a special event or achievement.

2 cloves garlic
3 to 5 anchovies (or to taste)
⅓ cup olive oil
2 eggs
½ cup freshly grated Parmesan cheese
3 tablespoons fresh lemon juice
Freshly ground pepper to taste
1 tablespoon prepared mustard
3 quarts romaine lettuce, torn apart
Homemade French bread herbed croutons
½ cup butter, melted
½ cup crumbled bleu cheese

Rub the inside of a wooden bowl with the garlic cloves then mince them. Mash the anchovies in the bowl, add the olive oil, eggs, Parmesan cheese, lemon juice, pepper, and prepared mustard. Blend well. Toss in the Romaine lettuce. Toss in the homemade croutons, and top with crumbled bleu cheese. Yields 4 to 6 servings.

Note: Homemade croutons are made by cubing French bread and tossing the cubes in a pan with ½ cup melted butter seasoned with your favorite herbs. Brown slightly, then place on a cookie sheet and sprinkle with Parmesan cheese. Bake at 200° for 15 minutes or until toasted and crispy.

Laurel Schaefer, Miss America 1972

Warm Chicken Waldorf

4 5-ounce Teriyaki CHICKEN BY GEORGE® chicken breasts
¾ cup unsweetened apple juice
1 tablespoon cornstarch
2 red apples, coarsely chopped with the peel still on
1 cup sliced celery
3 tablespoons raisins
1 tablespoon sliced green onion

Cook the chicken in a skillet according to the package directions. Remove and keep warm. Combine the apple juice and cornstarch and pour it into the skillet. Bring the juice to a boil; boil and stir for 1 minute. Stir in the remaining ingredients and heat thoroughly. Top each chicken breast with the sauce. Yields 4 servings.

Phyllis George, Miss America 1971

Hot Chicken Salad

4 cups chopped, cooked chicken
2 10¾-ounce cans cream of chicken soup
2 cups chopped celery
1 cup slivered almonds
1 teaspoon salt
1 teaspoon pepper
1 cup mayonnaise
2 cans sliced water chestnuts, rinsed and drained
1½ cups grated Cheddar cheese
Crumbled potato chips

Cook chicken in salt water and chop into bite-size pieces. Preheat the oven to 350°. Combine all of the ingredients, except chips, in a 9 x 12-inch casserole dish. Sprinkle potato chip crumbs on top and bake until hot and bubbly, about 45 minutes. Yields: 10 to 12 servings.

Phyllis George, Miss America 1971

Lemon Herb Wild Rice Salad

3 5-ounce Lemon Herb CHICKEN BY GEORGE® chicken breasts, cooked and cut into strips
2 cups cooked wild rice
½ cup chopped carrots
½ cup coarsely chopped pecans
½ cup golden raisins
3 tablespoons olive oil
2 tablespoons sherry wine vinegar
1 garlic clove, minced
1 tablespoon finely chopped chives

Combine the first 5 ingredients in a large bowl. Combine the remaining ingredients in a small jar. Cover and shake vigorously. Pour the dressing over the chicken mixture and mix well. Yields 4 to 6 servings.

Phyllis George, Miss America 1971

Cranberry Tokay Salad

2 3-ounce boxes lime-flavored gelatin, dissolved according to package directions
1 16-ounce can whole-berry cranberry sauce
3 apples, thinly cut (2 with peel, 1 without peel)
3 oranges, peeled and cut up
1½ pounds tokay grapes, seeded and halved
½ cup chopped nuts

Combine all of the ingredients and chill in the refrigerator until firmly jelled. Yields 20 servings.

Nonnie Maffett, Mother of Debbie Maffett, Miss America 1983

Strawberry Salad

1 family-size package strawberry gelatin
2 cups boiling water
1 large can crushed pineapple, drained
1 16-ounce box frozen strawberries
3 small bananas
1 8-ounce carton sour cream

Dissolve the gelatin in the boiling water. Add the pineapple, strawberries, and bananas. Mix well. Put half of the mixture in the refrigerator and chill until set. Leave the remaining half of the mixture out. When the gelatin in the refrigerator has set, take it out and spread the sour cream over top. Add the remaining gelatin and chill until firm, about 1 hour. Yields 16 servings.

Shirley Cothran Barret, Miss America 1975

Mandarin Orange Salad

1 pound fresh spinach
2 heads Boston lettuce
2 avocados, peeled and cut into wedges
1 11-ounce can mandarin oranges, drained
1 Bermuda onion, thinly sliced

Dressing

1 cup vegetable oil
½ cup sugar
⅓ cup vinegar
1 tablespoon dry mustard
2 green onions, sliced

Combine the salad ingredients in a large bowl. Pour the oil, sugar, vinegar, and mustard in a blender; blend thoroughly. Stir in the green onions. Chill and pour over salad ingredients. Yields 8 to 10 servings.

Terry Meeuwsen Friedrich, Miss America 1973

Low-Cal Strawberry Salad

1 3-ounce box sugar-free strawberry gelatin
1 cup boiling water
2 small cans crushed, drained pineapple
1½ cups freshly sliced strawberries
3 bananas, mashed
1 cup chopped pecans
1 3-ounce package "lite" cream cheese, softened to room temperature

Dissolve the gelatin in 1 cup of boiling water. Add the fruit and nuts. Pour ½ of the mixture into a bowl and chill until firm. After the mixture has set, spread the cream cheese on top and add the remaining gelatin mixture. Chill until firm. Yields 4 servings.

Marlesa Ball Greiner, Miss Georgia 1986

Fantastic Fruit Salad

This is a great meal on a hot day or if you are dieting.

1 golden apple
1 peach
1 banana
¼ cup walnuts, chopped
½ cup peach yogurt (or your favorite)
1 teaspoon sugar or sugar substitute
1 teaspoon cinnamon
1 melon (any variety)

Chop all of the fruits into small bite-size pieces. Combine all ingredients, except melon, and mix until all the fruit is covered by the yogurt. Chill for 1 hour. Slice the chilled melon in half, scoop out the seeds, and fill with the fruit salad. Yields 1 to 2 servings.

Note: Use your own favorite fruits.

Melissa Aggeles, Miss Florida 1988

Blueberry Lemon Mold

1½ packages of lemon-flavored gelatin
¾ cup hot water
1 cup sour cream
¼ teaspoon vanilla extract
1 16-ounce can blueberries, with syrup reserved
Lemon drops, crushed

Dissolve ½ package of gelatin in ¾ cup hot water. Let cool. Add the sour cream and vanilla extract. Beat until fluffy and creamy. Pour into a 1 quart ring mold to set. Measure the blueberry syrup and add water to make 2 cups. Heat to boiling and add 1 package lemon gelatin. Chill; when the gelatin is beginning to set, add the blueberries and pour the mixture on top of the jelled sour cream mixture in the mold. Chill until firm. To serve, invert the mold onto a platter and sprinkle with crushed lemon drops. They lend not only a tartness, but a beautiful sparkle. Yields 6 to 8 servings.

Kay Taylor Sherk, Miss Iowa 1955

The White Glove Treatment . . .

By the end of the 1930s a disgruntled talent scout at the Miss America Pageant complained to *Holiday* magazine, "I'm telling you, culture and respectability have ruined the Miss America Pageant!"

Cinnamon Applesauce Salad

½ cup cinnamon red hots
1 cup boiling water
1 3-ounce package lemon-flavored gelatin
1 8-ounce package cream cheese, softened to room temperature
½ cup mayonnaise
1½ cups applesauce
½ cup finely chopped pecans (optional)

Stir the red hots in the boiling water until dissolved. (Or microwave for about 5 minutes.) Add the gelatin and stir until dissolved. Cream together the mayonnaise and cream cheese until mixed well. Add the cream cheese mixture and applesauce to the gelatin mixture and stir until well mixed. If adding nuts, chill until the mixture starts to thicken, add the nuts, and pour the gelatin into a bowl or mold; finish chilling until set—overnight or at least several hours. If not adding nuts, pour immediately into a bowl or mold and chill until firm. Yields 8 to 10 servings.

Darlene Compton Welch, Miss Kentucky 1974

Frozen Strawberry Banana Salad

1 21-ounce can strawberry pie filling
1 pint vanilla ice cream, softened
1 tablespoon lemon juice
3 medium bananas, chopped
¼ cup coarsely chopped toasted almonds

Combine the pie filling, ice cream, and lemon juice. Stir in the bananas and nuts. Turn into 8 individual molds or fill cupcake liners. Freeze until firm, several hours or overnight. Place in refrigerator 15 minutes before serving. Unmold onto lettuce-lined plates. Yields 8 servings.

Kimberly Kay Christiansen, Miss Colorado 1980

Ezee Fruit Salad

This recipe can be made in quantity to serve large crowds.

1 cup COLD pineapple juice
1 3.4-ounce package lemon-flavored instant pudding and pie mix
Fruit cocktail, drained
Sliced bananas
Mandarin oranges
Sliced kiwi fruit

Blend juice and pudding mix together thoroughly. Add a can of fruit cocktail to the pudding mixture. Then add sliced bananas and mandarin oranges. Top with thinly sliced kiwi fruit, cut in half to decorate the top. (It is best to add the kiwi at the last minute before serving because the seeds have a habit of flushing out and the salad looks like someone sprinkled coarse ground pepper over the top.) Yields 4 ½-cup servings.

Marion Rudeen Payne, Miss Minnesota 1939

LaMaize Sauce

This sauce was made famous when served over shrimp by a well-known Philadelphia hotel. Superlative on cold shrimp, lobster, crab meat, and cold fish, this is also good on salads (chef's salad in particular) and on cold hard-boiled eggs.

1 pint mayonnaise
1 pint chili sauce
½ cup Heinz India Relish
1 hard-boiled egg, chopped
1 teaspoon chopped chives
½ green bell pepper, finely chopped
1 pimiento, finely chopped
2 tablespoons finely chopped celery
1 tablespoon prepared Gulden's mustard
Salt and pepper to taste
1 tablespoon A-1 Sauce
Dash paprika

Combine all of the ingredients and blend well. Chill and serve. Preferably this should stand for at least 24 hours before it is served. It can be kept for up to a week in the fridge.

Frances Burke Kenney, Miss America 1940

Caesar Salad Dressing

Dressing

4 egg yolks
¼ cup coarse grain Dijon-style mustard
1 tablespoon chopped anchovies
1 tablespoon minced garlic
½ cup freshly squeezed lemon juice
1 tablespoon Worcestershire sauce
3 cups olive oil
Basil leaves to taste
Salt to taste
Ground white pepper to taste

Salad

Hearts of romaine lettuce, chopped
Garlic croutons
Parmesan cheese, freshly grated

Place the egg yolks, mustard, anchovies, garlic, lemon juice, and Worcestershire sauce in a mixer. Whip for 5 minutes. While mixing, gradually add the olive oil and basil. Season with salt and pepper. Place the romaine lettuce in a separate bowl and top with the croutons. Pour the salad dressing over the mixture. Top with Parmesan cheese and serve. Yields 1 quart of dressing.

Deanna Fogarty Hardwick, Miss California 1979

Pepper Cream Dressing

1 quart mayonnaise
1¼ cups half and half
⅛ cup grated Parmesan cheese
½ 1-ounce can black pepper
Salt to taste

. . . .

Combine all of the ingredients. Refrigerate until ready to serve. Yields about 5 cups.

Marie McLaughlin Cascone, Miss Pennsylvania 1976

Honey Salad Dressing

I am associated with the Miss Utah Pageant. Because Utah is known as the "Beehive State," this is a very appropriate recipe with honey.

1 teaspoon paprika
½ teaspoon powdered dry mustard
½ teaspoon salt
½ teaspoon celery salt
½ cup honey
3 tablespoons lemon juice
¼ cup vinegar
1 cup vegetable oil

. . . .

Combine the dry ingredients. Add the honey, lemon juice, and vinegar. Slowly add the vegetable oil, beating until well blended. Yields 2 cups.

Rosanne Tueller Nielsen, Miss District of Columbia 1963

Williamsburg Lodge Honey Dressing

½ cup vinegar
¼ cup sugar
¼ cup honey
1 teaspoon dry mustard
1 teaspoon paprika
1 teaspoon celery seed
1 teaspoon celery salt
1 teaspoon onion juice
1 cup vegetable oil

. . . .

Combine the vinegar, sugar, honey, mustard, and paprika. Boil 2 minutes and cool. Add the celery seed and celery salt, onion juice, and vegetable oil, and shake vigorously. Serve with any fresh or frozen fruit salad. Shake well before using. Store in the refrigerator. Yields 1¾ cups.

Nancy Glisson, Miss Virginia 1993

Cranberry Freeze

1 16-ounce can whole-berry cranberry sauce
1 8-ounce can crushed pineapple
1 cup chopped pecans
1 8-ounce carton sour cream
2 tablespoons mayonnaise
2 tablespoons sugar

. . . .

Combine all of the ingredients. Pour into cupcake papers placed in muffin tins. Freeze. Remove the papers and serve on bed of lettuce. Yields 8 servings.

Note: These can be wrapped in plastic wrap after they are frozen and stored in the freezer for unexpected guests.

Terry Meeuwsen Friedrich, Miss America 1973

Breads

Grandma's Creamed Cornbread

1 cup cornmeal
¾ cup all-purpose flour
2 tablespoons sugar
4 teaspoons baking powder
½ teaspoon salt
1 cup milk
1 egg, beaten
4 tablespoons melted butter, divided
1 16½-ounce can creamed corn

Preheat oven to 450°. Sift together the cornmeal, flour, sugar, baking powder, and salt. Add the milk, egg, and 2 tablespoons of butter, and mix well. Add the creamed corn and mix well. Grease a medium skillet with remaining butter. Pour the corn mixture in skillet and bake for 25 minutes. Let stand for 15 minutes before serving. Yields 6 servings.

Mary Shelby Bauer, Miss Passaic, New Jersey 1927

Jalapeño Cornbread

3 cups yellow cornmeal or cornmeal mix
1½ teaspoons baking powder (omit if a mix is used)
1 cup cream-style corn
1 teaspoon sugar
2 teaspoons salt
1 cup chopped onion
1⅓ cups grated cheese
1 cup vegetable oil
3 eggs
1¾ cups milk
½ cup chopped jalapeño peppers

Preheat oven to 350°. Combine all of the ingredients and pour into a greased 9 x 16-inch pan. Bake for 1 hour. Yields 10 to 12 servings.

Bob Wheeler, Miss Arkansas Pageant

Mexican Cornbread

1½ cups cornmeal
1 cup cream-style corn
1 cup buttermilk
½ cup vegetable oil
2 eggs, beaten
2 tablespoons diced green bell pepper
1 tablespoon baking powder
1 teaspoon salt
1 teaspoon sugar
2 jalapeño peppers, seeded and minced
¼ cup finely chopped onion
1 cup shredded Cheddar cheese

. . . .

Preheat oven to 350°. Combine all of the ingredients, except the cheese. Pour the batter into a large greased iron skillet and sprinkle the cheese on top. Bake for 30 minutes. Yields 6 to 8 servings.

Mrs. Kenneth Chapman, Miss Oklahoma Pageant

Mom's Cornbread

1 cup white cornmeal
½ teaspoon salt
½ teaspoon baking soda
2 teaspoons baking powder
⅓ cup all-purpose flour
2 tablespoons vegetable oil
2 eggs
1 cup buttermilk

. . . .

Preheat oven to 450°. Combine the dry ingredients. Add the oil, eggs, and buttermilk, blending well. Pour into greased 8-inch round pan. Bake for 20 minutes. Yields 8 servings.

Donna Axum Whitworth, Miss America 1964

Doctor Miss America

Call it one-in-a-million odds. When Tennessee's first Miss America (1947), Barbara Jo Walker, married an obstetrical student during her reign, who could have predicted that Mr. Miss America would go on to deliver Kellye Cash—an adorable baby girl who grew up to become Tennessee's second Miss America (1987).

World's Best Cornbread Dressing

2 cups chopped celery
3 cups chopped onion
2 sticks butter or margarine
2 8-inch pans cornbread (see Mom's Cornbread recipe at left)
6 slices white bread
2 to 3 cups canned chicken broth
6 eggs, beaten
Salt and pepper to taste
Poultry seasoning to taste

. . . .

Sauté the celery and onion in the butter until limp. Crumble the cornbread into the mixture. Tear the white bread into small pieces and add it to the mixture. Add 1½ to 2 cups of chicken broth and mix together. Add the eggs. Season to taste with salt, pepper, and poultry seasoning. Preheat oven to 350°. Spray a 3-quart casserole dish or two 9 x 13-inch pans with vegetable cooking spray. Pour the dressing into the pans and cover with foil. Bake for 45 to 50 minutes. Add more broth during cooking if the dressing seems too dry. Yields 10 to 12 servings.

Donna Axum Whitworth, Miss America 1964

Sunny Corn Muffins

1¼ cups yellow cornmeal
¾ cup sunflower seeds
½ cup all-purpose flour
2 tablespoons sugar
2 teaspoons baking powder
¾ teaspoon salt
1 cup milk
1 egg
3 tablespoons vegetable oil

. . . .

Preheat oven to 375°. Combine all of the dry ingredients and set aside. Combine the milk, egg, and oil well. Stir the wet mixture into the dry ingredients just enough to blend. Do not overmix. Spoon the batter into 12 greased muffin cups and bake for 20 to 25 minutes or until golden. Yields 12 servings.

Jean Kyle Nelson, Miss Minnesota Pageant

Hey, a Girl's Gotta Do What a Girl's Gotta do . . .

When Bess Myerson competed in the 1945 Miss America Pageant, contestants were assigned regulation swimsuits. Bess was issued a white bathing suit that fit like a glove. But, since Bess was 5′10,″ the suit's seat rode up on her derriere so provocatively that Lenora Slaughter, the Pageant's matronly director, reissued her a larger, green bathing suit. One look at the baggy, pea green number, and Bess knew it was curtains for her chances. Then her heftier big sister, Sylvia, came up with an idea: she'd sleep in the smaller suit to stretch it, detach the shoulder straps to add some length to the seat, and sew Bess back into it. Myerson won the Miss America crown hands down—wearing that sexy little white swimsuit under all her competition clothes.

Beer Bread

3 cups self-rising flour
¾ cup granulated sugar
1 12-ounce can beer

. . . .

Preheat oven to 350°. Combine the flour and sugar very well, then slowly pour in the beer. Stir well and pour the batter into a greased loaf pan. Bake for 1 hour. Best when served warm! Yields 6 to 8 servings.

Judy Dale, Atlantic City Hostess

Cave Hill Spoonbread

1¼ cups yellow cornmeal
3 cups milk, rapidly boiling
3 eggs, well beaten
2 tablespoons butter, melted
1¾ teaspoons baking powder
1 teaspoon salt

. . . .

Stir the cornmeal into the rapidly boiling milk. Cook until very thick, stirring constantly to prevent scorching. Remove from the heat and allow to cool until cold and stiff. Preheat oven to 375°. Add the remaining ingredients and beat with an electric mixer for 15 minutes. Pour into a buttered casserole dish and bake for 30 minutes. Serve by spoonfuls. Yields 4 to 6 servings.

Phyllis George, Miss America 1971

Oatmeal Muffins

I love these muffins with honey and butter. They are very good served with soup for a light meal.

1 cup oatmeal
½ cup firmly packed brown sugar
1 cup buttermilk
1 egg
1 stick margarine, melted
1 cup all-purpose flour
2 teaspoons baking powder
1 teaspoon salt
½ teaspoon baking soda

Preheat oven to 425°. Soak the oatmeal and sugar in the buttermilk. Add the egg and margarine and beat well. Sift together the dry ingredients. Fold the liquid mixture into the flour mixture. Pour into well-greased muffin tins. Bake for 15 to 20 minutes. Yields 16 muffins.

Moira Alice Kaye Ely, Miss Tennessee 1983

Angel Biscuits

5½ cups all-purpose flour
3 teaspoons baking powder
1½ teaspoons salt
1 teaspoon baking soda
3 tablespoons sugar
¾ cup shortening
1 ¼-ounce package dry active yeast
¼ cup lukewarm water
2 cups buttermilk
Melted butter

Sift all of the dry ingredients into a bowl. Cut in the shortening with a pastry blender. Dissolve the yeast in the warm water and add it to the buttermilk. Pour into the first mixture and stir with a wooden spoon just until blended. Refrigerate overnight, or until ready to use. Preheat oven to 400°. Roll out the dough to ½-inch thickness; cut with a biscuit cutter. Place on a greased baking sheet. Brush with melted butter and let rise until double in size (usually 1 to 1½ hours). Bake for 15 minutes. Yields 4 dozen biscuits.

Note: When time is a factor: roll and cut the biscuits, brush with butter, place them on a baking sheet and refrigerate until about 1½ hours before baking. Place the chilled biscuits in a warm spot to speed rising. The dough is easy to make, keeps well when refrigerated, and may be used as needed.

Gail Bullock Odom, Miss Georgia 1973

Dillie Bread

¼ cup warm water
1 ¼-ounce package dry active yeast
2 teaspoons sugar
1 cup cottage cheese
1 egg
1 tablespoon butter
2 teaspoons dill seed
¼ teaspoon soda
½ teaspoon salt
2½ to 3 cups bread flour

Combine the first 8 ingredients in a blender and blend for about 2 minutes. Pour into a large mixing bowl. Add the flour and knead until elastic. Shape into a ball. Cover and let rise. Punch down and place in 2 small loaf pans or 1 quart-size round glass dish. Let rise until doubled in size. Preheat oven to 350°. Bake for 40 to 45 minutes, or until tester inserted in center comes out clean. Yields 10 to 12 servings per loaf.

Helen Rose Gennings Musgrave, Miss Arkansas 1968

The 1940s—The Era of Rosie the Riveter and the War Bride

As the 1940s dawned, the winds of war were approaching as Hitler's troops stormed across Europe and Japanese kamikaze pilots took off for Hawaii. On December 7, 1941, Japan bombed Pearl Harbor, nearly destroying the American naval fleet and plunging the United States into World War II. Atlantic City was transformed into a major military facility, with Convention Hall its training center and the glamorous hotels converted into barracks.

With the city occupied by the military, the Pageant was nearly discontinued, but officials decided that Miss America boosted U.S. morale and should go on. As always, she became a reflection of the times. With lonely GIs prizing their shapely poster girls, but pining for the pretty gals they'd left waiting back home, Miss America blended the images to symbolize both. She was the wholesome girl-next-door who looked like a pinup. Aware of their power to contribute to the war effort, Miss Americas toured the country selling war bonds and contestants entertained departing GIs and visited the wounded in military hospitals. "Everyone was doing his or her part for the war effort," recalls Jean Bartel, Miss America 1943. "It was a very dramatic period in our lives when we really felt very emotional."

The quintessential 1940s glamour girl, Miss America 1941, California's Rosemary LaPlanche, later signed with RKO Pictures and appeared in 84 films. (The Miss America Organization)

World War II brought dramatic changes to women's lives. With the male population engaged in battle, over three million women came out of the kitchen to man factory assembly lines, birthing the nickname "Rosie the Riveter." As leading ladies like Joan Crawford, Bette Davis, and Katharine Hepburn popularized the smart, self-sufficient woman, the Pageant reflected the change. The selection of Jean Bartel, an accomplished UCLA student and a member of Kappa Kappa Gamma, as Miss America 1943 demonstrated the Pageant's maturation from a glamour-girl show to a program for wholesome college women. "Lenora was always trying to upgrade the Pageant," says Bartel, "and this gave her the opportunity to open it up to higher education. I was an all-American girl-next-door. I just happened to be the right girl, at the right time, for the next step."

Inspired by her new titleholder, Lenora Slaughter moved to offer entrants scholarships to pursue a college education rather than showbiz careers. Undaunted by the fact that scholarships were usually only offered to males, Slaughter approached 236 corporations asking for contributions to a women's scholarship program. Five companies donated $1,000 each, creating the Pageant's first $5,000 Miss America scholarship.

The original scholarship recipient was Bess Myerson, Miss America 1945, the first New Yorker to win and the first Jewish winner. Bess's victory was inspirational in light of servicemen battling to end Nazi atrocities against Jews overseas. She was a beautiful public symbol of the people U.S. troops would eventually free. By the end of Myerson's reign, the world war was over, concentration camps were closed, and victorious American GIs were on their way home.

The end of World War II also ushered in the era of the war bride. As GIs rushed home, thousands of couples flocked to the altar, making "Mrs." the title every little girl wanted to win. The marriage-mania reached its pinnacle in 1947 when Princess Elizabeth, the future Queen of England, married in a ceremony publicized worldwide. In a classic case of the Pageant mirroring the times, Barbara Walker, Miss America 1947, married during her reign in a lavish American royal wedding. When asked if she'd hoped for a Hollywood contract, she answered, "The only contract I'm interested in is the marriage contract!"

While Miss America's public image as a student and bride was well received by the public, Lenora's efforts to move Miss America away from the image of a swimsuit glamour girl met with resistance from the press. It was the era of Betty Grable pinups and reporters insisted that Miss America belonged in a bathing suit. When Slaughter announced that the winner would be crowned in an evening gown, reporters threatened a boycott, packed their photo equipment, and left town. Lenora called their bluff on a suspicion that editors would order their reporters right back. Sure enough, that night they were back to watch Minnesota's BeBe Shopp crowned in a modest gown. "I was just thrilled to a peanut that we won," Lenora says triumphantly, "and Miss America was never crowned in a swimsuit again."

Thus, the Pageant closed the decade with its winners having typified a spectrum of feminine images: bathing beauty, college girl, Rosie the Riveter, war bride, and wholesome girl-next-door.

Yeast Rolls for a Week!

1 ¼-ounce package dry active yeast
2 cups warm water
4 cups self-rising flour
½ cup sugar
¾ cup shortening, melted and cooled
1 egg, beaten

Dissolve the yeast in the warm water. Sift together the flour and sugar and add to the yeast mixture. Add the shortening and the egg. Chill, covered, for 24 hours. Preheat oven to 425°. Fill greased muffin cups ½ full and bake for 10 to 15 minutes or until browned. Wonderful and easy. Yields 2 dozen rolls.

Dianne Hensley, Miss Tennessee Pageant

Terre Haute Hotcakes

1 cup buttermilk or sour cream
1 egg, separated (yolk and white beaten separately)
½ stick butter, melted
1 tablespoon sugar
½ teaspoon baking soda
¾ cup all-purpose flour
¾ teaspoon salt

Combine all of the ingredients and mix well. The batter should be very thin and pourable. Cook on a hot griddle. Yields 2 servings.

Charles Welch, Miss Oklahoma Pageant

In 1940 the Pageant moved to Atlantic City's new Convention Hall, where Philadelphia's Frances Burke became the first winner to walk the now-famous runway. (The Miss America Organization)

The Worst-Dressed Award

The famous black-and-white striped knit bathing suits issued to Miss America contestants in 1948 easily qualify as the single worst swimsuit ever worn in the Miss America Pageant. "They were terrible, terrible!" exclaims BeBe Shopp, that year's winner. "No one could believe that's what we had to wear! We felt like a bunch of zebras on-stage!"

Grammie's Coffee Cake

I remember having this coffee cake every Sunday morning as a child. It's been in Grammie Russell's family for years! I'm not much for sweet breakfasts, which is why I like this recipe. It's just the right amount of sweet and it goes very nicely with a hot cup of coffee.

2 tablespoons butter or margarine
1 egg
1 cup sugar
1 cup milk
2 cups all-purpose flour
2 teaspoons baking powder
1 scant teaspoon salt (optional)
Sugar
Cinnamon
Nuts
Shredded coconut (optional)

Preheat the oven to 350°. Put the butter in a 9-inch square pan and put the pan in the preheating oven to melt the butter. Beat the egg with the sugar and milk. Sift together the flour, baking powder, and salt, and add them to the liquid mixture. Use the melted butter to grease the pan and then pour the remainder into the batter. Sprinkle with sugar, cinnamon, nuts, and coconut. Bake for approximately 30 minutes or until golden brown. Enjoy! Yields 8 servings.

Elizabeth Russell Brunner, Miss Illinois 1979

Greek Bread

1 ¼-ounce envelope dry active yeast
¼ cup warm water
1 tablespoon sugar
1 cup milk
½ stick butter
½ teaspoon salt
4 cups bread flour, sifted and divided
Melted butter
Sesame seeds (optional)

Dissolve the yeast in the warm water with the sugar. Heat the milk, butter, and salt to 115 °. In a food processor with a metal blade, add 3 cups of the flour and the yeast mixture. Process for about 5 seconds. Continue processing while pouring the milk mixture through the feed tube. Turn the dough out onto a floured board and knead until smooth and the dough no longer sticks to your fingers. Place in a greased bowl, turning to coat on all sides. Cover with waxed paper, and a tea towel; let the dough rise in a warm place until doubled in size (1½ to 2 hours). Punch down, knead, and allow the dough to rise for an additional 1½ hours. Knead and form into round loaves and place in greased round cake tins. Allow to rise for 1 hour. Preheat oven to 375°. Brush with melted butter and sprinkle with the sesame seeds. Bake for 45 minutes or until golden brown and bread sounds hollow when thumped. Yields 2 loaves.

Rena Michaelides, Miss New York State Pageant

Honey Whole Wheat Bread

This is the recipe I used when I baked my wheat bread entry in the 1975 4-H division of the Phillips County Fair. I received the grand prize purple ribbon and a trophy from the Montana Wheat Hearts Association for it.

2 packages dry active yeast
5 cups warm water (110°-115°), divided
6 tablespoons lard (or other shortening)
¼ cup honey
4 cups whole wheat flour, stirred before measuring
½ cup instant potato flakes
½ cup nonfat dry milk
1 tablespoon salt
6½ to 8 cups sifted all-purpose flour

. . . .

Sprinkle the yeast on ½ cup of warm water; stir to dissolve. Melt the lard in a 6-quart saucepan. Remove from the heat, add the honey and remaining 4½ cups of warm water. Combine the flour, potato flakes, dry milk, and salt. Add to the saucepan and beat until smooth. Add the yeast and beat to blend. Then use a wooden spoon to mix in enough all-purpose flour, a little at a time, to make a dough that leaves the sides of the pan. Turn onto a lightly floured board and knead until smooth and satiny and small bubbles appear, 8 to 10 minutes. Place the dough in a lightly greased bowl. Turn over to grease the top. Cover and let rise in a warm place until doubled in size, 1 to 1½ hours. Punch down the dough, turn it onto a board, and divide into thirds. Cover and let it rest for 5 minutes. Shape into 3 loaves and place them in greased 9 x 5-inch loaf pans. Cover and let rise until doubled in size, about 1 hour.

Preheat oven to 400°. Bake for about 50 minutes, or until a knife inserted in the center comes out clean. Remove the bread from the pans and cool on wire racks. Yields 3 loaves.

Lori Conlon Khan, Miss Montana 1979

Pomp and Strangulation

In 1943, when California's Jean Bartel, a UCLA student and a Kappa Kappa Gamma sorority sister, won the Miss America title, the band appropriately serenaded the bathing suit-clad student with the famous graduation song, "Pomp and Circumstance." Bartel loved the music—but hated the queen's robe. "When they played that song I must have smiled from ear-to-ear because I graduated to "Pomp and Circumstance." Then they changed the ribbons on me, put the crown on my head, and put this long red-velvet robe with ermine on me. It tied around the neck so every time I walked, I had to drag this long robe along—and it practically choked me!"

Monkey Bread

4 10-ounce cans uncooked biscuits
1½ tablespoons cinnamon
¾ cup sugar
½ cup nuts (and/or raisins, coconut)
1 stick margarine
1 cup firmly packed brown sugar

. . . .

Preheat oven to 350°. Cut each biscuit into 4 pieces. Put the sugar and cinnamon in a plastic bag. Add the biscuits and shake to coat. Put a layer of biscuits in a pan and sprinkle them with nuts. Layer until all of the ingredients are used. Bring the brown sugar and margarine to a boil. Pour the syrup over the biscuits. Bake for 30 to 45 minutes. Cool for 15 minutes. Turn upside down to serve. Pieces can be picked apart. Yields 10 to 12 servings.

Gail Bullock Odom, Miss Georgia 1973

In 1948, when officials announced that Miss America would be crowned in a gown rather than the customary swimsuit, reporters threatened to boycott the Pageant. The compromise was that Miss America 1948 (BeBe Shopp) was crowned in a modest gown while her runners-up appeared in swimsuits. (The Press, Atlantic City)

Le Pancake

1 cup milk
1½ tablespoons butter, melted
1 egg, beaten
¾ cup all-purpose flour
1¾ teaspoons baking powder
1½ tablespoons sugar
¼ teaspoon salt
1 tablespoon grated orange rind

. . . .

Add the milk and butter to the egg. Sift the dry ingredients together and add to the liquid mixture. Beat well with an egg beater. Makes a thin batter. Pour onto a hot greased griddle; turn to brown. Serve with steaming maple syrup. Yields 4 servings.

Note: Top these with fresh fruit for a hearty and delicious meal.

Vanessa Williams, Miss America 1984

Zucchini Bread

3 eggs
1 cup vegetable oil
3 cups all-purpose flour
2 cups sugar
2 teaspoons cinnamon
1 teaspoon salt
½ teaspoon baking powder
1 teaspoon baking soda
2 cups shredded zucchini
1 cup chopped nuts
1 cup raisins
1 teaspoon vanilla extract

. . . .

Grease and flour four 9 x 5-inch loaf pans and set them aside. Preheat oven to 325°. Beat the eggs and oil together. Combine the remaining ingredients in a separate bowl. Add the egg and oil mixture. Blend well. Place the mixture in the prepared pans. Bake for 1 hour. Cool 10 minutes before removing from pans. Yields 4 loaves.

Vonda Kay VanDyke Scoates, Miss America 1965

Strawberry Bread

2 10-ounce packages frozen sliced strawberries
4 eggs, beaten
1¼ cups vegetable oil
3 cups all-purpose flour
1 teaspoon baking soda
1 teaspoon salt
3 teaspoons cinnamon
2 cups sugar
1½ cups chopped pecans (optional)

. . . .

Thaw the strawberries in a bowl (including the juice) and add the eggs and oil. Mix well. Preheat oven to 350°. Sift together the dry ingredients in a separate bowl. Add the strawberry mixture to the flour mixture. Add the pecans, if desired. Mix well. Grease and flour two 9 x 5-inch loaf pans or three disposable aluminum foil pans (they are smaller). Pour the batter into the pans. Bake for 65 minutes for larger pans, or 40 to 45 minutes for smaller pans. Cool inverted on wire racks. After cooling, these may be frozen. Yields 2 or 3 loaves.

Judi Ford Nash, Miss America 1969

Now You See Them . . . Now You Don't

In 1947, at the height of the post-war pinup era, Miss America contestants wore two-piece swimsuits in the swimsuit competition for the first and only time. Considered racy at the time, the "bikinis" caught somebody's attention, because that year's Miss America became a "Mrs." before she'd even crowned her successor! The two-piecers were promptly discontinued the next year.

Sopaipillas

2 cups all-purpose flour
2 teaspoons baking powder
1 teaspoon salt
2 tablespoons lard or vegetable shortening
½ cup lukewarm water
Lard or vegetable shortening for frying

Stir the dry ingredients together. Work in the lard and lukewarm water to make a soft dough. Chill in the refrigerator. Roll out the dough on a floured surface to about ¼-inch thickness. Cut into 3-inch squares. Deep fat fry in hot (400°) lard a few at a time. Brown on each side and drain on paper towels. Serve piping hot. To eat, poke open the sopaipilla and pour in honey, or slather it with honey butter. Yields 6 to 8 servings.

Note: Honey butter for sopaipillas: Cream 1 cup butter or margarine. Gradually beat in ½ cup to 1 cup honey (If honey has begun to crystalize, you can use the larger amount). Cover and store in the refrigerator.

Mai Therese Shanley, Miss New Mexico 1983

Kringler

This is a Swedish sweet pastry.

2 cups all-purpose flour, divided
2 sticks plus 1 tablespoon butter, divided
1 cup plus 1 tablespoon water, divided
3 eggs
1 teaspoon almond extract, divided
1 cup confectioners' sugar
Cream

Preheat oven to 375°. Combine 1 cup of the flour, 1 stick of butter and 1 tablespoon of water. Mix to form a pastry. Pat onto a cookie sheet in 2 long strips, each 3 inches wide. Put the remaining water in a saucepan with 1 stick of butter. Heat to the boiling point. Remove from the heat and add the remaining flour. Stir until smooth. Add the eggs, one at a time, beating well after each addition. Add ½ teaspoon of almond extract. Spread the mixture over the pastry strips. Bake for 40 minutes. Make a frosting by combining the confectioners' sugar, the remaining butter, and a little cream to moisten. Stir in the remaining almond extract. Spread over the baked pastry. Yields 10 servings.

Vicki Train, Miss Nebraska 1991

Lemon Bread

1½ cups all-purpose flour
1 cup sugar
1 teaspoon baking powder
¼ teaspoon salt
Grated peel of 1 lemon
½ cup walnuts
½ cup milk
2½ tablespoons butter, melted
2 eggs, beaten

Topping

Juice of 1 lemon
¼ cup confectioners' sugar

. . . .

Preheat oven to 350°. Grease and flour a 9 x 5-inch pan. Combine the dry ingredients in a large bowl. Add the milk, butter, and eggs. Stir until well mixed. Pour the batter into the prepared pan. Bake for 45 to 50 minutes. Combine the ingredients for the topping and pour over the bread while it's still hot. Let the bread cool in the pan. Yields 1 loaf.

Laura Lynn Watters, Miss Kansas 1983

New England Banana Bread

2 cups sugar
2 sticks unsalted butter
5 well-ripened bananas
4 eggs
1½ cups all-purpose flour
1 teaspoon salt
2 teaspoons baking soda
1 cup chopped walnuts

. . . .

Preheat oven to 350°. Cream the sugar and butter in a large bowl until light and fluffy. Mash the bananas and add them to the sugar mixture. Beat the eggs well and blend them into the banana batter. Sift together the flour, salt, and baking soda in a separate bowl. Add the banana batter and blend well. Stir in the nuts. Pour into two greased and floured 9 x 5-inch loaf pans. Bake for approximately 45 minutes or until bread tests done. Cool in the pans for 5 minutes; then turn out on a rack. Cool completely before slicing. This bread freezes well and is also delicious toasted. Yields 2 loaves.

Jenna Wims Hashway, Miss Rhode Island 1988

Herb Patio Bread

2 cups warm water
2 ¼-ounce packages dry active yeast
2 tablespoons sugar
2 teaspoons salt
2 tablespoons margarine, softened
1 tablespoon dried rosemary leaves
4½ cups sifted all-purpose flour, divided

. . . .

Pour the water into a large mixing bowl. Sprinkle the yeast in the water. Stir to dissolve. Add the sugar, salt, margarine, rosemary, and 3 cups of the flour. Beat at low speed until well blended, then medium speed until smooth. Gradually add the rest of the flour until blended. Cover with waxed paper and then a towel. Let rise for about 45 minutes or until more than doubled in size. Preheat oven to 375°. With a wooden spoon, stir down the batter. Beat vigorously for 30 seconds; turn into a 2-quart casserole dish. Bake for 55 to 60 minutes or until nicely browned. Cut into wedges. Yields 6 to 8 servings.

Debbie Weuve Rohrer, Miss Iowa 1975

Entrées

Stir-Fry Beef and Snow Peas

1 pound boneless beef round steak, sliced across grain into thin strips
1 tablespoon dry sherry
2 tablespoons soy sauce
2 tablespoons cornstarch, divided
½ cup beef broth
2 tablespoons vegetable oil, divided
1 clove garlic, minced
2 cups fresh snow peas
1 cup fresh bean sprouts

Combine the steak, sherry, soy sauce, and 1 tablespoon cornstarch in a medium bowl. Dissolve remaining 1 tablespoon cornstarch in the broth and reserve. Heat 1 tablespoon of the oil in a large skillet. Add the beef and garlic. Cook over high heat, stirring constantly, until browned, about 3 minutes. Add the remaining tablespoon of oil. Add the snow peas and bean sprouts. Cover and simmer over medium heat 3 to 5 minutes. Add the beef broth mixture and cook, stirring until thickened, about 2 minutes. Yields 4 to 6 servings.

Note: Chopped mushrooms and celery are good in this, too.

Charlean Fuhrman Croxton, Miss South Dakota 1962

Barbecue Beef Brisket

Another great way to serve beef to lots of people is this recipe for brisket. It is my sister's recipe. She is an exceptional cook and has many opportunities to serve lots of people.

5 pounds beef brisket
¼ cup plus 2 tablespoons liquid smoke (3 ounces)
Celery salt to taste
Salt and pepper to taste
Worcestershire sauce to taste
¾ cup barbecue sauce

Place the brisket in a baking dish. Pour the liquid smoke over the brisket. Generously sprinkle celery salt on both sides of the meat. Cover and refrigerate overnight. Preheat oven to 275°. Add salt, pepper, and Worcestershire sauce. Cover with foil and bake for 5 hours. Uncover, pour the barbecue sauce over the brisket, and bake 1 additional hour. Remove from the dish, cool, and slice on the diagonal. Yields 8 to 10 servings.

Jane Jayroe, Miss America 1967

French Pot Roast

1 tablespoon vegetable oil
6- to 7-pound rump roast
4 cups dry red wine
1 10½-ounce can beef broth
1 8-ounce can tomato sauce
2 large garlic cloves, minced
1 teaspoon dried thyme
1 bay leaf
4 whole cloves
Parsley sprigs
2 teaspoons Tabasco sauce
16 small carrots
5 to 6 tablespoons butter, divided
1 pound medium mushrooms, cut in halves
20 small pearl onions, peeled
1 tablespoon sugar
Salt to taste
2 tablespoons cornstarch
Water
Chopped parsley

. . . .

Preheat oven to 325°. In a heavy pot, heat the oil, and brown the meat on all sides. Pour off the fat. Add the next 10 ingredients, cover and bring to a boil. Bake, covered, for 3 to 3½ hours. After the meat has cooked 2½ hours, boil the carrots in salted water to cover until tender. Drain. Add 2 to 3 tablespoons butter and sauté the carrots until lightly browned. Transfer to a serving platter and keep warm. Add the mushrooms to the same skillet. Cook until tender and add to the carrots. In a large pan, add the pearl onions with enough water to cover. Add 2 tablespoons butter, the sugar, and salt. Cook until all water evaporates. Shake the skillet to brown the onions. Place the onions on a platter with the roast. Skim the fat from the liquid in the roast pan. Blend the cornstarch with water and add it to the boiling liquid in the kettle; stir until thickened. (I usually skip the cornstarch and put sour cream into my gravy.) Sprinkle the meat with chopped parsley. Yields 12 to 14 servings.

Lori Smith-Madsen, Miss Texas 1977

Oklahoma Dad's Swiss Steak

This is a recipe from my grandfather, "Oklahoma Dad." He was a wheat farmer in the Oklahoma panhandle and in his later years, he became a great cook to the delight of his six adult children and their spouses and children.

5 pounds round steak or sirloin tips
Flour
Vegetable oil
3 large onions, chopped
½ bunch celery, chopped
1 green bell pepper, sliced into rings
1 tablespoon flour
1 8-ounce can tomato sauce
1 16-ounce can tomato juice
1 10¾-ounce can cream of mushroom soup
1 10¾-ounce can cream of celery soup

. . . .

Trim all fat from the meat. Slice and cut the meat into pieces. Flour the meat and brown it in oil. Place all of the pieces in a roaster or Dutch oven. Boil and drain the onions and celery and cover the steak with them. Add the sliced peppers. Preheat oven to 350°. Brown the 1 tablespoon of flour in oil, stir, add the tomato sauce, juice, and soups. Stir well, making a "gravy." Pour the gravy over the steak and vegetables. Cover the roaster and bake for 2 to 3 hours. Yields 8 to 10 servings.

Jane Jayroe, Miss America 1967

Lazy Day Beef Stroganoff

This recipe was given to me by my Wyoming chaperon, Vivian Hendrix, who went to Atlantic City with my mother and me. She is a delightful lady. She and her husband Jack are godparents to our three lovely daughters and an important influence on them.

2 pounds beef stew meat, cut into small cubes
2 onions, chopped
¼ to ½ teaspoon salt
Dash of pepper
1 10¾-ounce can cream of mushroom soup thinned with ½ can of water (I use Healthy Request low-fat soup and often use low-fat cream of tomato soup instead of mushroom)
1 cup reduced-fat sour cream
¼ to ½ cup finely diced dill pickle

....

Preheat oven to 275°. Place the stew meat, onions, salt, pepper, and soup in a casserole with a tight lid and mix well. Cover and bake for 4 to 5 hours. When ready to serve, remove from the oven, put over low heat on the stove, and add the sour cream and diced pickle. Heat through but do not boil. Serve over noodles or rice. Yields 4 to 6 servings.

Note: If using low-fat sour cream, it may be necessary to thicken by adding a bit of cornstarch or flour thinned with a dab of water before heating.

Carol Jean Held Chenoweth, Miss Wyoming 1948

Stuffed Green Peppers

This recipe is my mother Charla McMechan's.

3 green bell peppers, cut in half lengthwise, seeded and cored
¾ pound ground beef
⅓ cup quick-cooking rice, uncooked
1 teaspoon salt
¼ teaspoon pepper
1 egg
⅓ cup tomato juice
1 8-ounce can tomato sauce, divided
2 teaspoons Worcestershire sauce
2 tablespoons salsa

....

Place the peppers in a 12 x 7-inch baking dish. Combine the remaining ingredients, using only half of the tomato sauce. Spoon the mixture into the pepper halves. Spoon the remaining tomato sauce over the meat mixture. Microwave, covered with waxed paper, for 13 minutes, or until the meat is done and the peppers are of a desired softness. Yields 6 servings.

Joni McMechan Checchia, Miss Indiana 1988

Great Plains Stuffed Green Peppers

This recipe is a Kansas father-daughter favorite.

4 medium green bell peppers
1 pound Kansas lean ground beef
1 medium onion, chopped
⅓ cup cooked white rice
¼ cup Heinz 57 sauce
¼ cup ketchup

....

Preheat oven to 350°. Slice the stem ends from the peppers and clean out the seeds. Blanch the peppers in boiling water for 5 minutes and drain. Combine the beef and remaining ingredients. Stuff the peppers and arrange them in a greased baking dish. Top with extra Heinz 57 sauce. Bake for 45 to 50 minutes or until the tops are slightly crispy. Yields 4 servings.

Trisha Jo Schaffer, Miss Kansas 1994

Cabbage Patch Stew

This is a recipe that I received when my father died. To make a more healthy version, substitute ground turkey meat for the ground beef. There is absolutely no difference in taste.

1 small head cabbage, chopped
3 small onions, chopped
3 to 5 ribs celery, chopped
2 cans stewed tomatoes
1 or 2 regular-size cans cocktail juice (you may want to add more)
2 15-ounce cans Ranch-style Beans (These are barbecue beans)
Water
Salt to taste
1½ pounds ground beef
1 1¾-ounce envelope chili seasoning mix

. . . .

Combine all of the ingredients, except ground beef. Add water as needed for cooking slowly. Add salt to taste. Simmer for several hours. Brown the ground beef with ¼ to ½ of the seasoning packet and add the remainder of the packet to the stew pot. Add the beef to the pot. Simmer an additional hour or until you are ready to serve. This is very good as a "leftover" the next day. Yields 8 to 10 servings.

Mary Lou Butler Blaylock, Miss Texas 1965

Reuben Casserole

1 16-ounce can sauerkraut, drained
1 12-ounce can corned beef
2 cups shredded Swiss cheese
½ cup mayonnaise
¼ cup Thousand Island dressing
2 medium tomatoes, sliced
2 tablespoons butter or margarine
2 or 3 slices pumpernickel bread, crumbled

. . . .

Preheat oven to 350°. Place the drained sauerkraut in a 2-quart casserole dish. Break the corned beef into small pieces on top of the sauerkraut. Top with cheese. Combine the mayonnaise and dressing and spread over the cheese. Top with sliced tomatoes. Melt the butter and stir it into the bread crumbs; spread this mixture evenly over the tomatoes. Bake for 30 minutes. Let sit 5 minutes before serving. Yields 4 to 5 servings.

Elaine Rushlow Finan, Miss Rhode Island 1979

Baked Chow Mein

2 pounds ground beef
2 large onions, diced
4 stalks celery, diced
2 cups water
½ cup uncooked rice
1 10¾-ounce can cream of mushroom soup
4 tablespoons soy sauce
1 teaspoon oregano
4 drops of Tabasco sauce
1 tablespoon Worcestershire sauce
Toasted, slivered almonds

. . . .

Preheat oven to 350°. Brown the meat and onion; drain off excess drippings. Add all of the remaining ingredients except the almonds. Bake for 1 hour. Cover with foil for the first 30 minutes. Before serving sprinkle with almonds. Yields 8 servings.

Madonna Smith Echols, Miss Kentucky 1946

The 1950s—The Golden Era of Television

The 1950s heralded the golden era of television and launched the Pageant as a treasured annual television extravaganza viewed by millions. That important milestone occurred on September 11, 1954, when ABC aired the first live coast-to-coast broadcast of the Miss America Pageant. With television still a remarkable new discovery and Queen Elizabeth's coronation staged just a year earlier, "Miss America" was a match made in ratings heaven—the coronation of an American queen on live television. Of course, it didn't hurt to have a stellar panel of celebrity judges that included Grace Kelly, who would soon become the Princess of Monaco. At the close of the historic telecast, the panel awarded the crown to California's Lee Meriwether—who was so shocked that she couldn't stop sobbing. Finally, her mother, who had been brought onstage, snapped on the air, "Stop your sniveling, Lee!" The telecast was a huge success. "Everybody and his mother tuned in to see that Pageant," recalls Kenn Berry, a Pageant volunteer for four decades. "To think that folks out in Idaho could see this on television was amazing! It just knocked everything off the airwaves."

In 1954, 27 million viewers watched the first live coast-to-coast broadcast of the Miss America Pageant, aired by ABC. Miss California, Lee Meriwether, was crowned the winner. (The Miss America Organization)

The following year's broadcast was nearly as historic, introducing the song, "There She Is, Miss America," and Bert Parks. From the moment viewers first heard the ebullient emcee serenade Miss America to "There She Is," the pair became Pageant legends. Lee Meriwether recalls, "Bert really cared about the girls. Of course, he sang like gangbusters, but the personality of the man is what I remember as endearing."

In addition to bringing Miss America into homes from coast to coast, television also solidified her public image. No longer cheesecake, Miss America now personified the wholesome American debutante. "The fifties were the age of innocence," says Evelyn Ay, Miss America 1954, "and that's what they expected Miss America to be. Be friendly, be bright, and have that Doris Day, fresh-scrubbed look."

Indeed, the era's queens were so wholesome that the first winner of the decade, Yolande Betbeze, refused to pose in a swimsuit after she was crowned, asserting that she was an opera singer—not a pinup girl. Alas, Catalina was a major sponsor who had donated contestants' swimsuits for years and paid Miss Americas to tour the country modeling their swimwear in department stores. Stunned by Yolande's refusal, executives asked the Pageant to force Miss America to promote Catalina's products. When Lenora backed Yolande's decision, Catalina withdrew its sponsorship, and at the suggestion of Miss America 1949, created another contest to promote its swimwear. "I understand that that little devil, Jacque Mercer, told him, 'Why don't you go run another pageant?' " says Slaughter, "and he did—and that's Miss Universe!" The resulting Miss USA/Universe pageants, unlike Miss America, which has evolved into a talent/scholarship pageant, retained their status as true "beauty pageants."

Of course, there were exceptions to the prepackaged wholesomeness of the era, most notably blond bombshell Marilyn Monroe. In a legendary moment in pageantry, seductive Monroe and straight-laced Miss America came face-to-face when the screen goddess served as grand marshal of the Pageant's parade. There Marilyn created a sensation riding down the Boardwalk in a low-cut dress, blowing kisses to the crowd. "Wow, was it ever a big deal!" recalls Neva Langley, Miss America 1953. "It was embarrassing for the Pageant at the time because she wore the first dress anybody had ever worn, I suppose, that was cut down to her midriff. I actually think she was rather exposed several times!"

A few years later, one contestant blended Monroe's sex appeal with Miss America's trademark sweetness to win the crown. Marian McKnight, Miss South Carolina, a blond singer who developed laryngitis, decided to imitate Monroe as her talent. She recalls slinking on-stage in a gown that showed "as much cleavage as we could show then—or that we dared show then—and I just sort of fluffed my hair up the way Marilyn did, lowered the eyes, did the pout, and the whispery voice." Charmed, judges awarded her the 1957 Miss America title. Only later did she learn that Monroe's ex-husband, Joe DiMaggio, was in the audience watching her act with amusement. Stunned, she drawled, "I'm just so glad I didn't see him!"

By the end of the 1950s, aided by the magic of television, Miss America the person had become what every little girl wanted to be and every red-blooded boy wanted to marry—and Miss America the Pageant had emerged as one of the most successful shows on television and a true American institution.

Kay's Green Chili

Vegetable oil
2½ to 3 pounds fresh pork cut into bite-size pieces (roast, chops, tenderloin, etc.)
1 large onion, chopped
4 tablespoons all-purpose flour
4 cups water, divided
4 fresh tomatoes, chopped
2 7-ounce cans diced medium-hot green chilies or 1 pint roasted chilies
½ hot jalapeño pepper, diced (more or less according to taste)
Garlic salt to taste
Salt and pepper to taste

. . . .

Cover the bottom of a Dutch oven with oil. Add the pork pieces and onion, and brown slightly. Stir in the flour and 1 cup of water. Add the remaining ingredients and stir well. Cook on low heat for 2 to 3 hours. Serve as chili with tortillas, over eggs, or enchiladas; many uses. Yields 8 or more servings.

Kay Anne Goforth Gatz-Wilhelm, Miss Kansas 1952

Stuffed Pumpkin

1 small pumpkin
2 tablespoons butter or margarine
1 medium onion, cut up
2 pounds lean ground pork
1 pound lean ground beef
4 medium potatoes, boiled and mashed with a small pat of butter
1 cup bread crumbs
1 teaspoon cloves
Salt to taste
Dash of pepper

. . . .

Preheat oven to 375°. Slice the top off of the pumpkin and set aside. Remove all of the seeds inside. Melt the butter in a skillet. Add onion and sauté until transparent. Add the meat and cook until brown. Add the mashed potatoes and bread crumbs. Add the seasonings. Spoon the mixture into the pumpkin shell. Place the lid on the pumpkin and bake for 1 hour or until the pumpkin is soft when pricked with fork. Yields 6 to 8 servings.

Rose Brouillette Smith, Miss Rhode Island 1934

Meal in a Pumpkin

This recipe has been shared by a friend who saw me crowned "Miss Iowa." Some forty years later, and living in Phoenix, Arizona, we serve together on the Screen Actors Guild Board of Directors and take active parts in the community!

1 medium pumpkin
1 cup chopped onion
½ cup chopped green pepper
1½ pounds ground beef
2 tablespoons vegetable oil
1 teaspoon salt
Dash of pepper
1 bay leaf
4 cups chicken bouillon
2 cups rice
1 tablespoon margarine

. . . .

Preheat oven to 350°. Remove the insides of the pumpkin, rinse, and salt the inside. Put the top back on and bake on a cookie sheet for 1 hour. Meanwhile, cook the onion, pepper, and beef in the oil until browned. Add the seasonings, bouillon, and bay leaf. Bring the mixture to a boil. Add the rice and margarine and simmer for 15 minutes. Pour the mixture into the pumpkin and bake for an additional 15 minutes. Yields 4 to 6 servings.

Carolyn Hill Pain, Miss Iowa 1952

Magnanimous Mother Nature

On her way to becoming Miss America 1953, Georgia's Neva Langley was nearly frisked by chaperons after jealous contestants and their parents complained that she was padding and asked to have her checked. Only her chaperon's adamant assurances that Miss Georgia's curves were all due to Mother Nature's generosity spared Neva the indignity of being frisked.

A successor had the opposite problem. After Lee Meriwether placed a dismal twentieth in her state's swimsuit contest, her director ordered her a custom swimsuit with a strategically ruffled brassiere. "It hid a multitude of sins!" Lee quips. When Meriwether was named Miss America 1955, her sorority sisters couldn't resist sending her a teasing telegram: "Thought they checked you for falsies! Love Delta Phi."

Yum Yums

¾ cup ketchup
2 cups water
2 teaspoons chili powder
1 onion, chopped
2 tablespoons dry mustard
1½ pounds lean ground beef
Salt and pepper to taste
Buns, buttered and toasted

. . . .

Combine the ketchup, water, chili powder, onion, and mustard, and simmer for 5 minutes. Add the ground beef and season to taste. Simmer for another 45 minutes. To serve, spoon over buttered, toasted buns. Yields 12 to 16 servings.

Sharon Ritchie Mullin, Miss America 1956

Spicy Barbecue Joes

2 pounds ground beef
2 cups chopped onion
1½ cups ketchup
⅓ cup dark corn syrup
⅓ cup prepared spicy brown mustard
2½ tablespoons vinegar
1½ tablespoons chili powder
¾ teaspoon cayenne pepper

. . . .

Cook the ground beef and onion over medium heat until browned. Drain off excess fat. Stir in the ketchup, corn syrup, mustard, vinegar, chili powder, and cayenne pepper. Bring to a boil. Reduce the heat and simmer, stirring occasionally, for 30 minutes. Serve on hamburger buns or over hot dogs on buns. Yields 10 to 12 servings.

Note: Mixture may be frozen. Defrost and reheat over low heat.

Kit Field Kruger, Miss Indiana 1968

Mom's Barbecue Sauce

This recipe truly is a family secret!
I came from a farm and good meat was always a part of our lives. This barbecue sauce was always on the table. It has a tangy but slightly sweet taste, much better than any barbecue sauce sold commercially.
It is fantastic on pork, chicken, and beef.

1 large bunch celery
1 to 2 large onions
2 green bell peppers
1 gallon ketchup
2 cups firmly packed brown sugar
1 cup vinegar
1 to 2 teaspoons chili powder
Tabasco sauce to taste

¼ cup Worcestershire sauce
2 tablespoons oregano
2 tablespoons basil

. . . .

Finely chop or shred the celery, onion, and pepper. Combine the remaining ingredients and simmer for 2 to 3 hours, stirring frequently. Pour ½ cup over any meat before cooking or use it as a condiment. Yields 6 quarts.

Note: Can be frozen or canned.

Nancy Beatty Buschart, Miss Illinois 1977

Red Beans & Sausage

1 pound red beans
6 cups water
Pinch baking soda
5 slices bacon, chopped
1 large onion, chopped
1 piece green bell pepper
Pinch of thyme
Salt and pepper to taste
¼ cup chopped celery
1 3-ounce can Italian-style tomato paste
2 teaspoons Worcestershire sauce
¼ teaspoon Louisiana Red Hot Sauce
1 clove garlic, chopped
2 pounds cooked or smoked sausage, cut into bite-size pieces
Hot, cooked rice

. . . .

Soak the beans in 6 cups of water overnight. Drain. Place the beans in a pot and cover them with cold water. Bring to a boil. Add the baking soda. Add the remaining ingredients, except for the sausage and rice. Cover and cook slowly over low heat for 2 to 2½ hours. Add the sausage and heat through. Serve over steamed rice. Yields 6 to 8 servings.

Caroline Masur, Miss Louisiana Pageant

Lamb with Rosemary

Since I spend time in Canada, I've acquired a taste for lamb. This is easy and delicious. It is great with roasted potatoes brushed with butter or olive oil and sprinkled with rosemary and thyme, then roasted to a golden brown.

½ cup dry red wine
1 tablespoon olive oil
2 cloves garlic, minced
1½ teaspoons fresh rosemary, chopped (or ½ teaspoon dried rosemary)
4 lamb chops
4 tablespoons butter, divided
2 tablespoons minced shallots
½ cup lamb or beef stock
Salt and pepper to taste

. . . .

Combine the wine, oil, garlic, and rosemary. Pour the mixture over the meat and marinate for 1 to 2 hours. Remove the meat, reserving the marinade. Pat the meat dry with paper towels. In a large skillet, melt 2 tablespoons of butter over medium-high heat. Cook the meat for about 3 minutes on each side or to desired doneness. Remove the meat and keep warm. Pour off all but 1 tablespoon of the fat from the pan, and add the shallots. Sauté for 1 minute or until soft. Strain the reserved marinade and add it to the pan along with the stock. Over high heat, reduce the sauce slightly. Add any juices that have accumulated around the lamb. Whisk in the remaining butter and season with salt and pepper. Strain the sauce, if desired, and pour it over the chops. Serve with mint sauce or jelly. Yields 4 servings.

Kylene Barker, Miss America 1979

By the 1950s, Miss America's image had become the wholesome girl next door with a hint of sex appeal, as exemplified by Mary Ann Mobley, Miss America 1959, a church choir singer who won the talent competition performing a mock strip tease. Second from the left is singer Anita Bryant, who finished as Second Runner-Up. (The Miss America Organization)

Lamb Medallions with Madeira Sauce

2 large onions, chopped
1½ sticks butter, divided
¾ cup milk
2 tablespoons all-purpose flour
Bay leaf
Salt to taste
White pepper to taste
12 cooked artichoke hearts
12 French-cut lamb chops
¼ cup Madeira wine
½ cup beef stock

Boil the onions in water, simmer for 5 minutes, and drain. Melt 4 tablespoons of butter in a pan, add the onions, and cook for 10 minutes, but do not brown. In another pan, add the milk, 2 tablespoons of butter, and the flour. Stirring slowly, add the bay leaf, salt, and pepper. Bring to a boil. Add the sauce to the onions. Cover and simmer for 5 minutes. Purée in a food processor. Heat the artichokes. Remove the bone and fat from the chops and sauté. Add the Madeira wine and stock, swirl in the remaining butter, and season with salt and pepper. Arrange the chops on a platter, fill each artichoke heart with the onion sauce, and place it on top of a chop medallion. Drizzle Madeira sauce over top. Yields 12 servings.

Jeanne Cangemi Bishop-Parise, Miss Nevada 1979

Western Lamb Riblets

3 pounds lamb riblets
¼ cup water
3 tablespoons olive oil
¼ cup red wine vinegar
½ cup chili sauce or ketchup
3 tablespoons Worcestershire sauce
1 tablespoon dry mustard
1½ teaspoons salt
½ teaspoon pepper
2 tablespoons diced onion
1 clove garlic, diced

Preheat oven to 325°. Place the lamb riblets on a rack in a shallow pan. Bake for 1½ hours. Drain off the drippings. Combine all remaining ingredients, mix well, and simmer a few minutes in the microwave. Pour and brush sauce over the riblets. Continue baking for 1½ hours longer, basting occasionally with sauce. Turn the riblets twice to coat the undersides. Yields 12 servings.

Karen Whittet Mannoni, Miss Montana 1952

Nevada Lamb

1 6 to 7-pound boned leg of lamb
½ teaspoon crushed dried thyme (or more)
1 egg, beaten
¼ cup milk
1 clove garlic, crushed
¼ teaspoon salt
⅛ teaspoon pepper
½ cup chopped Italian parsley
⅓ cup pine nuts, chopped
¼ cup soft rye bread crumbs
½ pound ground cooked ham

Preheat oven to 325°. With knife, enlarge the cavity of the leg of lamb. Rub inside and out with thyme. Combine the egg, milk, garlic, salt, and pepper. Add the parsley, pine nuts, bread crumbs, and ground ham. (Instead of grinding, I sometimes use the Cuisinart to chop the ham.) Mix well and fill the cavity. Tie the lamb and place it on a rack in a shallow roasting pan. Bake for 2¼ to 2½ hours, or to desired doneness. (We prefer to barbecue it in a covered barbecue.) Yields 10 to 12 servings.

Karen Wastun-Martin, Miss Nevada 1969

Spareribs and Sauce

1 pound pork ribs per person
Rind of one small orange
½ cup maple syrup
½ cup ketchup
Garlic to taste
Juice from ½ orange
1 tablespoon vinegar
1 tablespoon vegetable oil
½ teaspoon mustard
½ teaspoon Worcestershire sauce
1 tablespoon butter
Salt and pepper to taste

Preheat oven to 325°. Cut the orange rind into strips and dice very small. Combine all of the ingredients, except for the ribs, and bring them to a boil. Set aside. Place the ribs in a roaster. Bake, covered, for 1 hour. After 1 hour, pour off the fat and baste with the sauce. Return to the oven, uncovered, at 400° for 45 minutes. Continue to baste. Make sure to bake the ribs without sauce for the first hour. Yields approximately 1 pound of ribs per person.

Lea Schiazza-Cantwell, Miss Pennsylvania 1985

Iowa Pork Roast

This recipe was given to me by my Miss Iowa chaperon and good friend, Linette Johnston. She also accompanied me to the Miss America Pageant in 1990.

1 teaspoon salt
½ teaspoon pepper
1 teaspoon marjoram
1 6-pound boneless pork loin roast
2 bay leaves
½ stick butter
6 shallots, thinly sliced
¼ cup all-purpose flour
2 cups dry white wine
1 pound sliced fresh mushrooms
2 onions, thinly sliced
1 cup sauerkraut with some juice
1 16-ounce carton sour cream
3 to 4 beef bouillon cubes
1 tablespoon chives
Salt and pepper to taste

. . . .

Preheat oven to 500°. Rub the salt, pepper, and marjoram into the roast. Place the roast in a roasting pan with bay leaves on top. Bake, uncovered, for 20 to 30 minutes. Remove and drain the fat. Reduce heat to 350°. Melt the butter in a skillet until it sizzles. Add the shallots and brown lightly. Stir in the flour and cook 2 more minutes. Add the wine and mix thoroughly. Stir in the fresh mushrooms, onion, sauerkraut, sour cream, bouillon cubes, chives, salt, and pepper. Blend well. Pour the sauce over the meat. Cover and continue baking an additional 2½ to 3 hours. Slice and serve with sauce. May be served with buttered noodles. Yields 10 to 12 servings.

Kerri Lynne Rosenberg Burkhardt, Miss Iowa 1990

Ham and Broccoli Bake

2 10-ounce packages frozen broccoli
1 cup chopped ham
1½ cups cubed cheese
1 cup Bisquick
1½ cups milk
4 eggs

. . . .

Defrost the broccoli. Preheat oven to 350°. Layer the ham, broccoli, and cheese in a 2-quart casserole dish. Combine the remaining ingredients and pour over top. Bake for 50 minutes. Yields 4 servings.

Mary Shelby Bauer, Miss Passaic, New Jersey 1927

Pork Chops with Dressing

3 to 4 slices bread, torn up or cubed (use dry or older bread)
1 10¾-ounce can cream of mushroom soup
Salt and pepper to taste
2 tablespoons melted butter
1 4-ounce can mushrooms, drained
Dried onions to taste
4 pork chops, cut 1-inch thick

. . . .

Preheat oven to 350°. Combine the first 6 ingredients. Arrange the pork chops in a large baking dish and place ¼ of the dressing on each chop. Bake for 1 hour or until the dressing is brown. Check during baking to make sure some juice remains in the bottom of the baking dish. If it is dry, add ¼ cup water. Yields 4 servings.

Linda Hagan Kvanbeck, Miss Minnesota 1972

Great Granite State Pork Chops

1 tablespoon vegetable oil
6 center-cut pork chops
1 cup sweet apple cider (NOT vinegar!!!)
½ cup New Hampshire pure maple syrup
½ cup ketchup
¼ teaspoon ground cloves
¼ teaspoon ground ginger
1 tablespoon minced garlic
½ teaspoon dried, crushed rosemary
1 green onion, chopped
3 apples, preferably McIntosh, peeled, cored, and sliced thin
Vegetable cooking spray

Place the vegetable oil in a large skillet. Over medium-high heat, brown the pork chops on both sides. Remove to a baking dish. Preheat oven to 350°. In the same skillet, combine the cider, syrup, ketchup, cloves, ginger, garlic, rosemary, and green onion. Over medium-high heat, stir until warmed through, about 2 to 3 minutes. Shut off the heat. Return the chops to the skillet, turning in the sauce to cover. Spray the baking dish with cooking spray and place the coated chops back in the baking dish. Set remaining sauce aside. Top the chops with the apples. Bake for 40 minutes. Pour the remaining sauce over the top of the apples and chops. Bake an additional 20 minutes. Yields 6 servings.

Cathy Burnham, Miss New Hampshire 1975

In 1960, in an historic Pageant reunion, Miss America 1921, Margaret Gorman, and four of the Pageant's original directors, William Fennan, Louis St. John, Harry Latz, and Harry Godshall, gathered in Atlantic City.

Hungarian Ham Squares

6 eggs
¾ cup sour cream
½ teaspoon salt
1 cup finely chopped ham
½ tablespoon finely chopped green onion
½ cup shredded Swiss cheese
2 tablespoons butter, melted
¼ cup hulled sunflower seeds (optional)
Paprika (optional)

. . . .

Preheat oven to 350°. Beat the eggs until light; add the sour cream, salt, ham, onion, cheese, and butter. Pour into a buttered 9-inch square pan and sprinkle with the seeds and paprika. Bake for 10 to 15 minutes or until set. If desired, bake in advance and reheat in 350° oven until heated through. Recipe can be doubled and baked in 9 x 13-inch pan. Yields 2 dozen small squares.

Becky Schneberger, Miss Minnesota Pageant

Roast Pork and Sauerkraut

4- to 5-pound boneless pork roast (seasoned with salt, pepper, and garlic powder)
3 small onions, coarsely chopped
6 carrots, cut lengthwise into quarters
6 potatoes, cut into eighths
1 10¾-ounce can soup (tomato, onion, or cream of mushroom)
2 tablespoons tomato sauce
2 bags sauerkraut
1 cup firmly packed brown sugar

. . . .

Preheat oven to 350°. Place the roast in a roasting pan, add the remaining ingredients, adding the sauerkraut and brown sugar last. Cover and roast for 3 hours, or until the pork is fork-tender. Remove the roast from the oven. Place the meat on a serving platter . Let stand for a few minutes. Cut into slices. Arrange the sauerkraut around the meat, then top with the vegetables. Yields 8 to 10 servings.

Maxine Waack Field, Miss Ohio 1948

Pierogis

In memory of my brother, Nick Rafko.
This was his favorite meal.

4 eggs
2 teaspoons salt
1 tablespoon vegetable oil
1 cup water
4½ to 5 cups flour
8 potatoes, boiled and mashed with butter, salt, and pepper
1 8-ounce package cream cheese
1 16-ounce carton ricotta cheese
1 16-ounce carton dry curd cottage cheese
1 pound salt pork
Melted butter
Sour cream

. . . .

Beat the eggs, then add the salt, oil, and water. Add the flour and knead until smooth. Roll the dough out on a floured board to a thickness slightly thinner than a pie crust. Cut into 3½- to 4-inch circles. Mash the next 4 ingredients together and place a heaping tablespoon of the mixture in the center of each circle. Fold over to form a half-circle. Seal with a little water and pinch the edges. Drop into boiling salted water until the pierogis rise to the top. Drain. Cut the salt pork in small pieces and fry it. Combine salt pork and pierogis and top with melted butter or sour cream. Yields 8 to 10 servings.

Kaye Lani Rafko Wilson, Miss America 1988

The Case of the Royal Two-Timer

During the televised onstage interviews at the 1958 Miss America Pageant, two miffed finalists informed a startled Bert Parks that they had discovered they shared a common bond—the same two-timing air force cadet boyfriend! As millions of armchair viewers watched in amusement, Miss Iowa pronounced judgment on the philandering cadet. "I think he now has two ex-girlfriends!" "She said it very well," seconded Miss California.

Chicken Noodle Casserole

Whenever we go to visit my husband's grandmother, we always pray this is what she will make.

4 boneless, skinless chicken breasts
2 or 3 onion slices
1 8-ounce package extra wide noodles
1½ 10¾-ounce cans cream of chicken soup
Pepper to taste
Buttered bread crumbs

. . . .

Cook the chicken gently in water with the onion for about 1 hour. Put the chicken aside. If there is any fat, skim it off the broth. Cut the chicken into small cubes. Cook the noodles for about 10 minutes in the same water used for the chicken. If needed, add a little water. Preheat oven to 325°. Place the noodles on the bottom of a greased 9 x 13-inch pan. Add the chicken and spread the soup over top. Add pepper to taste and a little water. Top with buttered bread crumbs. Bake for 1 hour. Yields 10 to 12 servings.

VanNessa Straub-Krueger, Miss North Dakota 1991

Miss Vermont Busy Day Gourmet Chicken

4 chicken breasts, skinned
1 bottle Dijon-style Italian dressing
Frozen seedless grapes, taken off the stem

. . . .

Preheat oven to 350°. Place the chicken breasts in a glass baking dish. Pour ¾ of the dressing over the chicken. Marinate overnight or for at least 4 hours. Place the chicken on a broiler rack or barbecue grill. Bake for 25 minutes or until done, basting with the remainder of the dressing. Yields 4 servings.

Note: After dinner, pass a small platter of frozen grapes. They clean the palate prior to dessert much like Italian ice (with 75 percent fewer calories).

Wendy Masino Stebbins, Miss Vermont 1960

Fail-Proof Chicken

12 chicken thighs or breasts
1 10¾-ounce can cream of chicken soup
1 package onion soup mix
1 cup red wine
Hot, cooked noodles
Biscuits

. . . .

Preheat oven to 350°. Arrange the chicken on a flat pan. Combine the cream of chicken soup, onion soup mix, and red wine in a bowl and pour it over the chicken. Bake for 1½ hours. The chicken will be brown with lots of gourmet gravy. Serve the gravy over noodles or biscuits. Yields 12 servings.

Patricia Hill Burnett, Miss Michigan 1942

Chicken Teriyaki

⅔ cup soy sauce
¼ cup sherry
⅓ cup vegetable oil
1 tablespoon brown sugar or honey
2 tablespoons lemon juice
2 tablespoons minced onion
½ teaspoon ginger
1 clove minced garlic (or ½ teaspoon garlic salt)
Dash of pepper
8 chicken breasts, cut in half (or boneless, skinless chicken strips)

. . . .

Blend all of the ingredients except the chicken. Pour the mixture over the chicken and marinate overnight in the refrigerator. Grill over a medium fire 5 minutes per side. Yields 8 servings.

Nancy Humphries, Miss South Carolina 1987

Chicken Teriyaki Stir-Fry

1 10½-ounce can chicken broth
3 tablespoons soy sauce
2 tablespoons cornstarch
½ teaspoon ground ginger
1 tablespoon vegetable oil
4 5-ounce packages Teriyaki CHICKEN BY GEORGE®, cut into ½-inch strips
1 16-ounce package frozen vegetable medley, thawed

. . . .

Combine the chicken broth, soy sauce, cornstarch, and ginger in a small bowl. Heat the oil in a wok or large skillet. Add the chicken to the wok and stir-fry for 3 to 4 minutes. Add the vegetables and broth. Cover and cook for 3 to 4 minutes or until the vegetables are hot.

Phyllis George, Miss America 1971

Miss Georgia's Chicken in the Clay Pot

Oregano to taste
½ teaspoon dry mustard
½ teaspoon ground cloves
4 tablespoons butter
3 tablespoons currant jelly
Salt and pepper to taste
1 5-pound chicken

. . . .

Preheat oven to 350°. Melt the spices, butter, and jelly over low heat. Salt and pepper the chicken. Place the chicken in a clay pot. Pour the butter and jelly mixture over the chicken. Bake for 1½ hours. Enjoy! Yields 8 servings.

Tammy Fulwider, Miss Georgia 1983

Apricot Chicken

1 teaspoon salt
⅛ teaspoon white pepper
½ cup all-purpose flour
1 4-pound fryer chicken, cut up
½ stick butter
¾ cup dark rum, divided
1 large onion, finely chopped
2 pinches of ginger, divided
½ cup chicken broth
1 cup apricots
½ cup water
1 tablespoon brown sugar

. . . .

Lenora Slaughter, national director from 1941 until her retirement in 1967, improved Miss America's image from glamour girl to college girl, and developed the Pageant's scholarship program, now the world's largest private scholarship fund for women. (Candid Camera of Atlantic City)

Add the salt and pepper to the flour and roll the chicken pieces in it. Melt the butter in a heavy frying pan and brown the chicken well on both sides. Pour in ½ cup of rum and ignite. (The rum ignites more easily if warmed over a low flame before pouring over the chicken.) When the flame has burned down, add the chopped onion and a pinch of ginger. Cook for 5 minutes, then add the chicken broth. Cook over low heat for 40 minutes or until the chicken is tender. Meanwhile, cook the apricots in water for 15 minutes, or until barely tender. Add the apricots to the chicken with the remaining rum, the brown sugar, and a pinch of ginger. Blend well and cook 1 minute longer. Pour sauce over the chicken and apricots. Yields 8 to 10 servings.

Laura Jean Emery, Miss California 1947

Barbecue Apricot Kabobs

1 onion, cut into 1-inch chunks
1 tablespoon olive oil
½ teaspoon sugar
32 dried apricots
3 5-ounce packages Mesquite Barbecue CHICKEN BY GEORGE®, cut into 32 cubes

Combine the onion, oil, and sugar and let stand at room temperature. Place the apricots in a small bowl and cover with warm water. Let stand for 30 minutes. Drain. Alternate chicken, apricots, and onion, four of each, on 8 skewers. Broil 4 inches from heat source, turning once, for 10 to 12 minutes or until chicken is browned and no longer pink inside. Yields 4 servings.

Phyllis George, Miss America 1971

Southern Fried Chicken

1 fryer chicken
Salt and pepper to taste
¾ cup all-purpose flour
1 teaspoon salt
¼ teaspoon pepper
Vegetable oil or shortening

Cut the chicken into pieces and salt and pepper each piece liberally. Combine the flour, salt, and pepper in a plastic bag. Shake each chicken piece in the bag, one at a time, to coat well with flour. Fry in deep fat, covered for the first 5 minutes, then uncovered until golden brown (about 15 minutes total cooking time). Turn the pieces occasionally. Yield: 8 servings.

Laura Sue Humphress, Miss Kentucky 1994

Chicken and Peppers Piccata

2 to 3 tablespoons olive oil
2 large red bell peppers, cut into squares
2 large onions, cut into wedges
1½ pounds boneless chicken breasts, cut into 1-inch cubes
2 large cloves garlic, minced
1 dried hot red pepper, crumbled
Grated rind and juice of 1 lemon
2 tablespoons butter
2 tablespoons finely chopped parsley
Salt and pepper to taste
Hot, cooked noodles

Heat the oil in a large skillet. Sauté the red pepper and onion until they begin to soften. Remove the vegetables from the oil with a slotted spoon and set them aside. Brown the chicken in the same skillet, adding additional oil if necessary. When the chicken is lightly browned, add the garlic and hot pepper. Reduce the heat slightly and cook, covered, for 2 minutes. Using a wooden spoon, stir in the lemon rind and juice. Stir well to dissolve any brown particles in the skillet. Add the butter, blending it well into sauce. Return the cooked pepper and onion to the skillet; sprinkle with chopped parsley. Season with salt and pepper. Heat well. Serve over cooked noodles. Yields 4 servings.

Jenna Wims Hashway, Miss Rhode Island 1988

Chicken Casserole

3 medium-sized chicken breasts
Water
2 chicken bouillon cubes
2 tablespoons celery leaves
1 cup uncooked chicken-flavored rice and seasonings
1 cup chopped celery
2 tablespoons butter
1½ 8-ounce cans water chestnuts, diced
1 10¾-ounce can cream of chicken soup
⅔ cup mayonnaise
1 tablespoon diced onion
1½ cups cornflakes
1 stick butter
Slivered almonds (optional)

Boil the chicken in a pot of water along with the bouillon and celery leaves. Cook the rice according to package directions. Sauté the celery in 2 tablespoons butter until partially cooked, not limp. Drain the chicken and cut it into bite-sized chunks. Combine the chicken, rice, and celery with the water chestnuts, soup, mayonnaise, and onion. Pour the mixture into a casserole and chill. Preheat oven to 350°. Crush the cornflakes and sprinkle over top. Melt the remaining 1 stick of butter and pour it over the casserole. Sprinkle almonds on top, if desired. Bake, uncovered, for 40 minutes, or until browned. Yields 8 servings.

Sharon Ritchie Mullin, Miss America 1956

Cyprus Chicken with Spaghetti

1 4-pound chicken, washed
1 28-ounce can stewed tomatoes, chopped
⅓ cup sunflower oil
2 cubes or 1 heaping teaspoon chicken bouillon
Dash of salt
½ teaspoon cinnamon
1 pound spaghetti, uncooked
¼ cup olive oil
¼ cup lemon juice
Dry grated ricotta or Parmesan cheese
Parsley or mint sprigs

Cut the chicken into serving pieces. Boil the chicken in a large pot of water. Add 2 or 3 tomatoes to the water. Boil for 40 minutes on medium-high heat. Remove and drain the chicken in a colander. In a wok or frying pan, heat the sunflower oil and add the chicken, browning each side for 15 to 20 minutes. Add the bouillon to a separate half-full pot of boiling water. Add the remaining tomatoes, salt, and cinnamon. Crack the spaghetti in half and cook it to the *al dente* stage. Turn off and cover with a lid. Then allow the spaghetti to soak up all the liquid in the pot. Remove the chicken from the pan and pour the oil over top. Add the lemon juice. Arrange nicely on a large platter and garnish with parsley or mint. Place the spaghetti in bowls. Serve with grated cheese. Yields 4 to 6 servings.

Debbie Giannopoulos Mustafa, Miss Oklahoma 1972

Baked Chicken Breasts

4 chicken breasts
4 slices bacon
Chipped beef

Sauce:

1 10¾-ounce can cream of mushroom soup
½ pint sour cream

Preheat oven to 300°. Wrap each chicken breast in a slice of bacon and place in a casserole dish that has been generously lined with chipped beef. Combine the soup and sour cream. Cover the chicken withthe mixture. Bake, uncovered, for 3 hours. Yields 4 servings

Cody Marie Neville Mazuran, Miss Wyoming 1963

Miles on the Runway

At the 1948 Miss America Pageant, future movie star Vera Miles competed as Miss Kansas (as Vera Ralston). Her "talent" was talking about her plans to combine a career in Hollywood movies with raising a family of twelve children. Fortunately, her performance in the swimsuit competition was more memorable, where despite wearing the notorious zebra striped bathing suit required that year, her curves handily earned her the swimsuit trophy. Still, it wasn't enough and she was beaten by a marimba-playing Minnesota farm girl. Vera fared well enough, going on to appear in Hitchcock's thriller, *Psycho*.

Chicken Breasts Supreme

2 16-ounce cans French-style green beans, drained
4 chicken breasts, halved
Seasoned salt to taste
Paprika to taste
1 10¾-ounce can cream of mushroom soup
⅓ cup milk or chicken broth
1 cup grated Cheddar cheese
1 teaspoon parsley flakes
¼ cup chopped pimiento

Preheat oven to 325°. Place the green beans in a greased 2½-quart casserole or baking dish. Arrange the chicken on top of the beans, skin-side up. Sprinkle the seasoned salt and paprika over the chicken. Combine the mushroom soup and milk (and pour over the chicken. Sprinkle with cheese. Place parsley and pimiento on top. Cover and bake for 1½ hours. Remove the cover and bake for an additional 15 minutes or until cheese has browned. Yields 4 servings

Carlene F. Peterson, Miss Maine 1973

Hawaiian Chicken

4 whole chicken breasts, boned
Vegetable oil
1 cup pineapple juice
1 tablespoon honey
2 tablespoons brown sugar
⅓ cup soy sauce

. . . .

Preheat oven to 325°. Cut each chicken breast into 2 pieces. Lightly brown the chicken in the cooking oil. Do not overcook. Place the chicken in a casserole dish. Combine the remaining ingredients and pour the mixture over the chicken. Cover and bake for 1 hour. This can be prepared in advance and tastes better when left to marinate. Yields 8 servings.

Marjorie Kelly Shick, Miss Canada 1952

Hungarian Chicken Paprikas and Huluska

I am of Hungarian descent and my mother and grandmother made this every Sunday for dinner. When my daughter brings home a new friend, this is always what she requests. Obviously, it isn't a diet recipe, but we find that if we only eat it occasionally, it does no harm.

2 tablespoons vegetable oil
½ onion, finely chopped
1 tablespoon paprika
½ teaspoon salt
2½- to 3-pounds chicken pieces
2 teaspoons Tone's Chicken Soup Base (or 2 bouillon cubes)
Huluska
1 8-ounce carton whipping cream
1½ tablespoons all-purpose flour

. . . .

Heat the oil in a Dutch oven or large deep pot, add the onion and cook over low heat until the onions are clear, not browned. Stir in the paprika and salt. Add the chicken pieces and soup base. Stir until the chicken is fully coated with the paprika mixture. Cover with a tight-fitting lid and cook slowly over low heat. Check and stir about every 10 minutes. If natural juices don't develop enough in the bottom of the pot, add a little water (¼ cup). Total cooking time should be about 45 minutes. When the chicken is done, remove it from the pot. Make the Huluska. Combine the cream and flour until smooth. Add this mixture to the drippings and simmer for 2 minutes over medium heat until thickened. Add the Huluska to the sauce. Serve at once with the chicken. Yields 4 servings.

Huluska

3 eggs
½ cup milk
2 quarts water
2 teaspoons salt, divided
2½ cups all-purpose flour

. . . .

Beat the eggs together with the milk and 1 teaspoon of the salt. Add the flour and mix to form a soft dough. Bring the water to a boil, add the remaining salt, and drop the dough by scant teaspoonfuls into the boiling water. Boil until the dumplings rise to the top and float. Drain.

Kathleen Oros Reed, Miss Illinois 1965

Chicken Breasts in Wine Sauce with Brown Rice

Salt and pepper to taste
4 large chicken breasts, split, boneless, and skinless
Margarine or butter
2 10¾-ounce cans cream of mushroom soup
2 cups light sour cream
½ cup cooking sherry (optional)
1 8-ounce can mushroom pieces, drained (optional)
Hot, cooked Brown Rice

. . . .

Preheat oven to 300°. Salt and pepper the chicken, then brown in the margarine. Arrange the chicken in a baking dish in a single layer. Combine the remaining ingredients in the skillet with the chicken drippings. Pour the mixture over the chicken pieces and cover with foil. Bake for 1½ hours. Turn the oven up to 350° and bake for an additional 30 minutes, uncovered. Serve hot over Brown Rice. Yields 6 to 8 servings.

Brown Rice

1 cup uncooked rice
1 10¾-ounce can beef consommé soup
1 stick light margarine
2 tablespoons chopped onions

. . . .

Combine the ingredients in a greased 2-quart casserole dish. Bake at 350° for 1 hour.

Jane D. Briggeman Sype, Miss Nebraska 1969

Where's the Stake?

After three contestants dragged the poor audience through identical scenes from *Joan of Arc* in 1959, Pageant officials adopted a first-come-first-served rule allowing only one contestant to perform any given talent selection.

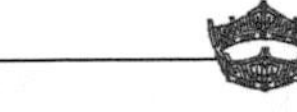

Breast of Chicken Normandie

4 green apples, peeled and sliced
1½ cups apple cider or juice
6 chicken breast halves, skinned and boned
All-purpose flour
Salt and pepper to taste
4 tablespoons sweet butter
4 tablespoons minced shallots
1½ cups whipping cream
¼ cup brandy
1 teaspoon Spice Islands chicken stock

. . . .

Poach the sliced apples in the apple juice. Remove the apples and set aside. Cut each chicken breast lengthwise and flatten between oiled waxed paper. Dust with flour, salt, and pepper. Sauté lightly in butter. Set aside. In the same pan, add the chopped shallots and sauté until clear. Add the apple juice from poaching the apples. Reduce by half; add the cream, brandy, and chicken stock. Simmer until the sauce is thickened. Cool. Return the chicken and apples to the sauce. Heat and serve. Yields 6 servings.

Marian McKnight Conway, Miss America 1957

Chicken Orange

This makes a very good dish for company that can be prepared in advance.

8 to 12 boneless chicken breasts, halved
Pancake mix
1 stick butter, melted
Celery salt to taste
Garlic salt to taste
Chopped parsley
Pepper to taste
2 cups orange juice
Juice of 1 lemon
¼ cup firmly packed brown sugar
1 teaspoon Worcestershire sauce
1 teaspoon salt
1 tablespoon molasses

. . . .

Preheat oven to 275°. Roll the chicken breasts in dry pancake mix. Coat with butter and place in a casserole dish. Sprinkle with the celery salt, garlic salt, parsley, and pepper. Bake, covered, for 2 hours. Remove from oven and lower oven temperature to 250°. Combine the orange juice and lemon juice, sugar, Worcestershire sauce, salt, and molasses. Pour over the chicken. Bake, uncovered, for 1 additional hour. Yields 8 to 12 servings.

Neva Jane Langley Fickling, Miss America 1953

Quick Chicken Vermouth

1 6-ounce box Uncle Ben's long grain and wild rice
1 pound fresh mushrooms, sliced
Butter
4 split boneless chicken breasts
1 8-ounce carton sour cream
1 10¾-ounce can cream of mushroom soup
½ cup vermouth

. . . .

Cook the rice according to package directions. Spread the prepared rice in the bottom of a large shallow baking dish. Melt the butter in a skillet and sauté the mushrooms. Remove the mushrooms and set them aside. Sauté the chicken in butter until brown. Arrange the chicken on top of the rice. Top with the sautéed mushrooms. Preheat oven to 350°. Combine remaining ingredients and pour over top of the chicken. Bake for 45 to 60 minutes. Yields 4 servings.

Note: This can be refrigerated until ready to cook.

Vonda Kay VanDyke Scoates, Miss America 1965

Baked Chicken Parmesan

¼ teaspoon garlic powder
¼ teaspoon paprika
⅛ teaspoon thyme
1 tablespoon parsley
¼ cup Parmesan cheese
⅓ cup bread crumbs
1 chicken, cut into serving pieces
⅓ cup water
1 tablespoon vegetable oil
½ stick margarine, melted

. . . .

Preheat oven to 350°. Combine the first 6 ingredients and use to coat the chicken. Pour water into a greased roasting pan and arrange chicken in the pan. Sprinkle with the oil and melted margarine. Bake, uncovered, for 30 minutes. Cover the dish with foil and bake for an additional 15 minutes at 325°. Remove the foil and bake for an additional 10 minutes. Yields 4 to 6 servings.

Shirley Cothran Barret, Miss America 1975

Chicken Parmesan

½ stick butter or margarine
4 chicken breast halves
1 tablespoon all-purpose flour
1 tablespoon lemon juice
¼ cup dry sherry
1 cup heavy cream
6 tablespoons grated Parmesan cheese
1 tablespoon butter or margarine
Rice (optional)

. . . .

Melt ½ stick butter in a skillet, add the chicken, and brown well. Cover the skillet, lower the heat, and cook for approximately 30 minutes, or until tender. Remove the chicken from the skillet and blend the flour into the butter remaining in the skillet. Cook over very low heat for about 10 minutes and stir in the lemon juice. Add the sherry and cream and reduce to make a sauce. Arrange the browned chicken breasts in a shallow serving dish and pour the sauce over the chicken. Sprinkle with the Parmesan cheese and dot with 1 tablespoon butter. This is good served over rice. Yields 4 servings.

Barbara Walker Hummel, Miss America 1947

Tortilla Chicken Casserole

This dish should be prepared a day ahead.

4 whole boneless chicken breasts
Salt and pepper to taste
Oregano to taste
1 10¾-ounce can cream of chicken soup
1 10¾-ounce can cream of mushroom soup
1 soup can milk
1 onion, grated
1 to 1½ 12-ounce cans Ortega Chile Salsa
12 corn tortillas
4 cups grated Cheddar cheese

. . . .

Preheat oven to 400°. Season the chicken breasts with salt, pepper, and oregano. Wrap the breasts in foil and bake for 1 hour. Cool the chicken, reserving all juices, and cut it into large chunks. Combine soups, milk, onion, and salsa. Pour 2 to 3 tablespoons of the chicken juices into a greased baking dish. Place a layer of tortillas in the dish. Cover with a layer of chicken, layer of soup mixture, then a layer of cheese. Repeat the layers until all ingredients are used. Refrigerate for 24 hours. Preheat oven to 325°. Bake until the cheese is melted thoroughly. Yields 6 to 8 servings.

Lee Meriwether, Miss America 1955

Roasted Chicken

1 fryer chicken
1 onion, halved
Parsley
Garlic salt to taste
Onion salt to taste
Paprika to taste
1 14½-ounce can chicken broth
Potatoes
Carrots

. . . .

Preheat oven to 375°. Skin the chicken and place in a large baking pan. Stuff the chicken with ½ the onion, a large handful of parsley, and then another ½ onion. (That's the secret! The stuffing, which is not to be eaten, makes the chicken so very moist.) Season with garlic and onion salt, and paprika. Pour in the chicken broth. Add potatoes and carrots. Roast, uncovered, for 1½ to 2 hours. Yields 4 to 6 servings.

Marilyn Van Derbur Atler, Miss America 1958

The late Bert Parks, the Pageant's master of ceremonies for a quarter of a century (1955 to 1979), was famous for his inimitable rendition of "There She Is, Miss America." (The Miss America Organization)

Mexican Chicken Kiev

8 chicken breast halves, skinned and boned
1 7-ounce can diced green chilies
4 ounces Monterey Jack cheese, sliced
½ cup fine dry bread crumbs
¼ cup grated Parmesan cheese
1 tablespoon chili powder
½ teaspoon salt
¼ teaspoon cumin
¼ teaspoon black pepper
¾ stick butter, melted
Tomato sauce

. . . .

Pound the chicken breasts to ¼-inch thickness. Place 2 tablespoons of the chilies, and 1 slice of cheese on each breast. Roll up and tuck the ends under. Combine the bread crumbs, Parmesan cheese, chili powder, salt, cumin, and pepper. Dip the chicken in the melted butter, roll it in the crumb mixture, and place it, seam-side down, in an oblong baking dish. Drizzle with the remaining melted butter. Cover and chill 4 hours or overnight. Preheat oven to 400°. Bake, uncovered, for 20 minutes. Serve with tomato sauce, seasoned to taste. Yields 8 servings.

Tawny Godin, Miss America 1976

Onion Baked Chicken

This dish is easy and makes its own gravy.
Great served over white or brown rice.

1 chicken, boned and cut up in medium pieces, or 4 to 5 whole chicken breasts
1 cup Bisquick
1 teaspoon salt
½ teaspoon pepper
¼ teaspoon paprika
4 teaspoons butter or margarine
1 package dry onion soup mix
2 cups hot water

. . . .

Preheat oven to 325°. Combine the Bisquick, salt, pepper, and paprika in a bowl or plastic bag. Coat the chicken with the mixture and arrange in a 3-quart casserole dish. Dot with margarine. Combine the dry onion soup with the hot water and pour over the chicken. Cover the casserole dish and bake for 1 hour. Yields 4 to 5 servings.

Donna Axum Whitworth, Miss America 1964

Party Chicken

6 chicken breasts, halved, skinned, and boned
4 ounces boiled ham, sliced thin
6 slices bacon, cut in half
2 10¾-ounce cans cream of mushroom soup
1 pint sour cream
½ cup chablis (optional)

Preheat oven to 275°. Place each chicken breast on 1 ham slice folded in thirds. Lay a slice of bacon on top of each chicken breast. Place the chicken and ham in a casserole dish. Combine the soup with the sour cream and chablis and pour half over the chicken. Bake for 2 hours. Cover with the remaining sauce and bake for 1 additional hour. Yields 6 to 8 servings.

Note: This may be made ahead and refrigerated.

Ruth Malcomson Schaubel, Miss America 1924

The late Albert Marks, Jr. led the Pageant into the television age and served as chairman and chief executive officer for 25 years before retiring in 1987. (The Miss America Organization)

Vegetable and Chicken Stir-Fry

From the kitchen of my godmother, Patricia Stone Motes.

¾ cup chicken broth
2 teaspoons cornstarch
2 whole boneless, skinless chicken breasts, cut in thin strips (¾ to 1 pound)
1 tablespoon soy sauce
2 teaspoons salt-free seasoning, divided
2 tablespoons vegetable oil, divided
2 cups fresh broccoli florets
1 medium red or green bell pepper, cut into thin strips
1 medium onion, cut into thin strips
1 cup sliced fresh mushrooms
Hot cooked rice or pasta

Mix the broth and cornstarch, set aside. Combine the chicken strips, soy sauce, and 1 teaspoon salt-free seasoning in a medium bowl. Heat 1 tablespoon oil in a large skillet over medium-high heat. Add the chicken mixture and stir-fry for 2 to 3 minutes or until done. Remove the chicken from the skillet to a serving dish. Heat the remaining oil in the same skillet over medium heat. Add vegetables and remaining salt-free seasoning. Stir-fry until crisp-tender. Return the chicken to the skillet. Stir the broth-cornstarch mixture to blend and add it to the chicken and vegetables. Bring the mixture to a boil, stirring constantly. Cook for 1 minute or until the sauce is bubbly and slightly thickened. Serve over steamed rice or pasta. Yields 4 to 6 servings.

Kimberly Aiken, Miss America 1994

Chicken Enchiladas with Sour Cream

4 cups diced, cooked chicken
2 cups (or more) grated Cheddar cheese
1 pint sour cream
12 flour tortillas
Vegetable oil
2 10-ounce cans crushed or minced tomatoes with green chilies

. . . .

Preheat oven to 350°. Combine the chicken, cheese, and sour cream. Cook the tortillas in ½-inch of oil one at a time, briefly on each side. Dip each tortilla into the tomatoes and chilies, then fill with the chicken mixture. Roll. Place the rolls close together in a flat, greased casserole dish. Pour the remaining sauce over all. Bake for 10 to 15 minutes. Yields 12 servings.

Sharlene Wells Hawkes, Miss America 1985

Chicken Enchiladas

1 onion, chopped
½ stick butter
2 10¾-ounce cans cream of chicken soup
1 soup can water (or chicken broth)
1 can mild green chilies
2 cups chopped cooked chicken
1 12-ounce bag Doritos, crushed
Grated cheese

. . . .

Preheat oven to 350°. Brown onion in butter. Add soup, water, and green chilies. Heat and add chicken. Sprinkle the Doritos in the bottom of a casserole dish. Top with chicken mixture, then with grated cheese. Bake for 20 minutes. Yields 4 to 6 servings.

Susan Powell, Miss America 1981

Chicken Dijon

6 chicken breasts, boned and skinned
1 package Pepperidge Farm seasoned croutons
1 16-ounce jar Dijon-style mustard
1 pint sour cream
1 stick butter

. . . .

Preheat oven to 400°. Rinse the chicken and pat it dry. Crush the croutons. Spread both sides of the chicken liberally with mustard, dip in sour cream, and roll heavily in the crushed croutons. Place the chicken in a greased baking dish and dot with butter. Cover the chicken with foil and bake for 30 minutes. Remove foil and bake at 450° for 15 minutes longer. Yields 6 servings.

Susan Perkins Botsford, Miss America 1978

Chicken-Broccoli Casserole

1 cup uncooked small elbow macaroni
6 small green onions, chopped
½ stick butter
American cheese
2 10-ounce packages frozen chopped broccoli
2 cups cubed boiled chicken
½ teaspoon salt
½ cup milk
1 10¾-ounce can cream of chicken soup

. . . .

Cook the macaroni and sauté the onions in butter. Preheat oven to 375°. Put macaroni in a well-greased 9 x 13-inch baking dish. Layer sliced American cheese over macaroni. Break up uncooked broccoli and layer it over the cheese. Sprinkle onion on broccoli then layer boiled chicken on top. Mix salt, milk, and soup, and pour over top. Top with American cheese. Bake for 30 minutes. Yields 6 servings.

Laura Lynn Watters, Miss Kansas 1983

Chicken Divan

3 whole chicken breasts
Onion
Celery
Carrot
1 bay leaf
Peppercorns
Salt to taste
2 10¾-ounce cans cream of chicken soup
1 8-ounce carton sour cream
1 cup mayonnaise
1 cup grated sharp Cheddar cheese
1 tablespoon lemon juice
Salt and pepper to taste
Paprika to taste
3 10-ounce packages frozen broccoli, cooked and drained
Parmesan cheese
Butter

. . . .

Cook the chicken breasts by simmering in water with onion, celery, carrot, bay leaf, peppercorns, and salt. Combine soup, sour cream, mayonnaise, grated cheese, lemon juice, and seasonings. Arrange broccoli in the bottom of a greased flat 3-quart casserole. Sprinkle generously with Parmesan cheese. Preheat oven to 350°. Remove the skin from the chicken and take the chicken from the bone; pull into pieces and spread over the broccoli. Sprinkle again with Parmesan and paprika. Dot with butter. Cook for 30 to 40 minutes, or until bubbly and hot throughout. Yields 4 to 6 servings.

Note: This can be made ahead and refrigerated or frozen and cooked later.

Terry Meeuwsen Friedrich, Miss America 1973

Miss America's Moral Crusade

BeBe Shopp, Miss America 1948, was the first queen to travel overseas during her reign, where she made headlines after innocently answering reporters' questions about falsies and the shocking new "bikini" worn on the French Riviera. "Well, I don't know what to say," the nineteen-year-old farm girl responded, "except that I don't think they're proper for American girls to wear." Within hours she was in international headlines, "Miss America on Moral Crusade!" "Well, I got to Europe and all the papers said I was on a crusade to clean up Europe," BeBe recalls, chuckling. "I mean, I wasn't saying anything—but they felt they couldn't have a Miss America going to sightsee and do appearances. She had to be 'on a crusade!'" Her father blamed the bad press on communists seeking to blemish the reputation of his daughter and fine American girls.

Chicken Parisienne

2 10-ounce packages broccoli, partially cooked
1 1.2-ounce package dry onion soup mix
1 pint sour cream
1 cup whipping cream, whipped
2 cups cooked chicken
1 tablespoon Parmesan cheese

. . . .

Preheat oven to 350°. Place the broccoli in a baking pan. Combine the soup mix with the sour cream and spoon half of the mixture over the broccoli. Fold the whipped cream into the remaining half of the sauce. Place the chicken breasts over the broccoli. Spoon the remaining sauce over top. Sprinkle with cheese. Bake for about 20 minutes. Yields 4 servings.

Marilyn Van Derbur Atler, Miss America 1958

Cumin Chicken Casserole

5 to 6 chicken breasts, skinned
Butter
Paprika to taste
3 cups water
1½ cups rice
½ onion, chopped
½ cup chopped green bell pepper
Salt to taste
1 teaspoon cumin

Brown the chicken in butter. Sprinkle paprika on the chicken. Preheat oven to 350°. Combine the water, rice, onion, green pepper, salt, and cumin and pour the mixture into a 9 x 13-inch pan. Place the chicken on top. Cover pan with foil. Bake for 45 minutes or until chicken is tender. Yields 5 to 6 servings.

Note: Chicken breasts may be cut in half to yield 10 to 12 servings.

Carene Clarke Jordan, Miss Idaho 1957

Chicken Divine

4 chicken breasts
¼ teaspoon salt
¼ teaspoon black pepper
1 10-ounce package frozen broccoli, cooked
1 tablespoon butter
Hot cooked rice (optional)

Sauce

1 10¾-ounce can cream of chicken soup
½ cup mayonnaise
½ teaspoon lemon juice
½ teaspoon curry powder
½ cup grated Cheddar cheese
¼ cup bread crumbs

Cover the chicken breasts with water. Add the salt and pepper. Simmer for 1 hour. Butter a casserole dish and arrange the chicken in the bottom of the dish. Top with the broccoli. Preheat oven to 350°. Combine all the sauce ingredients except the cheese and bread crumbs. Pour the sauce over the chicken and broccoli and sprinkle with cheese and bread crumbs. Bake for 30 minutes. Broil for 3 minutes to brown the top. Serve over rice, if desired. Yields 4 to 6 servings.

Valerie Ann Crooker, Miss Maine 1980

Baked Chicken Breasts Supreme

1 pint sour cream
¼ cup lemon juice
4 teaspoons Worcestershire sauce
4 teaspoons celery salt
2 teaspoons paprika
2 teaspoons garlic salt
4 teaspoons salt
½ teaspoon pepper
6 to 8 chicken breasts
2 cups seasoned bread crumbs
1 stick butter
½ cup shortening

Combine the first 8 ingredients in a bowl. Add the chicken, turning to coat. Marinate, covered, in the refrigerator overnight. The next day, roll the chicken in the bread crumbs. Arrange the chicken in a single layer in a baking dish. Preheat oven to 350°. Melt the butter and shortening and pour them over the chicken. Bake for 45 to 60 minutes, basting occasionally. Yields 6 to 8 servings.

BeBe Shopp Waring, Miss America 1948

Char's Chicken Tetrazzini

Remember the creamy noodle casserole you loved as a kid? It smelled and tasted so delicious after a long day at school! Now you can recreate that comforting one-dish meal in half the time with the help of your microwave oven. This tangy tetrazzini takes only 30 minutes from pasta to plate.

6 ounces fusilli (or spaghetti), broken
½ green bell pepper, chopped
1 small onion, chopped
1 8-ounce carton plain yogurt
2 tablespoons all-purpose flour
1 tablespoon plus ½ teaspoon paprika
¾ cup chicken broth
½ pound chicken, cooked and diced
1 4½-ounce jar mushrooms, drained
¼ cup grated Parmesan cheese
2 tablespoons water or white wine

. . . .

Cook the pasta according to the package directions. Cook the pepper and onion in a few tablespoons of water in a covered 2-quart microwave-safe casserole on HIGH power for 2 to 4 minutes, or until crisp-tender, stirring once. Drain. Combine the yogurt, flour, and 1 tablespoon of the paprika in a small bowl. Add this to the pepper mixture, and stir in the broth. Cook, uncovered, on HIGH for 6 to 8 minutes or until bubbly, stirring every minute until thickened, then every 30 seconds. Stir in the chicken, mushrooms, 2 tablespoons of cheese, and the water. Add the pasta and toss gently to coat. Cook, covered, on HIGH for 5 to 7 minutes or until hot, stirring once. Combine the remaining cheese and paprika and sprinkle over top. Yields 5 to 6 main-dish servings.

Charlene Woods Faber, Miss Colorado 1941

The Winning Bluff

In 1957, Marilyn Van Derbur's sorority sisters "drafted" her into a local pageant. She gamely went along with it until she learned a talent was required. With no idea what to perform, Marilyn taught herself to play one medley, "Tea for Two" and "Tenderly," on an organ. It was the only tune she could play, but she bluffed so convincingly that she won not only the local title, but the state and national titles as well. The day after she was crowned Miss America, Marilyn arrived on the set of the *Steve Allen Show* where the host informed her that when they went on live television in a few minutes she was to play "Night and Day!" Shocked and unable to convince the host to switch to "Tea for Two," Miss America gamely went on the air and pretended to play as Allen carried the tune on the piano.

Honey Suz Cornish Hen

½ medium onion, chopped
1 cup chopped green bell pepper
½ cup chopped mushrooms
3 tablespoons butter
1½ cups cooked brown rice
2 Cornish hens (1½ to 2 pounds each)
Salt, pepper, and Ac'cent to taste
½ cup golden honey

. . . .

Sauté the onion and green pepper in a skillet. Add the mushrooms when the onion and pepper are medium soft. Add the butter and rice. Mix thoroughly. Preheat oven to 325°. Prepare the hens by sprinkling them with salt, pepper, and Ac'cent. Stuff the hens with the rice mixture and place in a baking pan. Roast for 1 hour. Remove from the oven and glaze with honey. Return to the oven for 10 minutes. Yields 4 servings.

Suzette Charles, Miss America 1984

Pheasant in Sour Cream Sauce

½ stick butter
1 to 2 pheasants, cut into serving pieces
1 cup sour cream
1 teaspoon dry mustard
½ teaspoon salt
½ teaspoon pepper
¼ cup white wine
2 cloves garlic, crushed

Preheat oven to 350°. Melt the butter in a heavy casserole dish and brown the pheasant on all sides. Remove the casserole from the heat. Combine the sour cream, dry mustard, salt, pepper, wine, and garlic. Pour the mixture over the pheasant. Cover and bake for 1 to 1½ hours, or until tender. Yields 4 servings.

Note: Serve with wild rice, a green vegetable, a citrus/leafy salad, and a yeast roll. The sour cream sauce is wonderful over the wild rice as well.

Donna Axum Whitworth, Miss America 1964

Barbecued Turkey Breasts

1 cup vegetable oil
2 cups Seven-Up
1 cup soy sauce
1 tablespoon dehydrated horseradish
1 tablespoon garlic powder
5 pounds boneless turkey breast

Combine the first 5 ingredients in a large plastic container, and stir thoroughly. Place turkey in marinade and marinate for 8 hours before barbecuing. Barbecue slowly. Do not overcook or burn. Turn frequently, basting with barbecue sauce with each turn of the meat. Cook until the meat is white when cut with a knife. Yields 10 to 12 servings.

Karen Herd Talbot, Miss Idaho 1971

Kentucky's Original Hot Brown

Cheese Sauce

2 tablespoons butter
¼ cup all-purpose flour
2 cups milk
½ cup grated sharp Cheddar cheese
¼ cup grated Parmesan cheese
¼ teaspoon salt
½ teaspoon Worcestershire sauce

Sandwiches

8 slices trimmed toast
1 pound sliced cooked turkey breast
8 slices tomato
8 slices bacon, partially cooked (or ¼ pound baked country ham, thinly sliced)
4 ounces grated Parmesan cheese
Parsley sprigs

Melt the butter in a saucepan and blend in the flour. Add the milk, cheeses, and seasonings, stirring constantly until smooth and thickened. Set aside. Preheat oven to 400°. Cut the toast into triangles and arrange it in baking dishes. Place the turkey slices on top of the toast and cover with the hot cheese sauce. Top with tomato and bacon. Sprinkle with Parmesan cheese. Bake until bubbly. Garnish with parsley sprigs. Yields 8 servings.

Note: To freeze Kentucky Hot Browns, omit the tomato slices and wrap the sandwiches in aluminum foil. When ready to bake, remove the foil and bake at 375° until hot and bubbly.

Tonya Dee Virgin, Miss Kentucky 1993

Confetti Spaghetti

1 green bell pepper, chopped
12 scallions or 1 onion, diced
4 to 5 cloves garlic, minced
1 teaspoon basil
2 teaspoons parsley
1 teaspoon oregano
1 teaspoon salt
Red pepper flakes (optional)
1 jar capers (optional)
⅓ cup olive oil
⅓ cup balsamic or red wine vinegar
1 tablespoon Worcestershire sauce
2 to 3 tomatoes, diced
1 2-ounce tin anchovies plus oil, diced
6 ounces pitted black olives, halved
1 16-ounce package frozen peas, thawed and drained
¼ pound salami, cut in strips
¼ pound Provolone cheese, cut in strips
¼ pound prosciutti or other ham, cut in strips
4 to 6 ounces sweet pickled peppers or pimientos, diced
1 16-ounce box spaghetti, broken
3 to 4 ounces grated Parmesan or Romano cheese
8 to 10 romaine or lettuce leaves

. . . .

Sauté the green pepper, onion, garlic, and herbs in olive oil for no more than 2 minutes. Place this warm mixture in a large bowl and add the remaining ingredients except for the pasta, cheese, and lettuce. Toss. Cook the pasta to the *al dente* stage; drain. While hot, toss with warm herb mixture; add the grated cheese. Arrange in a large serving bowl lined with lettuce leaves. Serve immediately as a main dish or chill to serve as an antipasto or salad. Yields 4 to 6 main dish servings, or 8 to 10 side salad servings.

Lois Janet Piercy Hurley, Miss Pennsylvania 1959

Sweet 'n Simple

It may be a legend today, but the song, "There She Is, Miss America," began as a sudden impulse. A year before the first live telecast of the Miss America Pageant, songwriter Bernie Wayne (of "Blue Velvet" fame) read an article about the upcoming telecast. Although he had never seen a pageant before, Wayne sat down and penned the tune—in one hour.

Tosca's Pasta

This is my sainted mother's recipe.
Our fresh crab on the southern Oregon coast
makes this recipe even better tasting than
it was in Nevada.

4 tablespoons olive oil
3 medium potatoes, peeled and diced
2 onions, sliced
1 32-ounce can tomatoes
Salt and pepper to taste
2 tablespoons chopped parsley
½ pound crab meat
1 16-ounce box seashell pasta
4 quarts salted water, boiling
½ cup grated pecorino cheese

. . . .

Heat the oil in a large saucepan; add the potatoes and onions. Cook for 10 minutes, stirring constantly to prevent burning. Add the tomatoes, salt, pepper, and parsley. Cover and cook over low heat for 25 minutes. Add the crab meat during the last 3 to 5 minutes. Meanwhile, cook the pasta in rapidly boiling water until tender. Do not overcook. Drain. Place in a large hot bowl. Add the potato and crab mixture and the cheese. Mix thoroughly. Serve hot. Yields 6 servings.

Tosca Carolyn Masini Means, Miss Nevada 1950

Linguine Toscano

8 ounces whole wheat linguine
2 teaspoons olive oil
1 small onion, chopped
4 large cloves garlic, minced coarsely
1 14- to 16-ounce can crushed tomatoes
⅛ to ¼ teaspoon cayenne pepper
2 teaspoons oregano
2 large tomatoes, cut into wedges and then into strips
6 black olives, pitted, and sliced into thin circles
2 scant teaspoons grated Parmesan cheese per portion

Prepare the pasta according to package instructions or personal preference. If the pasta is done before you are ready, drain and keep it warm. Sauté the onion and 1 to 2 teaspoons of the minced garlic in 1 teaspoon of the olive oil. Add the crushed tomatoes, cayenne, and oregano. Simmer, uncovered, for 10 to 15 minutes. When ready to serve, sauté the remaining garlic in the remaining oil over medium heat for about 30 seconds. Add the tomato strips and increase the heat to medium-high. Toss over the heat for 1 to 2 minutes. Add the prepared tomato sauce. Simmer 1 to 2 minutes more and correct the seasonings. Add the cooked pasta. Blend with the sauce, being careful not to damage the noodles. Serve with black olive slices and Parmesan cheese sprinkled over each serving. Yields 6 servings.

Wendy Masino Stebbins, Miss Vermont 1960

For years, judges interviewed contestants over meals, changing tables every few minutes when officials rang a bell. Evelyn Ay, Miss America 1954, recalls, "It seemed that the minute you would pick up a fork of [food] and put it in your mouth, that's when the judge would ask you a question." (Fred Hess & Son)

Italian Spaghetti and Meat Sauce

2 pounds ground beef
1 medium onion, finely chopped
1 green bell pepper, finely chopped
2 15-ounce cans tomato sauce
2 12-ounce cans tomato paste
2 envelopes Italian-style spaghetti sauce mix
3 cups water
1 tablespoon sugar
1 teaspoon crushed oregano
2 cloves garlic, crushed
1 bay leaf, finely crushed
1 16-ounce package Italian-style spaghetti, cooked

Cook and stir the ground beef, onion, and green pepper in a large pan until the meat is brown and the vegetables are tender. Stir in the remaining ingredients, except for the spaghetti. Simmer, uncovered, for 1½ hours, stirring occasionally. Serve over hot spaghetti. Sauce can be refrigerated overnight before serving. Yields 4 to 6 servings.

Debbie Weuve Rohrer, Miss Iowa 1975

Chicken Spaghetti

1 chicken, boiled and cubed
1 package spaghetti, boiled in chicken broth
1 can tomatoes
1 bell pepper, diced
1 onion, diced
2 10¾-ounce cans cream of mushroom or cream of chicken soup
1 or 2 cloves garlic, chopped
1 teaspoon chili powder
1 jar sliced pimientos
1 cup diced celery
Salt and pepper to taste
Grated cheese

Preheat oven to 350°. Drain the spaghetti and combine all the ingredients, except the cheese. Add some of the chicken broth, if needed. Sprinkle generously with grated cheese. Bake for about 30 minutes. Yields 4 to 6 servings.

Tammy Copeland, Miss Delaware 1983

Spaghetti Cheese Pie

1 8-ounce package spaghetti
½ stick butter
1 cup cottage cheese
1 8-ounce package cream cheese, softened to room temperature
3 eggs
2 teaspoons dried dill
1 teaspoon dried chives
1 teaspoon salt
¼ teaspoon pepper
3 ounces Cheddar cheese slices

Cook the spaghetti according to the package directions. Drain and toss with ¼ cup butter. Place in a greased 1½-quart shallow casserole and shape into a "crust" pushing it up against sides to form a full border. Preheat oven to 350°. Beat the cottage and cream cheeses until smooth. Beat in the eggs, dill, chives, salt, and pepper. Pour the mixture into the spaghetti shell. Bake for 30 minutes or until set. Arrange the cheese slices on top of the pie. Return to the oven for a few minutes until the cheese is melted. Yields 4 to 6 servings.

Lisa Somodi, Miss Iowa 1991

Quicky Spaghetti and Meatballs

1½ pounds ground chuck
1 package hamburger seasoning (any brand)
½ teaspoon salt
½ teaspoon pepper
1 8-ounce jar pimiento-stuffed olives
2 tablespoons vegetable oil
1 package Lawry's Spaghetti Sauce mix
1 6-ounce can tomato paste
2½ cups water
¼ to ½ cup white wine
1 or 2 packages spaghetti

Place the ground chuck in a mixing bowl and add the hamburger seasoning, salt, and pepper. Mix thoroughly by hand. Form meatballs and place a stuffed olive in the center of each one. Balls should be 1½-inches in diameter. Brown meatballs on all sides in a skillet, using the oil to prevent sticking. Combine the Lawry's Spaghetti Sauce mix, tomato paste, water, and white wine, and stir well. Add this mixture to the meatballs. Bring to a boil, lower the heat, and simmer for 30 minutes, stirring several times. Prepare the spaghetti according to the package directions. Serve the sauce and meatballs over top. Yields 4 to 6 servings.

Anne Morse Bryant, Miss South Carolina 1946

Sensational Siblings

Neva Langley, Miss America 1953, and one of the most beautiful of all winners, recalls the unexpected downside of having her twenty-eight-year-old sister travel with her as her chaperon. "One thing that happened every now and then that wasn't funny at all at the time," Neva recalls, "was that we would get off an airplane and people would look at us and they wouldn't know which one of us was Miss America. It would just infuriate me! I would think, 'My gosh, how could they think she's Miss America? She's twenty-eight years old!' Well, when I turned twenty-eight, I called my sister and I said, 'Let me tell you something. Now I know exactly why they thought you were Miss America!"

Pasta alla Puttanesca

1 pound mild Italian sausage
6 tablespoons olive oil
2 cloves garlic, minced
2 28-ounce cans Italian plum tomatoes, drained and chopped
2 cups pitted black olives, halved
2 tablespoons capers
½ teaspoon red pepper flakes
1 can minced anchovies
½ cup fresh minced parsley
2 tablespoons fresh oregano (or 2 teaspoons dried)
Salt to taste
Freshly ground pepper to taste
1 pound spaghetti, cooked
Parmesan cheese

Cut the sausage into ½-inch slices; brown in skillet on all sides. Drain off all fat. Add the remaining ingredients except the spaghetti and cheese. Cook over medium-high heat, stirring often, until the sauce thickens slightly, about 10 minutes. Spoon over spaghetti that has been cooked in 1 gallon of boiling salted water until just tender. Serve with Parmesan cheese and extra red pepper flakes if desired. Yields 4 servings.

Nancy Fleming, Miss America 1961

N. Rokos/C P News

Practice Makes Perfect. Every moment viewers see in the Pageant must be perfectly timed, from complex production numbers to the "spontaneous" banter of the hosts.

Live from Atlantic City! At last, the telecast begins and Regis Philbin and Kathie Lee Gifford welcome fifty-five million viewers.

J.M. Frank/C P News

N. Rokos/C P News

Preliminary Winners. The announcement of the winners in the talent and swimsuit competitions offers a promising hint of who may make the Saturday night finals. Kathleen Farrell (left), Miss Illinois, learns that Catherine Lemkau (right), Miss Iowa, won the swimsuit competition in 1992.

N. Rokos/C P News

A Dream Comes True. As the auditor hands the emcee the official results, fifty state titleholders hold their breath. For Trisha Schaffer, Miss Kansas, Lea Mack, Miss Ohio, and Jennifer Makris, Miss New Jersey (left to right), who have just been selected as national semifinalists, the dream has become reality.

K.A. Frank/C P News

The Top Ten. Out of the thousands of entrants who dreamed of this moment in the spotlight, only ten contestants earned the right to compete in the nationally televised finals of the 1989 Miss America Pageant.

J.M. Frank/C P News

She's back! It is always a thrill for Miss America to return to the stage a year later. Debbye Turner, Miss America 1990, stars in a glittering production number.

J.M. Frank/C P News

Leading Man. Special guest star, vocal legend Kenny Rogers, serenades the national contestants and the audience.

N. Rokos/C P News

Communicating to Win. As millions of viewers look on, Heather Whitestone, Miss Alabama, explains her platform, "Anything is Possible," to emcee Regis Philbin.

S. Jaslecki/C P News

Proving that Anything IS Possible. Heather Whitestone reacts to the news that she is the first woman with a physical disability ever to earn the Miss America title.

J.M. Frank/C P News

Miss America Meets the Public. During her year, Miss America appears on dozens of talk shows. Leanza Cornett (1993) appeared on *Regis and Kathie Lee* soon after her victory.

J.M. Frank/C P News

Miss America Meets the Press. As the spokesperson for the largest private women's scholarship program in the world, Miss America's responsibilities include promoting the program during hundreds of press interviews.

K.A. Frank/C P News

The Final Walk. After an unforgettable year in the national spotlight, Gretchen Carlson, Miss America 1989, returns to Atlantic City to take her final walk on the famous runway that changed her life forever.

Spaghetti Pie

6 ounces spaghetti
2 eggs, beaten
¼ cup grated Parmesan cheese
2 teaspoons butter or margarine
½ cup chopped green bell pepper
⅓ cup chopped onion
1 cup sour cream
1 pound Italian sausage
1 6-ounce can tomato paste
1 cup water
4 ounces mozzarella cheese, cut into strips

. . . .

Break the spaghetti in half and cook according to the package directions. Drain. While the spaghetti is still warm, combine with the eggs and Parmesan cheese. Place the spaghetti in a well-greased 10-inch pie plate or 9 x 12-inch pan. Press up around the sides of the pan to form a crust. Melt the butter in a pan; add the green pepper and onion. Sauté until the onion is transparent. Add the sour cream. Spoon the mixture over the spaghetti. Remove the sausage from its casing. Crumble into the skillet and cook until done. Drain off the excess grease. Add the tomato paste and water to the sausage mixture. Simmer for 10 minutes. Preheat oven to 350°. Spoon the sausage over the sour cream mixture. Bake for 25 minutes. Add the mozzarella cheese strips and return to the oven until the cheese melts, about 5 minutes. Yields 5 to 6 servings.

Kimberly Kay Christiansen, Miss Colorado, 1980

Spinach Lasagna (or Vegetarian Lasagna)

1 medium to large onion, chopped
Margarine or olive oil
2 cloves garlic, minced
6 to 8 ounces mushrooms (fresh or canned), sliced
1 6-ounce can tomato sauce
1 6-ounce can tomato paste
1 teaspoon basil
1 teaspoon oregano
6 to 8 lasagna noodles
4 eggs (or Egg Beaters), divided
2 cups fat-free small curd cottage cheese
⅔ cup Parmesan cheese
2 10-ounce packages frozen chopped spinach, thawed
6 to 8 ounces low-fat Monterey Jack cheese, grated
6 to 8 ounces mozzarella cheese, grated

. . . .

Sauté the onion in a small amount of margarine or olive oil. Add the garlic and mushrooms and sauté. Add the tomato sauce, tomato paste, one can of water, and the spices. Stir together and simmer for at least 15 minutes. Boil the noodles until soft but not pasty. Rinse the noodles and drain. Add 2 beaten eggs to the noodles and mix gently. Combine the cottage cheese, Parmesan cheese, remaining eggs, and spinach, and mix well. Preheat oven to 350°. Grease the bottom of a 9 x 13-inch pan or baking dish. Spoon a small amount of sauce in the bottom of the pan and spread it around. Place a layer of noodles, a layer of filling, half of the Monterey Jack cheese, more sauce, noodles, filling, Monterey Jack cheese, and sauce. Bake the lasagna, covered with foil, for 45 minutes. Then turn the oven heat up to 450°, sprinkle the mozzarella cheese over the top, and return the dish, uncovered, to the oven for 5 minutes, or until the cheese has browned slightly. Yields 6 to 8 servings.

Marian Cox Hampton, Miss Illinois 1955

Elizabeth's Lasagna

2 28-ounce cans Italian-style peeled tomatoes
4 8-ounce cans tomato sauce
4 teaspoons salt, divided
3 teaspoons dried oregano
2 teaspoons onion salt
2 cups minced onion
2 cloves garlic, minced
⅓ cup olive oil
2 pounds ground chuck roast or round
2 teaspoons monosodium glutamate
2 tablespoons cooking or olive oil
¾ pound lasagna noodles
¾ pound ricotta cheese
½ pound thinly sliced or crumbled mozzarella cheese
½ pound grated Parmesan cheese

. . . .

Combine the Italian tomatoes, tomato sauce, 2 teaspoons salt, oregano, and onion salt in a large saucepan. Cook and start to simmer. Meanwhile, sauté the onions and garlic in ⅓ cup olive oil. When the onions are translucent, add the meat, monosodium glutamate, and the remaining salt. Cook until the meat loses its red color. Add to the tomato sauce and simmer for 2½ hours. Fill a large pot with water and add the oil. When the water comes to a boil, add the noodles and cook for 25 minutes, stirring occasionally. Drain and separate the noodles. Combine the ricotta, mozzarella, and Parmesan cheeses and set them aside. Preheat oven to 350°. Put a thin layer of sauce in bottom of two 12 x 8 x 2½-inch baking dishes, then crisscross a layer of lasagna noodles and a layer of the cheese mixture. Repeat the process twice with the sauce, noodles, and cheese. Bake for 40 minutes. Remove from the oven and let stand for 10 minutes. Yields 16 servings.

Elizabeth Ward, Miss America 1982

Pam's Lasagna

3 tablespoons olive oil
3 tablespoons butter
2 tablespoons chopped yellow onion
2 tablespoons chopped celery
2 tablespoons chopped carrots
1 clove garlic, minced
1½ pounds lean ground beef
2 tablespoons plus ½ teaspoon salt, divided
1 cup dry white wine
½ cup milk
½ teaspoon nutmeg
1 10-ounce can Italian tomatoes, roughly chopped with juice
1 8-ounce can tomato sauce
1 tablespoon parsley flakes
2 tablespoons sugar
½ teaspoon crushed basil
1 pint cottage cheese
½ cup grated Parmesan cheese, divided
½ teaspoon crushed oregano
8 ounces lasagna noodles, cooked and drained
8 ounces mozzarella cheese, sliced

. . . .

Brown the onions with all the oil and butter in an earthenware, heavy enameled, or cast-iron pot. When the onions have become translucent, add the celery, carrots, and garlic. Cook gently for 2 minutes. Add the ground beef, crumbling it in the pot with a fork. Add 2 tablespoons of salt and cook until the meat has become brown. Add the wine, turn the heat up to high, and cook until the wine has evaporated. Turn the heat down to medium and add the milk and nutmeg. Cook until the milk has evaporated. Then add the tomatoes, tomato sauce, parsley, sugar, and crushed basil. Cover and cook on low for 5 to 7 hours. Combine the cottage cheese, ¼ cup of the Parmesan cheese, the remaining salt, and crushed oregano. Preheat oven to 350°. Layer half the cooked noodles, sauce, mozzarella cheese, and cottage cheese mixture in a 9 x 13-inch pan.

Repeat, reserving enough sauce for a layer on top. Sprinkle with the remaining Parmesan cheese. Bake for 45 minutes. Yields 8 to 10 servings.

Pam Eldred, Miss America 1970

Veal Parisienne

2 2½-pound veal cutlets, sliced into thin scallops
Salt and pepper to taste
Flour
2 to 3 eggs, lightly beaten with 2 to 3 tablespoons water
Fine bread crumbs
Butter and vegetable oil (equal portions for sautéing veal)
2 tablespoons lemon juice
3 tablespoons butter
2 to 3 tablespoons parsley, minced
Scalloped lemon rounds for garnish

....

Place the veal between sheets of plastic wrap and pound thin without breaking the meat. Slice into neat scallops. Season lightly on both sides with salt and coarsely ground pepper. Dip into flour and shake well. Dip into the beaten eggs, letting the excess drip off. Coat well on both sides with fine bread crumbs and press with a spatula so that the crumbs adhere. Chill for 20 to 30 minutes to set the coating. Heat the butter and oil in a large skillet. Add the veal and cook briefly, browning on each side, and turning once only. When browned, remove to an ovenproof serving dish and keep warm. Add lemon juice to the skillet and deglaze by scraping up any brown bits from the bottom of the pan. Cut the remaining 3 tablespoons of butter into pieces and swirl into the pan bit by bit, letting the juices thicken. When the sauce is the consistency of heavy cream, add the minced parsley. Pour the sauce over the scallops. Garnish the platter with scalloped lemon rounds and serve very hot. Yields 6 servings of 4 to 6 ounces each.

Note: Scallops may be prepared ahead. Refrigerate until ready to cook. They also may be wrapped airtight and kept frozen for one month. Alternate or additional garnishes may be used. Suggested garnishes are: toast crescents sautéed in parsley butter; hard boiled eggs, sieved with the whites separated from the yolks and placed in toast cups or on lettuce; puff pastry crescents; cherry tomatoes filled with spinach or tiny peas. Chicken may be used in place of veal.

Dorothy Benham McGowan, Miss America 1977

Patio Cassoulet

1 medium onion, diced
½ pound Italian sausage
2 tablespoons vegetable oil
1 3½-pound fryer chicken, cut into serving pieces
½ teaspoon salt
1 16-ounce can plum tomatoes
1 green bell pepper, cut into rings
1 20-ounce can white kidney beans (cannellini beans)
½ teaspoon hot pepper sauce
1 teaspoon Worcestershire sauce

....

Cook the onion and sausage in oil until browned. Brown the chicken in a separate skillet and set aside. Preheat oven to 350°. Add the salt, tomatoes, and green peppers to the sausage. Pour into a casserole dish. Add the beans, hot pepper sauce, and Worcestershire sauce. Mix well. Add the chicken. Bake, covered, for 1 hour. Yields 4 servings.

Note: This can be assembled in the morning or the day before.

Patricia Donnelly Harris, Miss America 1939

Alaska Joins the Union

In the late 1950s when Alaska became a U.S. state, it sent its first representative to the Miss America Pageant. When Bert Parks introduced the state queens in alphabetical order during the parade of states, Miss Alaska suffered a severe case of stage fright and refused to walk on-stage. "I called, 'Alaska,' and nothing happened," Parks recalled. "Then we got to the end, and I was thinking she would never come, but someone finally coaxed her into coming out after Miss Wyoming. It gave me a grand opportunity to say, 'Ladies and gentlemen—Alaska has at last joined the Union!' "

Fast and Easy Crustless Quiche

We served this hot dish at my Miss New Jersey Pageant reception on a sweltering evening in July and none of the hearty pageant people noticed the heat one bit.

4 eggs
½ cup vegetable oil
¾ cup Bisquick
¼ cup grated Parmesan cheese
¼ cup Swiss cheese
½ small onion, chopped
1 cup cooked spinach

. . . .

Preheat oven to 350°. Combine the eggs, oil, and Bisquick. Add the remaining ingredients and pour into a 9-inch pie or quiche dish. Bake for 20 minutes in an electric oven, or for 30 minutes in a gas oven. Yields 8 servings.

Note: For a spicier quiche, use ½ cup jalapeño cheese, ¼ cup Parmesan cheese, ¼ cup pepper rings, and a small jar of mushrooms.

Linda Gialanella Giordano, Miss New Jersey 1972

Green Chili Quiche

Fresh green chilies are a staple in New Mexico. They are used in almost every type of dish from salads to desserts. Roye Sue Bradford, business manager for Miss New Mexico in 1990, shared this recipe with me. It originated in a local Mexican restaurant outside of Santa Fe.

3 tablespoons butter
2 medium onions, finely chopped
1½ tablespoons all-purpose flour
2 eggs
⅔ cup whipping cream
½ cup tequila
1 teaspoon salt
Pinch of nutmeg
Pinch of paprika
Pinch of sage
¾ cup grated Swiss cheese, divided
½ cup diced green chilies (fresh or canned)
9-inch pie shell, baked
⅛ teaspoon ground black pepper

. . . .

Melt the butter and sauté the onions until tender and golden brown in color. Sprinkle flour over the onions and cook over low heat, stirring constantly, until the onions are coated with flour. Remove from the heat and let cool. Preheat oven to 375°. Beat the eggs. Beat the cream, tequila, salt, pepper, nutmeg, paprika, and sage into the eggs. Stir in onions, ½ cup of the cheese, and the chilies. Pour into the pie shell and sprinkle with the remaining cheese. Bake for 20 minutes or until done. Yields 6 servings.

Jana McCoy, Miss New Mexico 1990

New Mexico Chalupas

6 large tortillas
Vegetable oil
Salsa to taste
1 cup refried beans
½ cup minced onion
1 cup grated longhorn cheese
1½ cups shredded lettuce
1 medium tomato, chopped
1½ cups guacamole
½ cup sour cream
Ripe olives

. . . .

Fry the tortillas one at a time in hot oil. Hold the center of the tortilla down in the oil with a wooden spoon so the tortilla forms a saucer shape. Drain on paper towels. Preheat oven to 375°. Mix bottled or homemade salsa with the beans to taste. Spread each tortilla with the bean mixture, sprinkle with onions, and cover with grated cheese. Place in oven for about 10 minutes. Use a cookie sheet or ovenproof plates to serve. Top each tortilla with lettuce and tomatoes. Spoon the guacamole on top. Decorate with a spoonful of sour cream and ripe olive slices. Serve immediately. Yields 6 servings.

Teresa E. Anderson-Glynn, Miss New Mexico 1980

Chilies Relleño Bake

2 4-ounce cans whole green chilies
3 cups grated Monterey Jack cheese
1 cup grated sharp Cheddar cheese
2 eggs, beaten
1 tablespoon all-purpose flour
2 tablespoons milk

. . . .

Preheat oven to 375°. Cut the chilies into thin strips, removing any seeds. Alternately layer the chilies and cheeses in a slightly oiled 9-inch baking dish. Combine the eggs, flour, and milk, and pour the mixture over the chilies and cheese. Bake for 50 minutes or until firm. Cool for 5 minutes and cut into squares. Yields 6 servings.

Note: This recipe may be doubled and baked in a 9 x 13-inch dish. It can also be cut into smaller squares and used as a hot appetizer.

Marion Rudeen Payne, Miss Minnesota 1939

Fettuccine Lafitte

1 cup cubed ham
2 tablespoons olive oil
1 8-ounce carton whipping cream or half and half
2 tablespoons tomato paste
½ teaspoon red pepper
½ teaspoon white pepper
¼ cup grated Parmesan cheese
Hot, cooked fettuccine

. . . .

Lightly brown the ham in the olive oil in a medium hot skillet. Reduce the heat to low and add the cream, tomato paste, both peppers, and Parmesan cheese. Allow the mixture to thicken and blend. If it is too thick, add milk to dilute. If too thin, add more Parmesan cheese. Pepper may be increased to make the dish spicier. Pour the sauce over cooked fettuccine and serve immediately. Yields 4 to 6 servings.

Note: This dish can be used as an entrée or side dish with fish or chicken.

Karen Hopson Hall, Miss Mississippi 1981

Spa Pizza

A healthy, low-calorie, easy, quick appetizer or entrée. You can always add other ingredients too, like black olives or fresh spinach. Be creative!

Soft flour tortillas
Zucchini
Onions
Oregano to taste
Basil to taste
Garlic to taste
Pepper to taste
Low-cholesterol oil
Tomato sauce
Low-fat mozzarella cheese, grated

. . . .

Preheat oven to 350°. Place the flour tortillas in the oven until crispy. Sauté the zucchini, onions, and spices in oil. Add just enough tomato sauce to coat the zucchini mixture nicely. Spread evenly onto the crisp tortillas. (Be careful not to overload.) Sprinkle with cheese and broil for just a few minutes until the cheese is melted. (Watch carefully so as not to burn.)

Elizabeth Russell Brunner, Miss Illinois 1979

Tarte Epinard à la Grecque

½ 16-ounce package phyllo pastry leaves
2 sticks butter, divided
½ cup finely chopped onion
3 eggs
½ pound feta cheese, crumbled
2 tablespoons fresh dill (or 1 tablespoon dried dill weed)
1½ tablespoons fresh parsley (or 2 teaspoons dried parsley)
1 teaspoon salt
3 10-ounce packages frozen chopped spinach, thawed and well drained
1½ sticks butter, melted

. . . .

Thaw the pastry leaves according to package directions. Melt ½ stick of butter in a skillet and sauté the onion until brown. Remove from heat. Beat the eggs in a large bowl with a mixer, stir in the cheese, dill, parsley, salt, and pepper. Add the spinach and sautéed onion; mix well. Melt the remaining butter. Brush a 13 x 9-inch baking pan with some of the melted butter. Preheat oven to 350°. Layer 8 phyllo pastry leaves, one by one, in the bottom of the pan, brushing the top of each with a little of the melted butter. Spread evenly with the spinach mixture. Cover with 8 more layers of pastry leaves, brushing each with butter. Pour any remaining butter over top. Trim any uneven edges off pastry. Bake for 30 to 35 minutes or until the crust is puffy and golden. Yields 6 servings.

Deborah K. Davids, Miss Colorado 1982

Quiche Bretagne

¼ cup diced celery
¼ cup diced onion
1 tablespoon butter
½ cup mayonnaise
2 tablespoons all-purpose flour
2 eggs, beaten
2 tablespoons heavy cream
¼ cup white wine
Dash of garlic salt
3 cups crab meat or shrimp
8 ounces grated Swiss cheese
9-inch pie crust

. . . .

Preheat oven to 350°. Sauté the celery and onion in butter until limp. Add the next 8 ingredients and pour the mixture into the pie crust. Bake for 40 minutes. Yields 6 to 8 servings.

Bob Wheeler, Miss Arkansas Pageant

Sunday Brunch

8 slices egg bread, crust removed
2 cups cubed ham
2 tablespoons minced onion
2 tablespoons minced green bell pepper
4 cups shredded Cheddar cheese
1 tablespoon all-purpose flour
6 large eggs
2 tablespoons Dijon-style mustard
3 cups whole milk
1 teaspoon garlic salt

. . . .

Arrange the cubes of bread in a buttered 9 x 13-inch glass dish so that the bottom is completely covered. Top with the ham, onion, and pepper. Cover with shredded cheese and sprinkle flour on top. Beat the eggs, add the mustard, milk, and garlic salt, and blend well. Pour the eggs over the bread and cheese. Cover and refrigerate overnight. Preheat oven to 350°. Bake, uncovered, for 1 hour, or until the mixture is set in center. (A metal pan may be used.) Yields 6 to 8 servings.

Note: There are all sorts of variations for this dish. Use your own creations.

Jean Bartel, Miss America 1943

Rockport Eggs

Best made the night before.

18 eggs
¼ cup milk
1 stick butter, melted
1 10¾-ounce can cream of mushroom soup
¼ cup sherry
4 ounces grated Cheddar cheese
2 6½-ounce cans crab meat

. . . .

Combine the eggs, milk, and butter. Combine the soup, sherry, Cheddar cheese, and crab meat in a separate bowl. Combine the egg mixture with the crab meat mixture. Pour the blended mixtures into a shallow baking dish. Chill overnight. Preheat oven to 350°. Bake for 1 hour. Yields 10 to 12 servings.

BeBe Shopp Waring, Miss America 1948

There He Is . . . and How to Catch Him

The mid-century was the era of matrimony—as reflected by the Pageant's almost debutante focus on the subject. It seemed that the bulk of the emcee's questions revolved around landing a good husband, and viewers could pick up some handy dating advice. In 1958, when Mississippi's Mary Ann Mobley was asked to share her dating strategy, she replied, "The first thing that they say is get him to talk about himself, so the first thing I ask is, 'Do you play football?' or 'What sport are you interested in?' Then if he doesn't say anything, you say, 'What are your hobbies?' and you go down the line from there. And if you can't get him to answer you on any of those, then you're just quiet for the rest of the evening." (It was a moot point, as she married Gary Collins, whose profession is talking.)

A year later Bert asked Lynda Lee Mead, the eventual winner, about her dating psychology. "You're proficient at golf or tennis. You know you can beat your date. Would you? Should you?" The southern belle drawled, "I wouldn't, and I shouldn't, because I did once—and I never saw him again!" (She didn't repeat the mistake—and married a handsome surgeon.)

Smithfield Egg Casserole

Do all the work the night before.
A real Christmas morning delight.

5 tablespoons butter, divided
2 tablespoons all-purpose flour
1 cup milk
½ cup grated Cheddar or Swiss cheese
¼ pound Smithfield ham, chopped
¼ cup chopped green onions
12 eggs, lightly beaten
1 4-ounce can sliced mushrooms, drained

Melt 2 tablespoons of butter in a small saucepan and stir in the flour. Gradually add the milk and cook, stirring constantly, until the mixture thickens. Add the cheese and stir until melted. Set aside. Sauté the ham and onions in the remaining butter. Add the eggs, stirring constantly, and cook over medium heat until set. Stir in the mushrooms and cheese sauce. Spoon into a greased 9 x 13-inch baking dish. Chill overnight. Preheat oven to 350°. Bake for 20 to 30 minutes. Yields 8 servings.

Dona Pillow Forehand, Miss Virginia 1972

Cheese Soufflés by "Dearie"

This recipe comes from my grandmother on my father's side of the family, Rose H. Mayer. We called her "Dearie" because she was an elegant, charming, and gracious lady. This was a very special recipe because it was served on special occasions . . . like Sunday night "supper," birthdays, and during the Jewish holidays.

2 tablespoons butter
2 tablespoons all-purpose flour
Salt and pepper to taste
1 cup milk
1 cup grated sharp cheese
4 eggs, separated

Preheat oven to 350°. Cream the butter, flour, and seasonings in a saucepan. Add the milk and cook until the mixture thickens. Add the cheese, stirring well. Beat the egg yolks and egg whites separately. Fold the yolks into the whites. Fold the egg mixture into the thickened milk mixture. Turn into a buttered baking dish. Set the dish in a pan of water. Bake for 40 to 60 minutes, or until puffy and golden. Serve immediately or it may fall. Yields 6 servings.

Jacquelyn Mayer Townsend, Miss America 1963

Seafood

Easy Lobster Newburg

2 cups cooked and cubed lobster meat
4 tablespoons butter or margarine, melted
2 tablespoons all-purpose flour
1½ cups milk, scalded
¼ teaspoon salt
⅛ teaspoon pepper
½ cup light cream or half and half
2 egg yolks, slightly beaten
2 tablespoons sherry (optional)

Sauté the lobster in butter for about 3 minutes. Remove the lobster. Blend the flour into the butter until smooth. Gradually stir in the milk. Cook in a double boiler over hot water, stirring constantly, until thick and smooth. Add the salt, pepper, and lobster. Cook an additional 5 minutes. Combine the cream, egg yolks, and sherry, and add to the mixture. Cook 2 more minutes. Yields 6 servings.

Note: I use Pepperidge Farm pastry shells but this could be served on toast points. It goes well with twice-baked potatoes, crusty bread, and a simple salad.

Virginia Gregory Belanger, Miss Rhode Island 1954

Colonel Bill's Shrimp and Clam Stew

Colonel Bill, William J. May from New Bern, North Carolina, is my husband. His daughter, Kathy, is married to my son, Richard Peterson.

3 pounds of red potatoes, scrubbed
2 pounds Polish sausage, cut in 1½-inch slices
6 tablespoons seafood seasoning
Salt to taste
1 lemon, cut in half
12 ears fresh shucked corn, broken in half
5 pounds large shrimp
3 dozen cherrystone clams (in shells)

Start with an extra large pot filled half full of water. Simmer the potatoes and sausage for about 20 minutes. Add the seafood seasoning, salt, and lemon. Add the corn and cook for 10 minutes. Check seasonings and add more if needed. Add more water if needed. When water is boiling again, add the shrimp and then the clams. Cook for 2 to 3 minutes, or until the shrimp are pink and the clams are open. Drain and serve hot. Yields 10 to 12 servings.

Joyce Earle Perry Peterson May, Miss South Carolina 1951

Vermont Fish Stew

1 large onion, chopped
1 large clove garlic, minced
2 tablespoons olive oil
¼ cup uncooked brown rice
2 large tomatoes, peeled and cut into chunks
2 tablespoons tomato paste
½ teaspoon marjoram
1 small bay leaf
Black pepper to taste
6 cups vegetable stock
1 large sweet potato, cut into bite-size chunks
1 cup peas
1 cup corn
½ cup coarsely chopped red bell pepper
½ cup coarsely chopped green bell pepper
2 pounds scrod fillets, cut into bite-size chunks
Yogurt

. . . .

Sauté the onion and garlic in olive oil in a large pot until translucent. Add the rice, tomatoes, tomato paste, marjoram, bay leaf, and black pepper. Stir and simmer a few minutes, then add the vegetable stock. Bring to a boil, add the potato, lower the heat, and simmer for 45 minutes. Add the peas, corn, peppers, and fish. Let simmer 5 more minutes. Serve with a dollop of yogurt. Yields 12 servings.

Wendy Masino Stebbins, Miss Vermont 1960

Maine Lobster Stew

2 cups cooked lobster, cubed with liver, fat, and roe
1 stick butter
4 cups milk
2 cups cream

. . . .

Sauté the lobster meat in the butter in a double boiler. Add the milk and cream. Heat until hot. Do not boil. Stir constantly while heating to improve the flavor. If time permits, cool the stew by placing it in the refrigerator overnight, this also improves the flavor. Reheat when ready to serve. Yields 4 servings.

Note: To prepare the lobster, place the live lobsters in 2 or more quarts of boiling water with ¼ cup salt. Boil for 20 minutes. Cool the lobsters and remove meat. Include the lobster liver (green), eggs (orange), and white fat inside of shells.

Lisa Kent, Miss Maine 1988

Maine Fish Chowder

1 pound uncooked fish fillets
½ cup chopped onion
2½ cups diced potatoes
1½ cups water
4 cups milk
2 cups heavy cream
1 stick butter
1 teaspoon salt
⅛ teaspoon pepper

. . . .

Place the fish, onion, potatoes, and water in a pan. Simmer for 15 to 20 minutes or until tender. Place in a double boiler and add the milk, cream, butter, salt, and pepper. Heat thoroughly. Do not boil. Yields 4 servings.

Note: If time permits, cool the chowder by placing it in the refrigerator overnight. This improves the flavor. Reheat when ready to serve.

Lisa Kent, Miss Maine 1988

Seafood Gumbo Alabama

This gumbo was served at a dinner party in my home for Luciano Pavarotti. He adored it!

3 tablespoons vegetable oil (or canola)
4 tablespoons all-purpose flour
2 large onions, chopped
6 ribs celery, chopped
1 large green bell pepper, chopped
2 20-ounce cans tomatoes
1 pound okra, sliced
4 quarts water
4 to 6 crabs (optional)
½ teaspoon garlic salt
2 to 3 crushed bay leaves
1 tablespoon salt
Black or red pepper to taste
1½ tablespoons Worcestershire sauce
1 pound crab meat (and/or crab claws)
1½ pounds raw peeled shrimp
Tabasco sauce to taste

....

Make a dark golden roux with the oil and flour in a heavy skillet. Stir in the onions, celery, green pepper, and simmer a few minutes, stirring constantly. Add the undrained tomatoes and okra. Simmer until the okra is tender. Place the mixture in a large soup pot. Add the water, crabs, and seasonings. Cook very slowly over low heat for several hours, stirring constantly. Add the crab meat, crab claws, and shrimp during the last 15 minutes of cooking time. Adjust the seasonings if needed. Serve over hot rice in soup bowls. Yields 8 to 10 servings.

Yolande Betbeze Fox, Miss America 1951

Seafood Gumbo

8 tablespoons shortening
4 tablespoons all-purpose flour
1 large onion, chopped
2 pounds okra, cut
6 green onions, chopped
2 cloves garlic, chopped
½ green bell pepper, chopped
1 cup canned tomatoes
Water
2 tablespoons minced parsley
1 bay leaf
1 piece thyme (or a good pinch)
5 drops Louisiana Hot Sauce
2 teaspoons Worcestershire sauce (or to taste)
5 pounds shrimp
3 cracked crabs (or 1 pound crab meat)

....

Heat the shortening until it is very hot. Add the flour and brown it well. Add the onions, okra, garlic, and green pepper. Brown over low heat, stirring often. Add the tomatoes and simmer, adding enough hot water to keep the ingredients from sticking. Add 5 cups of hot water, cover, and cook very slowly. Add the remaining ingredients, cover, and cook another hour. Add more water and seasonings if needed and cook another 20 minutes. Oysters may be added (2 dozen with 1 cup of oyster liquor). Excellent over steamed rice. Yields 10 to 12 servings.

Caroline Masur, Miss Louisiana Pageant

Shrimp Scampi

1 pound large shrimp (about 24; 6 to a serving)
4 tablespoons butter
½ teaspoon salt
6 cloves garlic, peeled and crushed
2 tablespoons chopped fresh parsley, divided
1 teaspoon grated lemon peel
2 tablespoons fresh lemon juice
Lemon wedges
Hot cooked rice or fettucini

. . . .

Shell the shrimp, leaving the tails on. Devein and wash well. Drain. Melt the butter in a 9 x 13-inch baking dish in a 400° oven. Add the salt, garlic, and 1 tablespoon of the parsley. Mix well. Arrange the shrimp in a single layer. Bake, uncovered, for 5 minutes. Turn the shrimp, sprinkle with lemon peel, juice, and remaining parsley. Bake for 8 to 10 minutes, or until the shrimp are tender. Pour the garlic drippings over the shrimp and garnish with lemon wedges. Serve over rice or fettucini. Yields 4 servings.

Marie Meyer, Miss America Pageant

Shrimp on the Grill

1 pound fresh or frozen large uncooked shrimp, in the shell
½ cup peanut oil
½ cup lemon juice
1 teaspoon seasoned salt
½ teaspoon seasoned pepper
¼ cup soy sauce
¼ cup thinly sliced scallions

. . . .

Wash, thaw, and dry the shrimp and place in a bowl. Combine the peanut oil, lemon juice, seasoned salt, seasoned pepper, soy sauce, and scallions. Pour mixture over the shrimp. Marinate the shrimp overnight or for several hours. Grill the shrimp for 10 minutes, turning, until pink. Reserve the marinade for dipping. Yields 4 servings.

Note: Shell the shrimp before serving which makes eating far less messy. If you eat outdoors, share the fun of shelling!

BeBe Shopp Waring, Miss America 1948

Chet's Baked Shrimp Casserole

1 pound cooked shrimp
1 tablespoon lemon juice
3 tablespoons vegetable oil
½ cup chopped green bell pepper
½ cup chopped onion
3 tablespoons butter
3 cups cooked rice
1 teaspoon salt
½ teaspoon pepper
½ teaspoon nutmeg
1 10¾-ounce can condensed tomato soup
1 cup whipping cream
½ cup dry sherry
½ cup slivered almonds, divided

. . . .

Place the shrimp in a 2-quart casserole. Marinate in lemon juice and oil for a few hours in the refrigerator, stirring occasionally. Preheat oven to 350°. Sauté the onion and green pepper in the butter until soft; add to the shrimp. Add the rice, salt, pepper, nutmeg, tomato soup, whipping cream, sherry, and ¼ cup of the almonds. Sprinkle the remaining almonds on top and bake, uncovered, for 25 minutes. Yields 8 servings.

Note: This freezes well.

Marian McKnight Conway, Miss America 1957

The 1960s—The Era of Camelot, Moon Walks, and Social Revolution

The 1960s began in storybook fashion as the era of Camelot dawned in Washington and President John F. Kennedy and his First Lady, Jacqueline, reigned as American royalty. Jackie's elegant image was the rage, inspiring imitators across the globe. "Jackie developed a style," recalls Miss America 1961, Nancy Fleming. "Instead of having that kind of soft, sexy 'movie star' look, she was elegant, and even young women began to look more sophisticated." So did Miss Americas, with ten consecutive brunette winners mirroring her style. Like the First Lady, Miss America personified American royalty and every little girl dreamed of wearing the crown.

In the 1960s, Miss Americas resembled First Ladies. After ten brunette Jacqueline Kennedy lookalikes, the decade closed with Judi Ford, a ringer for President Nixon's daughter Tricia.

While little girls fantasized about walking the famous runway, men dreamed of walking on the moon. They took a major step in that direction during Fleming's reign, when Alan Shepard became the first American in space. By a twist of fate, Nancy was in the astronaut's hometown as he took his historic flight. "This was the first time and nobody really knew if it was going to work or not so there was tremendous anxiety—and then equally tremendous thrill that it had worked and he was safe," she recalls. "They had a wonderful impromptu parade through the streets of his hometown and I got to ride with his parents, who were out of their minds with relief. It was such a special day and I felt that in my own small way I was a part of its history."

Ironically, Miss America was also nearby on November 22, 1963, for another momentous event in American history—the day the glowing Camelot era was extinguished by the assassination of President Kennedy. At that fateful instant, the reigning titleholder, Donna Axum, was in Dallas attending a convention only a few miles away. As guests heard the horrifying news that JFK had been shot, "we said a prayer for President Kennedy and they dismissed the convention," Donna recalls. Soon after they learned of the President's death. "It was a very somber day," she says softly, "as you can well imagine."

As if ripped from its foundation that day, the nation began to rock under the colliding influences of the Vietnam War, hippies, rock music, the sexual revolution, a drug epidemic, the assassinations of Martin Luther King and Senator Robert Kennedy, the removal of prayer from public schools, school desegregation, and the civil rights and women's movements. In 1968, feminists staged a protest during pageant week, hurling bras into a burning "freedom trash can," as FBI antiriot agents had them under surveillance.

At the time, the Vietnam War was the crux of the cultural collision, with long-haired antiwar protestors pitched against clean-cut, patriotic teens. Like every youth in the country, Miss America had to choose sides. Conservatism won. "I was a small town person from rural America and I felt like I was speaking for my people," recalls Debra Barnes, Miss America 1968, "because we still did believe in patriotism and the American Dream and all the things that we were raised to believe in." While their counterparts camped out at Woodstock and stormed administration buildings, Miss Americas toured Asia with USO troupes entertaining young and frightened GIs. "A main focus of my year was going to Vietnam," says Pamela Eldred, who won in 1969, "and seeing what our men had to go through. As we were performing in Vietnam, they had to stop the show in mid-performance because the enemy forces were getting so close that they wanted to get us out of there. As they evacuated us in tanks, I kept thinking about the poor guys who had to go back to it."

A year earlier, the conflict was so intense that Miss America's tour of military bases was changed to Korea. "I was glad, because the attention was on Vietnam and the guys in Korea were almost forgotten," says Debra Barnes. "We went to the Freedom Bridge, near the DMZ, and we saw a scouting party go out that night," she says, adding softly, "They didn't come back." The titleholders ignored taunts about their hawkish "involvement" in the war, instead emphasizing Miss America's role as a giver. "I didn't know enough politically to know whether I was for or against the war," says Jane Jayroe, Miss America 1967. "I just knew that I was for the people who were there. To think that we weren't supportive of them after their great sacrifice was a further tragedy."

Balancing the trauma of Vietnam was the extraordinary moment on July 20, 1969, when U.S. astronauts became the first men to walk on the moon, taking "one small step for man—one giant leap for mankind." During the 1960s, the United States and her people came a long way from the innocence of Camelot. It was an era of radical changes that altered a nation—and the lives of ten young women who wore the glittering symbol of a nation now under social siege.

Crab-Shrimp Casserole

1 cup diced onions
1 large green bell pepper, diced
1 cup diced celery
1 to 2 pounds shrimp, boiled and cleaned
1 12-ounce can crab meat

Sauce
1 cup mayonnaise
1 tablespoon Worcestershire sauce

. . . .

Preheat oven to 350°. Combine the onions, bell pepper, celery, shrimp, and crab meat, and place in a casserole dish. Combine the mayonnaise and Worcestershire sauce and spread over the top of the shrimp and crab mixture. Bake for 30 minutes. Yields 4 to 6 servings.

Dean Herman Maguire, Miss Florida 1981

Shrimp Creole

1½ cups chopped onion
1 cup finely chopped celery
2 medium green bell peppers, finely chopped
2 cloves garlic, minced
4 tablespoons butter or margarine
1 15-ounce can tomato sauce
1 cup water
2 teaspoons snipped parsley
1 teaspoon salt
⅛ teaspoon cayenne pepper
2 bay leaves, crushed
1 pound fresh or frozen raw shrimp, cleaned
3 cups hot cooked rice

. . . .

Sauté the onion, celery, green pepper, and garlic in butter until the onion is tender. Remove from the heat and stir in the tomato sauce, water and seasonings. Simmer, uncovered, for 10 minutes. Add more water if needed. Stir in the shrimp. Heat to boiling. Cover and cook over medium heat for 10 to 20 minutes or until the shrimp are pink and tender. Serve over rice. Yields 6 servings.

Julie Meusburger Parsons, Miss Nebraska 1985

Easy Cajun Crawfish Etouffée

1 stick butter or margarine
½ cup chopped onion
¼ cup chopped green onion
1 4-ounce can sliced mushrooms
1 10¾-ounce can cream of mushroom soup
1 3-ounce can tomato sauce
½ 10-ounce can diced Ro-Tel tomatoes and chilies
1 pound cooked and peeled crawfish tails (shrimp may be substituted)
Pinch of red pepper
Salt to taste
Garlic powder to taste
Chopped parsley to taste
Paprika to taste
Hot cooked rice

. . . .

Melt the butter in a large pot. Sauté the onions and sliced mushrooms. Add the soup and tomato sauce. Mix well and add the Ro-Tel (more if you like it hotter). Add the crawfish, mixing well while you add the seasonings to suit your taste. Simmer for 20 minutes. Serve hot over rice. Yields 6 to 8 servings.

Becky Wilson Lewis, Miss Louisiana 1975

Suzette's Pig Dinner, or Steamed Clams with Marinara Sauce

This recipe came from the Italian part of my heritage. I was about eight years old when I first learned of the "Pig's Bowl." Now it is called Suzette's special secret. I serve Suzette's Pig Bowl to people I want to get to know. An invitation for dinner spells casual: Dress to sit on the floor and leave all table manners at the door.

3 cloves garlic, finely chopped
Parsley, chopped
Olive oil
1 quart marinara sauce (any brand)
Fresh mushrooms, sliced
½ green bell pepper, cut into strips
Tabasco sauce
2 dozen clams, soaked in cold water and scrubbed to remove sand
3 scallions, chopped with the green tops
1 loaf Italian bread

Sauté the garlic with a handful of parsley in the olive oil. When slightly brown, add the jar of marinara sauce. (I "doctor" this with a small scoop of sugar, if the sauce is tart.) Add the mushrooms and green pepper. Simmer for about 30 minutes. Add Tabasco sauce according to taste. (I add 2 tablespoons and it is spicy enough.) While the sauce is simmering, steam the clams in another pot. Fill the pot about ¾ full with cold water. Add the clams and cover the pot. Begin with a high flame for steaming. Decrease the heat to medium after the water comes to a boil. The clams take about 10 minutes to open. Remove the clams and place them in a LARGE PIG BOWL (a spaghetti platter is suitable). Pour the marinara sauce over the clams. Sprinkle the scallions over top. Yields 2 servings.

Note: Leave all table manners aside. While eating the clams, dip the Italian bread in the sauce. This recipe should be enough for two people unless you are both avid clam eaters, then steam another dozen for good measure.

Suzette Charles, Miss America 1984

By the late 1960s, the tailored silhouette had softened into flowing chiffon designs in a rainbow of colors and the beehive coiffure was the rage. Debra Barnes, Miss America 1968, is third from left. (The Miss America Organization)

Imperial Crab

1 pound crab meat, cleaned and picked over
⅓ cup green bell pepper, chopped
1 small pimiento, chopped
1 egg, beaten
⅓ cup mayonnaise
¼ teaspoon pepper
½ teaspoon salt
1 teaspoon dry mustard
Pastry shells

. . . .

Preheat oven to 350°. Combine the crab meat gently with the next 7 ingredients. Place the mixture in pastry shells. Bake for 15 minutes. Yields 4 servings.

Keri Baumgardner Schroeder, Miss Alaska 1992

Chesapeake Bay Crab Cakes

1 pound backfin crab meat, cleaned and picked over
12 saltine crackers, crushed
2 teaspoons Old Bay seasoning
Salt and pepper to taste
1 egg
2 tablespoons mayonnaise
2 teaspoons dry mustard
Vegetable oil

. . . .

Place the crab meat in a bowl and sprinkle it with crackers. Combine the seasonings, egg, mayonnaise, and dry mustard and beat until thoroughly mixed. Pour the sauce over the crab meat. Shape into cakes and deep fry, or pan fry in oil until golden brown. Yields 4 to 6 servings.

Holly Jereme Wright, Miss Virginia 1980

There She Is . . . In Mime!

In 1967, during the victory walk of the newly crowned Miss America, Debra Dene Barnes, Bert Parks accidentally yanked the microphone cord out of its socket while serenading the winner to "There She Is, Miss America." Unaware of the mishap, the emcee continued to bellow into a dead microphone, giving the first mime performance of the famous song. According to the Chicago *Tribune,* when Parks and his wife returned to their hotel room, she received a phone call from a southern fan. "Miz Parks," the lad asked, "How come your husband sang that song for the rest of the country, but not for us folks down here?"

Miss Maryland Crab Cakes

This recipe was a favorite of my great-grandmother and was served on special occasions at the family plantation on Chesapeake Bay. This region of Maryland has been recognized since colonial days for its savory seafood.

1 pound backfin crab meat, picked over
1 teaspoon dry mustard
1 tablespoon mayonnaise
¾ tablespoon salt
1 teaspoon pepper
1 egg, well beaten
8 saltine crackers, crumbled
Vegetable oil or butter

. . . .

Combine all the ingredients except the oil, being careful not to break up any large lumps of crab meat. Form the mixture into 4 to 6 patties. Chill in the refrigerator for 1 hour. Deep fat fry or sauté the cakes in butter for 5 minutes, or until golden brown. Yields 4 to 6 servings.

Jean Crow Kiser, Miss Maryland 1949

Ask a Dumb Question . . .

In the 1960s, one of the most comical portions of the Miss America Pageant was the on-stage questions. Take the archetypical ditty thrown at Miss North Carolina 1962, Maria Fletcher. "As Miss America, you have just been introduced at a women's club luncheon," intoned Bert Parks. "You discover the speech you brought with you is for the Cattlemen's Association meeting next week. What would you do?" Without a moment's hesitation, the future Miss America responded, "I think I would just go ahead and deliver the speech I had planned and hope they would think it was a comedy routine!"

Stuffed Mussels

2 dozen mussels
3 onions, chopped
2 stalks celery, including the leaves, chopped
1 carrot, chopped or grated
½ cup long grain or brown rice
¼ cup olive oil
1 teaspoon salt
½ teaspoon cinnamon
¼ teaspoon cloves
¼ teaspoon freshly ground pepper
¼ cup chopped parsley
¼ cup pignolia nuts
½ cup Marsala wine
Pinch of salt

. . . .

Soak, scrub, and remove the beards from the mussels using a brush. Cover the mussels with water, add salt, bring to a boil, and steam for 10 minutes. Discard any unopened mussel shells. In a frying pan, sauté the onion, celery, carrot, and rice in the olive oil for 4 to 5 minutes. Add the remaining ingredients , except the mussels, plus 1 cup of the mussel stock from the pot. Cook until the rice is done. Remove the mussels from the shells and add to the rice mixture. Fill the mussel shells with the mixture and serve. This also tastes delicious at room temperature. Yields 6 servings.

Rena Michaelides, Miss New York State Pageant

Mother's Seafood Casserole

My mother and father, Elizabeth C. and John E. Perry, always served Christmas dinner on Christmas Eve. They prepared this seafood casserole as the traditional Christmas feast. It was always the hit of the dinner.

1 pound crab meat, cleaned and picked over
1 pound cooked shrimp, peeled and chopped (or cut)
1 cup mayonnaise
1 cup chopped green bell peppers
1 cup chopped onions
1 cup chopped celery
1 cup bread crumbs
½ teaspoon salt
1 teaspoon Worcestershire sauce
Butter
2 cups crushed potato chips

. . . .

Preheat oven to 400°. Lightly combine all of the above ingredients, except for the crushed potato chips. Put this mixture into a buttered dish with the potato chips sprinkled on top. Bake for 20 to 30 minutes. Yields 8 to 10 servings.

Joyce Earle Perry Peterson May, Miss South Carolina 1951

Butter Herb Baked Fish

½ cup sweet butter
⅔ cup crushed saltine crackers
¼ cup grated Parmesan cheese
½ teaspoon basil leaves
½ teaspoon oregano leaves
½ teaspoon salt
¼ teaspoon garlic powder
1 pound frozen flounder, sole, or perch fillets, thawed and drained

Preheat the oven to 350°. In 9 x 13-inch pan, melt the butter in the oven, for 5 to 7 minutes. Meanwhile, combine the cracker crumbs, Parmesan cheese, basil, oregano, salt, and garlic powder in a 9-inch pie pan. Dip the fish fillets in the baking pan butter and then in the crumb mixture. Arrange the fish fillets in the baking pan. Pour extra melted butter over top of the fillets. Bake near the center of the oven for 25 to 30 minutes, or until the fish is tender and flakes with a fork. Yields 2 to 4 servings.

Laurie Hixenbaugh, Miss Pennsylvania 1982

It's in the Cards

Then there was the year when poor Bert announced the wrong Top 10. During the afternoon rehearsals, pageant officials made up a practice set of announcement cue cards listing the previous year's Top 10. That night, moments before airtime, Bert's assistant handed the unsuspecting emcee the wrong Top 10 cue cards—the practice cards. As Bert began rattling off semifinalists' names, Pageant chairman Albert Marks realized to his horror that wrong states were being announced on live television! "Through no fault of Bert's, when he was announcing the Top 10, they were last year's!" Marks recalls. "We had contact with Bert out of the wings and stopped him cold. I picked up the telephone so fast, I almost broke it! Fortunately, the word got to him to stop, and he was given the right cards, but that happened on camera! We apologized," says Marks with a vaguely amused grin, "but those things happen. I hope on a very seldom basis—but they do happen."

Sole Stuffed with Shrimp and Mushrooms

½ cup finely chopped mushrooms
1 bunch green onions, chopped (white part only)
1 clove garlic, crushed
¼ cup minced green bell pepper
12 shrimp, cooked
1 tablespoon parsley
½ teaspoon salt
⅛ teaspoon pepper
4 2-ounce fillets sole
Lemon juice
Paprika

Place the mushrooms, onion, and garlic in a pan with a small amount of water. Cook until barely wilted. Add the green pepper and cook until no longer crisp. Dice the shrimp and add it to the pan along with the parsley, salt, and pepper. Place about 2 tablespoons of the shrimp mixture on each fillet. Roll and place the fish on a cookie sheet, rolled-side down. Tuck any leftover stuffing in the ends of the rolls. Chill for at least 10 minutes. Preheat oven to 350°. Place the rolled, stuffed fillets in a nonstick baking pan, sprinkle with lemon juice and a dash of paprika. Cover with foil and bake for 25 to 30 minutes or until barely flaky. Yields 4 servings.

Lynda Lee Mead Shea, Miss America 1960

Helluva Headline!

When Donna Axum, Miss America 1964, attended the Gator Bowl in Jacksonville, Florida, a fire broke out in the hotel where she and her traveling companion were staying. Twenty-one guests perished and Donna had to drag her unconscious chaperon to safety. Axum admits that in the midst of the peril, the disconcerting newspaper headline flashed across her mind: "Miss America Perishes in Fire, First Runner-Up Takes Over."

Lemon Baked Snapper

½ cup chopped onion, divided
¾ cup chopped fresh tomato
½ cup chopped celery
1 pound red snapper fillets
4 teaspoons Worcestershire sauce
1 tablespoon lemon juice
¼ cup chopped parsley
Lemon wedges

Preheat oven to 400°. Combine ¼ cup of the onion with the tomato and celery. Sprinkle over the bottom of an 8 x 8-inch baking pan. Arrange the fish fillets over the vegetables. Combine the Worcestershire sauce and lemon juice and spoon the mixture over the fish. Sprinkle with the remaining onion. Bake for 10 to 15 minutes, or until the fish flakes when tested with a fork. Sprinkle with parsley; serve with lemon wedges. Yields 2 servings.

Joni McMechan Checchia, Miss Indiana 1988

Northwest Grilled Salmon with Teriyaki and Papaya

Salmon caught in the Pacific Northwest is the best in the world (I am biased). My local pageant in Washington was the Miss Issaquah Pageant, and in our beautiful town, there is a salmon hatchery for Coho and Chinook salmon. Our local yearly festival is called Salmon Days, and it includes a gala event entitled Salmon-Enchanted Evening, and has "Sambassadors," who help put on the festival. The float that I rode in parades all around the state was a giant silver salmon.

This recipe has special meaning for me because it is a recipe my mother and I dreamed up for a celebration party after I won the Miss Issaquah title. Since then, it has become a tradition in our family to serve this recipe whenever we have something to celebrate.

1½ pounds salmon fillets, cut into 4 equal pieces
¼ cup soy sauce
¼ cup sugar
6 tablespoons dry sherry
3 thin slices fresh ginger (or ½ teaspoon ground ginger)
3 papayas, cubed
3 tablespoons lemon juice
¼ cup chopped cilantro

Grill the salmon briefly. Do not overcook. Combine the soy sauce, sugar, sherry, and ginger in a saucepan. Bring to a boil. Continue to cook until reduced by about half. Reduce the heat to a simmer to keep warm. Combine the papaya cubes, lemon juice, and chopped cilantro in a bowl. Spoon the sauce (about 1 tablespoon) on the salmon when serving, and top with the papaya mixture. Yields 4 servings.

Colleen Ann Kearney, Miss Washington 1992

Vegetables & Side Dishes

Mushroom-Artichoke Casserole

3 cups fresh mushroom halves
½ cup sliced green onions with tops
4 tablespoons butter or margarine
2 tablespoons all-purpose flour
⅓ teaspoon salt
Dash of pepper
¾ cup water
¼ cup milk
1 teaspoon instant chicken bouillon granules
1 teaspoon lemon juice
⅛ teaspoon ground nutmeg
2 10-ounce packages frozen artichoke hearts, cooked and drained
¾ cup soft bread crumbs (1 slice bread)
1 tablespoon butter or margarine, melted

Preheat oven to 350°. Cook the mushrooms and green onions in the butter. With a slotted spoon, remove the vegetables and set them aside. Blend the flour, salt, and pepper into the pan drippings. Add the water, milk, bouillon, lemon juice, and nutmeg. Cook and stir until bubbly. Add all the vegetables. Pour into a 1-quart casserole. Combine the bread crumbs and melted butter, and sprinkle them over top. Bake for 20 minutes. Yields 8 servings.

Marian McKnight Conway, Miss America 1957

Asparagus with Dijon Vinaigrette

3 pounds fresh asparagus, stiff ends trimmed
2 tablespoons Dijon-style mustard
4 tablespoons lemon juice
1 teaspoon sugar
½ teaspoon salt
½ teaspoon pepper
½ cup olive oil

Bring a large saucepan of salted water to a boil. Drop in the asparagus and cook, uncovered, until just tender, but still crisp. Have a large bowl of ice water ready. When the asparagus is cooked, plunge it into the ice water. This stops the cooking and keeps the asparagus a brilliant green color. Drain well and pat dry with paper towels. Refrigerate to chill. Meanwhile, put the mustard in a small bowl. Beat in the lemon juice, sugar, salt, and pepper. Continue to whisk or beat while slowly pouring in the olive oil. Keep beating until the mixture thickens. Taste and adjust seasonings if needed. When ready to serve, drizzle the sauce over the asparagus. Yields 8 servings.

Penny Tichenor Anthony, Miss Indiana 1974

Asparagus Slimmerette

1 13½-ounce can cooked asparagus
Bibb lettuce
1 tablespoon chopped scallions
2 tablespoons chopped pimiento-stuffed olives
2 tablespoons chopped pimiento
1 tablespoon olive oil
1 teaspoon lemon juice
1 tablespoon pimiento oil
2 tablespoons wine vinegar
Freshly ground pepper to taste

Place about 4 asparagus spears on a plate lined with lettuce. Scatter the scallions, olives, and pimiento on top of the asparagus. Combine the olive oil, lemon juice, pimiento oil, and vinegar. Pour the mixture over the asparagus and sprinkle with ground pepper. Chill. Yields 4 servings.

Ann Shirley Gillock Brooks, Miss Kentucky 1955

Vermont Baked Beans

1 16-ounce package dry soldier beans
1 onion, quartered
¾ pound sliced bacon
1½ cups maple syrup
½ cup molasses
3 tablespoons sugar

Soak the beans overnight. Drain and boil in fresh cold water for 1 hour. Drain the beans. Preheat oven to 300°. Place the onion quarters in the bottom of a bean pot. Add ½ of the beans, then the bacon slices, and the remaining beans. Stir in the remaining ingredients. Bake, covered, for 6 to 7 hours. Bake uncovered for 1 hour longer. Yields 10 to 15 servings.

Pati Papineau, Miss Vermont 1970

Baked Beans

My husband, Richard, hosted a surprise birthday party for me, and one of my friends brought baked beans. They were so tasty, and the mixture thick enough, that we were soon using these beans as a dip! It has become a family favorite with all our casual meals, especially when we are at our family ranch, kicking dirt, chasing armadillos, and building a Texas-size appetite.

1 pound ground beef
½ pound chopped bacon
1 onion, chopped
⅓ cup brown sugar
⅓ cup sugar
¼ cup ketchup
¼ cup barbecue sauce
½ teaspoon pepper
½ teaspoon salt
2 tablespoons dry mustard
2 tablespoons molasses
1 16-ounce can butter beans
1 20-ounce can pork and beans
1 16-ounce can red kidney beans
½ teaspoon chili powder

Preheat oven to 350°. Brown the ground beef, bacon, and onion, and drain. Add the rest of the ingredients. Bake in a casserole dish for 1½ hours or in a slow cooker on low for 3 hours. Yields 8 to 10 servings.

Shirley Cothran Barret, Miss America 1975

Marinated Green Beans

2 16-ounce cans whole green beans
2 4-ounce cans sliced mushrooms
1 16-ounce can artichoke hearts, cut up
1 4-ounce can black olives, cut up
1 8-ounce bottle Italian dressing
1 tomato, sliced

Combine all the ingredients, except the tomato, in a leak-proof container and marinate overnight. Turn the container upside down once. When ready to serve, arrange the tomato slices over top of the green beans. Yields 8 servings.

Terri Dodson Bachelor, Miss Missouri 1973

Green Bean Salad with Horesradish Dressing

1 pound green beans, trimmed
1 tablespoon bottled horseradish, drained
½ teaspoon Dijon-style mustard
2 tablespoons vegetable oil
¼ cup sour cream
Salt and pepper to taste
4 slices bacon

Steam the beans, then run cold water over them. Chill, covered, for at least 1 hour. Whisk together the horseradish, mustard, oil, sour cream, salt, and pepper in a small bowl and chill for at least 1 hour. Cook the bacon until it is brown and crisp. Drain on paper towels. Arrange the green beans in salad bowls, spoon the dressing over top or serve on the side, and sprinkle bacon on top. Yields 6 servings.

Note: Nonfat sour cream can be used and the oil can be cut in half to reduce fat.

Ellen Roseman, Miss Nevada 1964

Miss America's Moonshine

When Phyllis George competed as Miss Texas in the 1970 Miss America Pageant, she charmed the judges chattering about her singing dog and pet crab, Moonshine. After the judges awarded her the Miss America crown she showed up at her press conference toting along a small cage holding, you guessed it, Moonshine.

Scalloped Lima Beans

In the late 1960s my mother received this recipe from one of her friends and it became my favorite. When I arrived home in Hancock following my Miss America crowning, Mother made this dish. It was my only food request. Now she makes it every time we go home.

1 pound dry lima beans
1 stick margarine
½ cup all-purpose flour
1½ teaspoons salt
1 quart milk
½ teaspoon celery salt
1 pimiento or 1 tablespoon finely chopped red pepper
1 8-ounce package cream cheese, cubed
2 teaspoons grated onion
Buttered bread crumbs or crushed potato chips

Cook the dry lima beans as directed on the package until tender, not mushy. Preheat oven to 350°. Combine the margarine, flour, salt, and milk in a saucepan over medium-low heat. Blend in cream cheese and onion. When the sauce is thickened, mix it gently with the beans and pour it into a 9 x 13-inch baking pan. Sprinkle buttered crumbs or crushed potato chips over top. Bake for about 45 minutes. Yields 6 to 8 servings.

Rebecca King Dreman, Miss America 1974

All-American Broccoli Casserole

2 packages frozen chopped broccoli, cooked, and drained
2 tablespoons grated onion
2 eggs
1 cup grated cheese
1 10¾-ounce can mushroom soup
1 cup mayonnaise

. . . .

Preheat oven to 350°. Combine all of the ingredients. Place in a buttered casserole dish. Bake for 30 minutes. Yields 8 servings.

Marilyn Meseke Rogers, Miss America 1938

Broccoli Puff

½ cup chopped onion
2 tablespoons margarine
1 10¾-ounce can cream of mushroom soup
2 cups cooked rice
1 10-ounce package frozen chopped broccoli, cooked and well-drained
1 teaspoon Worcestershire sauce
¼ teaspoon thyme
4 eggs, separated
2 cups grated Cheddar cheese

. . . .

Preheat oven to 400°. Sauté the onion in margarine until tender. Stir in the soup, rice, broccoli, and seasonings. Turn into a greased, shallow 2-quart casserole. Bake for 20 minutes. Meanwhile, beat the egg yolks until thick and lemon-colored; add the cheese. Beat the egg whites until soft peaks form. Fold the egg yolk mixture into the egg whites. Remove the casserole from the oven and stir it. Spread the egg mixture over top. Bake 15 minutes longer or until golden brown. Yields 4 servings.

Debbie Weuve Rohrer, Miss Iowa 1975

Carrot Soufflé

1 pound carrots, peeled and cooked
3 eggs
⅓ cup sugar
3 tablespoons all-purpose flour
1 teaspoon vanilla extract
1 stick butter, melted
Dash of nutmeg

Topping

¼ to ½ cup crushed corn flakes or walnuts
3 tablespoons brown sugar
2 teaspoons butter, softened

. . . .

Preheat oven to 350°. Blend the carrots and eggs in a blender. Add the next 5 ingredients and blend well. Pour into a greased 1½-quart pan or soufflé dish. Bake for 40 minutes. Combine the topping ingredients and spread on top of the soufflé. Bake for an additional 5 to 10 minutes. Yields 6 servings.

Phyllis George, Miss America 1971

The 1970s—Protests, Pageantry, and Progress

The 1970s were an era of societal turmoil intensified by Watergate, President Nixon's resignation, and battles over the Equal Rights Amendment. It was the height of the civil rights movement, and the NAACP, irate that no black woman had ever made it to the nationals, asked the Pageant to encourage minorities to participate. In 1970, Cheryl Browne was named Miss Iowa, making her the first black woman to win a state title and compete in the Miss America Pageant. Her achievement was a historic milestone that paved the runway for a black woman to earn the Miss America title the following decade.

Vietnam and "women's liberation" continued to be the focus of social conflict, with Miss Americas, again, siding with conservative values and patriotism. It was an unpopular—and sometimes dangerous—stand. Laurel Schaefer, Miss America 1972, a conservative and a lieutenant commander in the ROTC Angel Flight program, faced death threats. "It was the era of Broadway's *Hair,* love beads, promiscuity, and drugs—and I did none of that. Being an ultra conservative then was the least popular thing you could be!" Laurel was dogged by feminist and antimilitary demonstrators and death threats. "The worst threat was when I had word that if I made an appearance I was going to be gunned down by a sniper. I realized that it wasn't me. It was against what Miss America stood for, traditional values. I believe the Silent Majority were in favor of those values, but we didn't hear about them. It was a very difficult time to be a Miss America, but I was the right person at the time for the job."

In 1974, two of the Pageant's most accomplished winners shared the spotlight as feminists protested the Pageant's "degradation" of women. Miss America 1974, Rebecca King, earned her law degree with Pageant scholarships, while her successor, Shirley Cothran, used her award to earn a doctorate. (Earle Hawkins)

Her successor, Terry Meeuwsen, took an equally strong stand, proudly wearing a POW bracelet and vowing not to remove it until the missing Wyoming GI was safely back in his family's arms. After her crowning, Terry met the missing serviceman's wife. "It was the first time we ever laid eyes on each other," she recalls, "and it was a very emotional experience."

In 1970, during the Pageant's Golden 50th Anniversary, Phyllis George was crowned with a commemorative golden crown—which she promptly dropped on live television. (AP/Wide World Photos)

In 1974, protestors returned to Atlantic City, this time staging a feminist convention to coincide with the Pageant. Ironically, as feminists attacked the Pageant as "degrading" to women, the two Miss Americas featured that week would became more accomplished than many of their detractors. Rebecca King, the reigning titleholder, used her pageant scholarships to attend law school, while the woman she crowned, Shirley Cothran, who already held a master's degree, used her award to earn her PhD. It was King, the no-nonsense future lawyer, who held the crown on August 8, 1974, when Richard Nixon, facing impending impeachment for obstruction of justice, became the first President of the United States ever to resign.

Despite the staggering controversies of the era, there were also lighter moments—most of them involving fashion trends. The "flip," the long, elaborately set and lacquered hairstyle, was the rage. Unfortunately, it was the worst possible hairdo a contestant could hope to maintain in Atlantic City's humid summer climate. "The hair spray came out, and pretty soon everyone was imitating each other and the broad shoulders were all covered with flips," says Rebecca King, smiling in recollection. "As the week went on things just got flippier and flippier around there!" King, the aspiring lawyer, couldn't be bothered and wore her hair straight down her back. She won, which effectively proved that, fashion or no fashion, the flip was finished at Miss America.

So were the emblems of royalty. Befitting the program's evolving image as a scholarship program, officials decided to eliminate the coronation robe and banner. "Frankly, I always hated both of them and I was glad when they got rid of them!" says Ruth McCandliss, the Pageant's perennial executive secretary, now retired. "Miss America is Miss America—and you don't have to stick a sign on her," she says, laughing, "and I thought the robe was a bit much, too."

However tumultuous, the 1970s inaugurated important changes. Society increasingly emphasized higher education and career pursuits for women and the Miss America Pageant, with its growing scholarship fund and academically accomplished titleholders, again mirrored evolving societal values.

Browned Butter Carrots

1 pound carrots, peeled and thinly sliced into coin shapes
2 teaspoons honey
¼ teaspoon ginger
4 tablespoons butter

Place the carrots in a saucepan and add a small amount of water. Bring to a boil and cook, adding additional amounts of water if necessary, until the carrots are soft but firm. Drain. Toss the carrots with the honey and ginger. Cover. Place the butter in a small saucepan and melt until brown. Pour the browned butter over the carrots and serve. Yields 4 to 6 servings.

Lynne Grote Tully, Miss Pennsylvania 1977

Cabbage and Noodles

My grandmother and my mother cooked this for the family. When I had my family, this was a favorite for them. Everyone still loves this very simple recipe which is nutritious and so delicious.

1 pound wide noodles
1 large head cabbage
2 sticks butter or margarine
Salt and pepper to taste

Cook the noodles until tender and then drain. Cut the cabbage into small pieces. Boil or microwave in water until done; drain. Add the butter. Great with applesauce, cottage cheese, and homemade bread. Yields 6 servings.

Ruth Douglas Kline, Miss Pennsylvania 1948

Carrots Grand Marnier

1 2-pound bag carrots
1 orange, peeled
⅛ cup Grand Marnier liqueur
⅛ cup orange juice

Slice the carrots into long strips. Slice the orange in rounds, then cut the rounds in half. Put the carrots and oranges in a microwave-safe dish. Pour the Grand Marnier and orange juice over the carrots. Cover and cook in the microwave to desired tenderness. Yields 6 to 8 servings.

Vonda Kay VanDyke Scoates, Miss America 1965

Cave Hill Corn Pudding

2 eggs
2 cups fresh corn, removed from the cob
1 cup heavy cream
1 tablespoon butter
½ green bell pepper, diced
1 teaspoon salt
1 tablespoon sugar
⅛ teaspoon black pepper

Preheat oven to 350°. Beat the eggs well and add the other ingredients. Pour into a greased casserole dish. Set dish into a larger dish. Add 1 inch of water to the larger dish. Bake for 45 minutes to 1 hour, stirring twice while cooking. Yields 4 servings.

Phyllis George, Miss America 1971

Who's the Reptile?

Talk about double trouble. Sharlene Wells Hawkes, Miss America 1985 and now an ESPN sportscaster, remembers the time a *People* magazine crew followed her around on a day when she had the flu. Late at night after an exhausting round of appearances, their photographer insisted they had to have a photo for their editor. "No big deal," said the photographer. "It's only a headshot. Throw anything on. Don't bother with your shoes." Famous last words. Always a good sport, barefooted Sharlene put on her crown and threw on the first thing in her suitcase—a dress in a reptile scale print. Later, Wells opened *People* to discover the "head shot"—a full-length portrait of Miss America with corn-pads decorating her bare feet. To add insult to injury, Mr. Blackwell named her to his infamous Worst Dressed List, describing her as "an armadillo in cornpads."

Baked Chili Cheese Corn

This recipe is a great accompaniment to grilled foods, especially beef tenderloin or steaks.

2 16-ounce cans Green Giant MexiCorn (or use 1 32-ounce bag frozen corn, thawed and drained, 1 green bell pepper, chopped, and 1 red bell pepper, chopped)
2 cups grated Cheddar cheese
1 8-ounce package cream cheese, softened to room temperature
1 7-ounce can diced green chilies
2 teaspoons chili powder
2 teaspoons cumin

Preheat oven to 350°. Butter a 1½ quart baking dish. Combine all the ingredients in a large bowl until well mixed. Transfer to the baking dish. Bake until bubbling, about 30 minutes. Yields 6 to 8 servings.

Mignon Merchant Ball, Miss Oklahoma 1986

Corn Stuffed Peppers

This is really delicious. The corn mixture can be stuffed into red peppers or baked in a casserole dish.

4 large red bell peppers
1 large zucchini
1 medium red onion
Olive oil
8 ears fresh corn
1 8-ounce package pepper Jack cheese
Tortilla chips

Preheat oven to 350°. Halve the red peppers. Remove the seeds and pulp, and set aside in a casserole dish. Cut the zucchini into bite-size pieces. Finely chop the onion and sauté in the olive oil. Combine the onion and zucchini in a large mixing bowl. Remove the corn from the cob and add to the zucchini mixture. Shred the cheese and add it to the mixture. Stuff the peppers with the corn mixture and top lightly with crushed tortilla chips. Bake for about 25 to 30 minutes. Yields 8 servings.

Susan Perkins Botsford, Miss America 1978

Festive Cranberry Relish

Great served with your Thanksgiving or Christmas turkey!

1 3-ounce box lemon-flavored gelatin
1 3-ounce box orange-flavored gelatin
3 cups boiling water
1 16-ounce bag fresh cranberries
2 apples (1 peeled, 1 unpeeled)
2 oranges (1 peeled, 1 unpeeled)
1 cup crushed pineapple
2 cups sugar
½ to 1 cup chopped pecans

Dissolve the gelatins into the boiling water. Grind the cranberries, apples, and oranges. Add the fruit to the gelatin. Add the pineapple, sugar, and nuts. Mix well and chill for several hours. Fills a large bowl. Keeps well. Yields 20 servings.

Note: This tasty treat in a festive Christmas jar with a bow is a lovely gift for friends.

Donna Axum Whitworth, Miss America 1964

What a Beauty!

When Kylene Barker, Miss America 1979, returned to Virginia as the state's first Miss America, the president of her alma mater, Virginia Tech, arranged for their celebrity graduate to be transported in style. "From what I understand," says Kylene, "he searched all over Virginia for the biggest, and best, and shiniest limousine he could find. I think it belonged to the governor or something. Well, this limousine had everything: a telephone, a bar, a television set. It was wonderful. So here I was, coming back as the newly crowned Miss America, and I'm perched atop this gorgeous limousine, waving and waving—and I could hear the crowd going, 'Look at that caaaaaar!' " She laughs. "I told the president, 'I owe you one for that!'"

French Onion Casserole

Great made a day ahead!

4 medium onions, sliced
3 tablespoons butter
2 tablespoons all-purpose flour
Dash of pepper
¾ cup beef bouillon broth
¼ cup dry sherry
1½ cups plain croutons
2 tablespoons butter, melted
2 ounces shredded Swiss cheese
3 tablespoons grated Parmesan cheese

Preheat oven to 350°. Cook the onions in 3 tablespoons of butter until tender. Blend in the flour and pepper. Add the bouillon and sherry; cook until thick. Place in a 1-quart casserole. Toss the croutons with the remaining butter. Sprinkle the onions with the Swiss cheese, croutons, and Parmesan cheese, in that order. Heat through or until the cheese is melted. Yields 4 to 6 servings.

Beth Guthmiller Hughes, Miss South Dakota 1976

Cottage Potatoes

10 pounds white potatoes
1 large onion, chopped
1 green bell pepper, finely chopped (optional)
8 ounces American cheese, cubed
Chopped parsley (optional)
1 2.5-ounce can pimiento, cut up
1¼ cups milk
2 sticks butter, melted
Salt and pepper to taste
1 cup crushed cornflakes (optional)

Preheat oven to 350°. Cook the unpeeled potatoes until nearly done. Peel and slice the potatoes into a large baking dish. Stir in the onion, green pepper, cheese, parsley, and pimiento. Cover with milk and butter. Add the salt and pepper and top with cornflakes. Bake for 1 hour. Yields 12 servings.

Elaine Pack Litster, Miss Idaho 1983

Pardon My Southern Accent!

Actress Delta Burke may have achieved fame and fortune in real-life for her acting skills, but her debut at the 1974 Miss America Pageant could have come straight out of a *Designing Women* episode. Delta, who competed as Miss Florida, planned to perform an English drama about King Henry VIII's soon-to-be-beheaded queen, Anne Boleyn. Unfortunately, after she picked up an accent from Miss Georgia, she portrayed the doomed British monarch—with a southern drawl! She missed the Top 10.

Ratatouille

1 large red onion, cubed
3 tablespoons extra-virgin olive oil
Salt and freshly ground pepper to taste
6 Japanese eggplants, cubed
3 large bell peppers, cut into large triangles (mixed colors are best)
6 to 8 cloves garlic, chopped
2 pounds summer squash, cut into thick wedges and slices
3 pounds Roma tomatoes, peeled and chopped
4 to 6 tablespoons chopped fresh basil

. . . .

Sauté the onion in the olive oil with salt and pepper until soft, about 5 minutes. Add the eggplant, bell pepper, garlic, and more salt and pepper. Sauté for 10 minutes over medium to low heat. Add the summer squash and tomatoes. Cook over low heat for 20 to 25 minutes, or until all of the vegetables are fork tender. Remove from the heat, add the basil and additional salt and pepper to taste.

Nancy Fleming, Miss America 1961

Potato Cheese Casserole

1 10¾-ounce can cream of chicken soup
½ pint sour cream
1 stick margarine or butter
1 cup milk
½ cup grated cheese
Salt to taste
Chopped onions
2 pounds potatoes, hashed or grated

. . . .

Preheat oven to 350°. Combine all the ingredients, except the potatoes. Place the potatoes in a greased casserole and cover with the soup mixture. Bake for 1 hour. Yields 8 to 10 servings.

Debbie Weuve Rohrer, Miss Iowa 1975

Roadhouse Potatoes

When I was growing up, after church on Sunday I would go to my grandparents' house to eat lunch. One of my grandmother's favorite things to make was Roadhouse Potatoes. As a kid, I liked just about anything. And while this dish isn't the most slimming, it sure does taste good!

3 cups half and half
1 stick butter
Pinch of salt and pepper
2 12-ounce packages shredded hashbrowns, thawed
¾ cup grated Parmesan cheese

. . . .

Preheat oven to 350°. Heat cream and butter together; add the seasonings. Place the potatoes in a 9 x 13-inch glass baking dish. Pour the cream mixture over the potatoes and sprinkle cheese on top. Bake, uncovered, for approximately 1 hour. Yields 6 to 8 servings.

Gretchen Carlson, Miss America 1989

Pennsylvania Dutch Potato Filling

Although I was Miss Delaware, I spent the first 13 years of my life in rural Lancaster County, Pennsylvania, where I lived in the heart of the Pennsylvania Dutch country. My nextdoor neighbors and playmates were Amish, and this side dish is a staple of the area at Thanksgiving, Christmas, and Easter—in the place of traditional bread stuffing or mashed potatoes. As with most Pennsylvania Dutch cooking, this dish is not easy on the waistline, but it is something to look forward to at the holidays!

2 pounds red potatoes, diced with skin on
2 sticks butter, divided
2 stalks celery, diced
1 large red onion, diced
3 slices stale bread, diced
2 eggs
Milk
Salt and pepper to taste
Parsley

. . . .

While the potatoes are boiling, fry the onion, celery, and bread in 1 stick of butter until brown. When the potatoes are soft (about 25 minutes) combine remaining butter, 2 eggs, and cooked potato mixture in a bowl. Blend well with an electric mixer. Add milk to the desired consistency, and salt and pepper. You can also toss in a little garlic powder if you like! Preheat oven to 400°. Pour the potato filling into a greased casserole dish. Bake until the top is brown. Garnish with a sprig of fresh parsley, if desired, and serve! Yields 8 to 10 servings.

Laura Ludwig Moss, Miss Delaware 1988

Healthful "Potato Chips"

2 large Idaho potatoes
Vegetable cooking spray

. . . .

Preheat oven to 450°. Slice the potatoes into thin medallions. Spray a cookie sheet with vegetable cooking spray. Line the potato slices on the cookie sheet so they touch one another. Bake for 45 minutes. Turn them over. Bake for another 15 minutes or until the potato slices are very brown. Yields 4 servings.

Marilyn Van Derbur Atler, Miss America 1958

Sweet Potato Balls

These are my favorite for the holidays. Try adding Grand Marnier for a festive taste. Because of the color it's a great addition to any plate.

1 large can sweet potatoes, drained
1 cup firmly packed brown sugar
1 stick butter or margarine, softened
9 or 10 large marshmallows
Shredded coconut (optional)

. . . .

Preheat oven to 350°. Combine all of the ingredients except for the marshmallows and coconut. Shape the mixture into approximately 3-inch balls around each marshmallow. Place in a lightly greased baking dish and sprinkle with coconut. Bake until the coconut has browned. Yields 4 to 6 servings.

Note: You can also use mini-marshmallows for the smaller balls.

Kylene Barker, Miss America 1979

Potato Casserole

1 2-pound bag hashbrowns, thawed
1 stick butter, melted
1 10¾-ounce can cream of mushroom soup
1 10-ounce block extra sharp Cheddar cheese, grated
1 tablespoon salt
½ tablespoon pepper
½ cup chopped onion
1 pint sour cream
2 cups cornflake crumbs
½ stick butter, melted

. . . .

Preheat oven to 350°. Combine the first 8 ingredients. Pour into a buttered 9 x 13-inch casserole. Coat the cornflake crumbs with the remaining butter and sprinkle over top of the casserole. Bake, uncovered, for 1 hour. You can mix and freeze for later, leaving off the topping until ready to bake. Yields 8 servings.

Jeanne Swanner Robertson, Miss North Carolina 1963

Southern Sweet Potato Casserole

This is both Southern and healthy.

3 cups peeled, cooked, and mashed sweet potatoes
½ cup sugar
2 eggs, beaten
½ stick low-fat margarine
½ cup milk
1½ teaspoons vanilla extract
1 teaspoon cinnamon
½ teaspoon nutmeg
½ cup firmly packed brown sugar
⅓ cup all-purpose flour
⅓ stick low-fat margarine
½ cup chopped pecans

. . . .

Preheat oven to 350°. Combine the first 8 ingredients well and place them in a casserole dish. Heat the remaining ingredients, stirring until margarine is melted. Blend well. Spread over the sweet potato casserole. Bake for 35 minutes. Yields 6 servings.

Nancy Humphries, Miss South Carolina 1987

Potato-Bread Filling

5 potatoes
1 egg, beaten
Salt and pepper to taste
2 tablespoons butter
½ onion, sliced
2 ribs celery, chopped
6 slices bread, cut into cubes
2 tablespoons chopped parsley
Butter

. . . .

Boil, skin, and mash the potatoes. Add the beaten egg and season well with salt and pepper. Preheat oven to 350°. Melt the butter in a skillet and brown the onion. Add the celery, bread cubes, and parsley. Stir, coating the bread cubes with butter. Add the potatoes and let cook for several minutes. Pour the filling into a generously buttered glass casserole and dot with butter. Bake, uncovered, for 45 to 50 minutes. This can also be used as a stuffing for poultry. Yields 6 to 8 servings.

Lynne Grote Tully, Miss Pennsylvania 1977

Creamy Rich Potatoes

This dish is always a smash with guests!

8 servings Potato Buds
1 8-ounce package cream cheese, softened to room temperature
1 cup sour cream
Garlic powder to taste
6 tablespoons butter, melted
Paprika

Preheat oven to 350°. Make the Potato Buds according to package directions. Blend together with the cream cheese and sour cream. Add the garlic powder. Pour into a buttered casserole. Bake for 30 minutes, or until set. Pour the melted butter over top either before or after baking. Sprinkle with paprika. Yields 8 servings.

Barbara Guthmiller Ausdemore, Miss South Dakota 1974

Kylene Barker, Miss America 1979, greets one of thousands of audiences she faced during her year in the national limelight. (Irv Kaar)

Kasha Varnishkes

My mother and grandmother have been making my favorite side dish, Kasha Varnishkes, for as long as I can remember. It is a simple dish originating from the Russian Jewish people. Because the name is a bit tricky, when I was a child my name for the dish was "Kasha and Veronica."

½ cup chopped onions
½ cup sliced mushrooms
2 tablespoons butter or margarine (optional)
2 cups broth, bouillon, consommé, or water
1 egg (or egg white)
1 cup coarse kasha
½ teaspoon salt (use less if you're using broth)
Dash of pepper
1 cup bowtie pasta

Sauté the onions and mushrooms in the butter or margarine. Set aside. Heat the broth to boiling. In a separate pan, lightly beat the egg with a fork. Add the kasha and stir to coat the kernels. Stir over medium to high heat for 2 to 3 minutes then reduce the heat to low. Stir in the sautéed onions and mushrooms, the broth, the salt, and the pepper. Boil the pasta until tender and add it to the kasha. Simmer for 10 minutes or until the kasha kernels are tender and the liquid is absorbed. Yields 4 servings.

Stacey Heisler Mason, Miss Michigan 1993

Kansas Wheat

1 onion, chopped
1½ cups bulgur wheat
2 tablespoons margarine, softened
1 clove garlic, minced
3 cups fat-free chicken broth
Pepper

. . . .

Sauté the onion and wheat in the margarine until golden. Add the garlic. Stir. Add the broth and pepper. Cover and simmer for 20 minutes. Yields 6 servings.

Mary Ann McGrew Trombold, Miss Kansas 1956

And in This Corner . . . Miss America!

For years, one of the most unnerving moments of being crowned Miss America was having Bert Parks stick a microphone in the winner's face as she was nearly hyperventilating from shock and ask something like, "What does it mean to you to be named Miss America?" "I remember thinking, *He can't ask me anything now. I don't even know my middle name!*" recalls Terry Meeuwsen, Miss America 1973. "As I look back on it now, how would I know? I'd only been Miss America for thirty seconds!" Then, finally, Miss America 1975, said what had been on winners' minds for ages. As she was being crowned, Bert asked Shirley Cothran, "How does it feel to be Miss America?" With a deceptively sweet smile she scolded, "How can you ask me questions at a time like this?" Parks was so taken aback that he later told a *Chicago Tribune* reporter, "I'd like to have punched her one!"

Company Rice

1 cup rice
1 cup water
1 cup beef bouillon
1 medium onion, sliced
1 8-ounce can mushrooms
1 stick butter

. . . .

Preheat oven to 350°. Place all the ingredients in a baking dish. Bake for 1 hour. Yields 4 to 5 servings.

Marie Nicholes, Atlantic City Hostess

Red Beans & Rice

2 cups dried red beans
1 ham bone
1 tablespoon dried green bell pepper flakes
1 tablespoon dried minced onion
2 teaspoons seasoned salt
1 teaspoon sugar
1 bay leaf
½ teaspoon dried minced garlic
¼ teaspoon cayenne pepper
½ teaspoon celery seed
¼ teaspoon crushed red pepper
1 teaspoon ground cumin
1 cup uncooked long grain rice
1 pound spicy smoked sausage, sliced into ¾- to 1-inch pieces

. . . .

Wash the beans. Place them in a Dutch oven and cover with water. Soak overnight. Drain. Add the ham bone and seasonings to the beans. Add water to cover the beans. Cook, partially covered, over medium-low heat for 3 to 4 hours. Cook the rice, according to package directions, 30 minutes before serving. Add the sliced sausage to the beans 20 minutes before serving. Salt and pepper to taste. Serve over hot rice. Yields 4 to 6 servings.

Debra Ann Ward Backus, Miss Louisiana 1973

Dirty Rice

This dish goes well with any meat.

1½ cups raw rice
½ cup vegetable oil
Giblets from 8 chickens, chopped
½ teaspoon thyme
½ teaspoon sage
1 tablespoon salt
3 cloves garlic, chopped
2 onions, chopped
1 teaspoon Tabasco or Louisiana Hot Sauce

Place the unwashed rice in an iron pot and drizzle with oil. Cook over medium heat until the rice is light brown. Stir often. Boil the giblets in a separate pot until tender. Save the water. Cut up the giblets and add them to the rice. Add all of the seasonings. Add water to the giblet liquid to make 3 cups. Add to the rice. Cover and cook until the moisture has evaporated and the rice is done. If it seems to be cooking too fast, add more hot water. Yields 6 to 8 servings.

Note: If you're having company, this can be started early in the day and finished up to 30 minutes before serving. Do everything up to adding water. Then cook when ready.

Caroline Masur, Miss Louisiana Pageant

Spanish Rice

¼ cup olive oil
1 onion, chopped
½ green bell pepper, chopped
1 clove garlic, minced
1 14-ounce can stewed tomatoes
1 teaspoon chili powder
Dash of Worcestershire sauce
1 cup rice, uncooked
2 cups water
Salt and pepper to taste

Sauté the onion, pepper, and garlic in the olive oil until the onion is transparent. Add the remaining ingredients. Bring to a boil, then simmer, tightly covered, on the lowest heat for about 20 minutes. Stir occasionally. Yields 4 to 6 servings.

Mai Therese Shanley, Miss New Mexico 1983

Open Mouth, Insert Foot

Tom Snyder once asked pageant CEO Albert Marks if he ever picked a favorite Miss America. Striving to be the picture of impartiality, he answered, "No, to me they all look like a plate of yesterday's mashed potatoes." It was an unfortunate analogy. After Miss Americas got wind of his remarks, he sheepishly clarified, "The sameness was what I meant—but it didn't come out that way." Sometime later, at a luncheon honoring former winners, Donna Axum, Miss America 1964, approached the podium and sweetly informed the Pageant patriarch, "Mr. Marks, please stay for a moment. We have something for you." Then, as Marks recalls, "She took her hand out from behind her back with a plate of cold mashed potatoes—and I got it!"

And the Geographic Genius Award Goes To . . .

One of the great traditions of the Miss America Pageant is the wall-sized "Miss America Map of America," where all fifty state representatives autograph their state. Nothing too demanding, here. Nevertheless, during the late 1970s, one Miss Rhode Island signed the map—only to realize that she had just put her John Hancock on the state of Massachusetts.

Mexican-Style Rice with Chili Peppers and Cheese

1 cup rice
2 cups water
2 cups sour cream (or plain yogurt)
Salt to taste
8 ounces Cheddar cheese, cut into small cubes
1 6-ounce can peeled and chopped or sliced green chili peppers, drained
Butter
½ cup grated Parmesan cheese (optional)

. . . .

Cook the rice in a tightly covered pot until just tender, about 20 minutes. Preheat oven to 350°. Combine the rice with the sour cream and season with salt. Spread half of the mixture in the bottom of a buttered casserole. Sprinkle the rice mixture with the Cheddar cheese and chili peppers. Top with the remaining rice mixture and dot with butter. Sprinkle with Parmesan cheese. Bake, uncovered, for 30 minutes. Serve immediately. Yields 6 servings.

Jo-Carroll Dennison, Miss America 1942

Spinach Casserole

1 10-ounce package frozen spinach
2 tablespoons butter
2 tablespoons finely chopped onion
2 tablespoons green bell pepper
¼ cup chopped celery
2 tablespoons all-purpose flour
1 cup milk
1 to 2 chopped hard-boiled eggs
2 teaspoons lemon juice
Salt and pepper to taste
½ cup grated cheese
½ cup buttered bread crumbs
Paprika

. . . .

Cook the spinach according to the package directions. Drain thoroughly. Preheat oven to 375°. Melt the butter. Sauté the onion, pepper, and celery until transparent, not brown. Add the flour and blend until smooth. Add the milk, stirring constantly. Cook until thick. Stir in the eggs, lemon juice, salt, and pepper. Turn into a well-greased baking dish. Top with cheese and bread crumbs. Sprinkle with paprika. Bake for 20 to 25 minutes, or until browned. Yields 6 servings.

Liz Barton, Miss Georgia Pageant

Spinach Soufflé

A microwave recipe

1 10-ounce package frozen chopped spinach
2 tablespoons all-purpose flour
2 eggs, beaten
1 3-ounce package cream cheese, cubed
¾ cup cubed American cheese
½ stick butter or margarine, cubed
1½ teaspoons instant minced onion
½ teaspoon salt

Topping

½ cup fine bread crumbs
½ stick butter
⅓ cup grated Parmesan cheese

Cook the spinach for 6 minutes on HIGH in a 1½-quart microwave-safe casserole dish. Stir once during the cooking. Drain. Stir in the flour. Add the next 6 ingredients and mix well. Cook on HIGH for 9 to 11 minutes, stirring twice during cooking. Combine the bread crumbs, butter, and Parmesan cheese. Cook on HIGH, stirring occasionally, until butter is melted. Spread topping over the spinach. Microwave on HIGH for an additional minute. Yields 4 servings.

Note: Do not double the topping for double the recipe of spinach.

Dorothy Wallin, Miss Pennsylvania Pageant

Spaghetti Squash

1 large spaghetti squash
Garlic or onion salt to taste
Roma tomatoes, cooked
Parmesan cheese, shredded

Preheat oven to 375°. Cut the spaghetti squash in half and bake for about 35 to 45 minutes, until tender. Be very careful not to overcook or the pasta-like squash will be mushy. With a fork, gently scrape out the squash. It will look very much like angel hair pasta. Add the garlic or onion salt, if desired. Cover with the tomatoes and cheese. Yields 4 servings.

Marilyn Van Derbur Atler, Miss America 1958

Royal Repartee

Bert Parks chats with Tawny Godin, Miss America 1976, as she is crowned:

Bert: "If I ever saw a happy girl, . . . Here is Tawny Godin, from New York.

Tawny: "I can't believe I'm not a five-year-old girl doing this to television anymore! It's really real!"

Bert: "What darling?"

Tawny: "I've been doing this ever since I was five years old."

Bert: "You've been doing what since you were five?"

Tawny: "Taking the walk with Miss America, of course."

Bert: "You mean watching the show? You never dreamed that you'd be here?"

Tawny: "No. But I should be good at it by now."

Zucchini Squash Casserole

2 pounds zucchini squash, sliced
¼ cup chopped onion
1 10¾-ounce can cream of chicken soup
1 cup sour cream
1 cup shredded carrots
Salt to taste
1 8-ounce package seasoned stuffing mix
1 stick butter, melted

Preheat oven to 350°. Cook the squash and onion in lightly salted boiling water for about 3 minutes. The squash should still be a little crisp; drain. Combine the chicken soup and sour cream. Stir in the shredded carrots, squash, onion, and salt. Combine the stuffing mix with the butter and place ½ in the bottom of a 12 x 7-inch baking dish. Spoon the vegetable mixture over top. Sprinkle the remaining stuffing mixture on top. Bake for 25 to 30 minutes. Yields 8 to 10 servings.

Debbie Weuve Rohrer, Miss Iowa 1975

During Pageant Week, contestants are assisted by the Miss America National Hostess Committee, a select group of more than one hundred New Jersey women volunteers. "The contestants are supervised about as well as you are in the Army!" Bert Parks once quipped. (Martin Photography)

Squash Casserole

3 cups parboiled squash
1 10¾-ounce can cream of chicken soup
1 cup sour cream
1 medium onion, chopped
1 2.5-ounce jar pimiento
1 8-ounce can sliced water chestnuts
1 stick margarine, melted
½ 8-ounce package Pepperidge Farm Herb Dressing

. . . .

Preheat oven to 350°. Combine the first 7 ingredients and place them in a casserole. Top with the dressing. Bake for 30 minutes. Yields 4 to 6 servings.

Gail Bullock Odom, Miss Georgia 1973

No Name Vegetable Dish

I never named this recipe.
I just got sick of the same old vegetables and dreamed it up one night.

½ pound bacon, diced
2 fresh tomatoes, quartered
1 16-ounce can whole asparagus
Salt and pepper to taste

. . . .

Fry the diced bacon in a skillet until crisp, remove, and drain. Place the asparagus in a skillet with the remaining bacon drippings, spread it around to cover the bottom of the pan. Place the tomatoes on top. Cover and simmer over low heat until the tomatoes are cooked through but not mushy. Place in a serving dish and sprinkle with the cooked bacon. Yields 4 servings.

Janice B. Walker-Molloy, Miss Alabama Pageant

Three Bean Casserole

2 10-ounce packages frozen lima beans
2 10-ounce packages frozen cut green beans
2 10-ounce packages frozen green peas
2 green bell peppers, diced
Butter
1 cup mayonnaise
1 cup half and half
1 cup grated Parmesan cheese
½ cup Ritz cracker crumbs

Cook the vegetables according to package directions; drain. Sauté the green peppers in butter. Preheat oven to 325°. Layer the beans in a casserole dish along with the green peppers. Combine the mayonnaise, half and half, and Parmesan cheese. Pour the mixture over the beans. Top with cracker crumbs and dot with butter. Bake for 20 minutes. Yields 6 to 8 servings.

Gail Broderick, Miss Iowa Pageant

Baked Cheese Grits

6 cups cooked grits, warm
5 eggs, beaten
1 cup half and half
1½ sticks butter
Salt and pepper to taste
1 6-ounce roll garlic cheese
¾ cup chopped green onions

Preheat oven to 350°. Combine the eggs and half and half. Fold into the warm grits. Add the remaining ingredients. Pour into a casserole dish and bake for 1 hour. Yields 8 servings.

Becky Smith Hyman, Miss South Carolina 1968

What a Target!

When Laurel Schaefer, Miss America 1972, and her USO tour troupe traveled to Vietnam to entertain the U.S. troops, they arrived on a military helicopter. The helicopter suddenly bounced around vigorously, but the pilot seemed nonchalant. Laurel casually asked, "Gee, what makes it do that?" Replied the pilot, "Oh, those are just heat-seeking missiles they're shooting at us."

Southern Cheese Grits

1½ cups hominy grits, uncooked
6 cups boiling water
1 stick butter
1½ cups milk
3 eggs, beaten
4 cups grated sharp Cheddar cheese
1 teaspoon garlic salt
3 teaspoons salt (or to taste)
2 green onions, chopped
Paprika

Preheat oven to 325°. Add the grits to the boiling water. Cook until they reach desired thickness. While the grits are still hot, add the remaining ingredients except the paprika. Mix well. Bake in a 9 x 13-inch glass baking dish for 1 hour. Sprinkle with paprika before serving. This can be frozen. Yields 4 to 6 servings.

Janice B. Walker-Molloy, Miss Alabama Pageant

Lowcountry Grits Casserole

Grits casserole is a Jenkins family tradition shared with family and friends on Christmas day.

1 cup grits, uncooked
½ teaspoon salt
4 cups boiling water
1 pound mild sausage, cooked, drained, and crumbled
2½ cups shredded New York-style sharp Cheddar cheese, divided
3 tablespoons butter
1 3-ounce package cream cheese
2 eggs, beaten
1½ cups milk
1 tablespoon Worcestershire sauce
1 tablespoon black pepper

. . . .

Slowly stir the grits into the salted, boiling water. Cook for 20 minutes over medium-low heat, stirring occasionally. Preheat oven to 350°. Spoon the sausage into a 13 x 9-inch baking dish. Combine the grits, 2 cups of the Cheddar cheese, the butter, and cream cheese. Stir until melted. Add the eggs, milk, Worcestershire sauce, and pepper. Pour over the sausage and sprinkle the remaining cheese on top. Bake for 1 hour. Yields 10 servings.

Note: Great with biscuits and preserves.

Jane Jenkins Herlong, Miss South Carolina 1979

Razorback Grits

1 cup water
Dash of salt
½ cup grits, uncooked
1 tablespoon butter
2 eggs
¾ cup milk
¾ cup grated Cheddar cheese

. . . .

Preheat oven to 350°. Boil the water and salt in a small saucepan; add the grits and butter, stirring constantly. Cook for 1 minute, then remove from heat. Beat the eggs lightly in a mixing bowl. Add the milk and cheese. Add the grits, mixing well. Pour into a greased 1-quart casserole. Bake for 35 to 40 minutes, or until set. Yields 4 servings.

Carole Lawson, Miss Arkansas 1987

Cakes & Pies

Crème de Menthe Cake

1 18¼-ounce box yellow cake mix
1 3-ounce pistachio-flavored instant pudding mix
1 cup vegetable oil
3 tablespoons crème de menthe plus enough water to make 1 cup
4 eggs
Green food coloring
1 2-ounce can chocolate syrup

Frosting

½ cup sugar
2 tablespoons butter
2 tablespoons milk
½ of 6-ounce package semisweet chocolate chips

Preheat oven to 350°. Combine the cake mix, instant pudding, oil, crème de menthe and water, eggs, and a few drops of green food coloring in a large mixing bowl. Mix well using an electric beater. Place ⅔ of the batter in a well-greased bundt pan. Add the chocolate syrup to the remaining batter. Mix well. Pour over the green batter. Make marble swirls through the batter with a knife. Bake for 1 hour. Cool for 20 minutes, then turn upside down onto a plate. Combine the sugar, butter, and milk in a saucepan. Bring to a boil and boil for 1 minute. Remove from the heat and add the chocolate chips. Stir until well blended. Drizzle over the cooled cake. Yields 12 to 16 servings.

Gretchen Carlson, Miss America 1989

Mystery Cake

1 box cake mix, any flavor
1 small can sauerkraut, rinsed, drained, and dried a little
1 teaspoon vanilla extract

Prepare the cake mix as directed on the box. Fold the sauerkraut into the cake batter; stir in the vanilla. Bake as directed on the box. Makes a fresh coconut-like cake. Best baked in layers. Use your favorite frosting. Yields 10 to 12 servings.

Marian Bergeron, Miss America 1933

Applesauce Cake

¾ cup sugar
½ cup shortening
1 egg
2 cups all-purpose flour
1 teaspoon baking soda
1 teaspoon ground cloves
1 teaspoon salt
1 teaspoon cinnamon
1 cup applesauce
1 cup raisins
1 cup chopped pecans

Preheat oven to 350°. Combine the sugar, shortening, and egg. Blend well. Add the remaining ingredients gradually. Blend thoroughly and pour into a greased and floured tube or loaf pan. Bake for 1 hour. Yields 20 servings.

HermaLoy Elliott Smith, Miss New Mexico 1962

Fresh Apple Cake

½ cup vegetable oil
2 cups sugar
2 eggs
2 cups all-purpose flour
1 teaspoon salt
1 teaspoon baking soda
2 teaspoons cinnamon
2 teaspoons vanilla extract
4 cups peeled and chopped apples
1 cup chopped pecans

Icing

1 8-ounce package cream cheese, softened to room temperature
½ stick margarine
1 tablespoon vanilla extract
2 cups confectioners' sugar

Preheat oven to 350°. Combine the oil, sugar, and eggs; beat well. Sift together, then gradually add the flour, salt, baking soda and cinnamon. Add the vanilla, apples, and pecans and mix well. Pour the batter into a greased loaf pan. Bake for 45 minutes. While the cake is baking, combine the ingredients for the icing, and mix well with an electric mixer. Spread on the cooled cake. Yields 10 to 12 servings.

Jane Jayroe, Miss America 1967

Torta Di Mele (Roman Apple Cake)

1 cup sugar
1½ cups all-purpose flour
¼ teaspoon salt
½ teaspoon baking powder
1 teaspoon baking soda
½ cup shortening
½ cup milk
1 egg
2 cups peeled and finely chopped apples

Topping

½ cup firmly packed brown sugar
2 tablespoons butter or margarine, softened
2 teaspoons all-purpose flour
2 teaspoons cinnamon
½ cup nuts, finely chopped
Whipped cream or ice cream, optional

Sift the dry ingredients together in a large mixing bowl. Add the remaining ingredients and blend on medium speed. Pour the batter into a 9 x 13-inch baking pan.

Preheat oven to 350°. Cream all the topping ingredients together. Pour over the cake batter. Bake for 45 minutes. Serve the cake topped with whipped cream or ice cream if desired. Yields 12 to 15 servings.

Kitsy Mangan, Miss Massachusetts Pageant

Grandma Russler's Easy Chocolate Cake

2 cups all-purpose flour
2 cups sugar
½ teaspoon salt
2 sticks margarine
1 cup water
4 tablespoons cocoa powder
1 teaspoon baking soda
2 eggs
1 cup sour cream

Frosting

1 stick margarine
4 tablespoons cocoa powder
5 tablespoons milk
1 teaspoon vanilla extract
1 16-ounce box confectioners' sugar

Preheat oven to 350°. Combine the flour, sugar, and salt in a bowl. Melt the margarine in a saucepan and add the water and cocoa powder. Bring the mixture to a boil and immediately pour it into a separate bowl. Beat in the baking soda, eggs, and sour cream. Add the dry ingredients. Pour the batter into a greased cookie sheet and one other small pan. Bake for 15 to 20 minutes or until the cake loses the "shiny look." Bring the margarine, cocoa powder, and milk to a boil. Stir in the vanilla and confectioners' sugar until well blended. Frost the cake while it is still warm. Yields 12 to 16 servings.

Heather Whitestone, Miss America 1995

Check Mate

In 1987, after a statistician predicted several Miss Americas by feeding their personal stats into a computer, Pageant officials discontinued publishing contestants' measurements in the program book. So there.

Heavenly Rum Cake

1 package butter cake mix
1 3-ounce package vanilla pudding
½ cup vegetable oil
½ cup light rum
4 eggs
½ cup water
½ to ¾ cup chopped nuts

Glaze

1 stick butter
1 cup sugar
¼ cup water
¼ cup rum

Preheat oven to 325°. Combine the first 6 ingredients with an electric mixer until well blended. Spray nonstick cooking spray in bundt pan. Pour the chopped nuts into the bottom of the pan. Pour in the batter and bake for 50 to 60 minutes until done. Remove from the oven and let cool in the pan for 10 minutes. The cake should fall easily from the pan after 10 minutes. While the cake is baking, combine the glaze ingredients in a saucepan. Cook over low heat for about 50 minutes, or until thickened, stirring often. Spoon over the warm cake. Yields 10 to 12 servings.

Donna Axum Whitworth, Miss America 1964

Ice Box Cake

42 macaroons, divided
1 quart chocolate ice cream, softened slightly
1 quart coffee ice cream, softened slightly
Chocolate sauce
Chocolate covered English toffee rolled in almonds (See's or Almond Roca is good), crumbled

. . . .

Grease an 8- or 9-inch spring-form pan. Crumble 28 macaroons in the bottom of the pan. Spread the chocolate ice cream on top of the macaroons. Drizzle with chocolate sauce. Sprinkle with toffee. Add 14 more crumbled macaroons. Add a second layer of coffee ice cream. Drizzle with chocolate sauce. Crumble more toffee over top. Put the pan in the freezer. Remove in time to soften slightly before serving. Yields 10 servings.

Jean Bartel, Miss America 1943

Carrot Cake

1 cup vegetable oil
4 eggs
2 cups sugar
2 cups all-purpose flour
2 teaspoons baking soda
1 teaspoon salt
2 teaspoons cinnamon
3 cups grated carrots
½ cup nuts

Frosting

¾ stick butter
1 8-ounce package cream cheese, softened to room temperature
2 teaspoons vanilla extract
1 16-ounce box confectioners' sugar

. . . .

Preheat oven to 300°. Combine the oil and eggs with the sugar. Add the dry ingredients and carrots. Add the nuts. Pour into a greased and floured 9 x 13-inch cake pan. Bake for 50 to 60 minutes or until the cake tests done. Allow cake to cool. Cream the butter, cream cheese, and vanilla together. Add the confectioners' sugar, a small amount at a time. Mix well and frost the cooled cake. Keep the cake in the refrigerator. Yields 10 to 12 servings.

Susan Perkins Botsford, Miss America 1978

Zucchini Cake

Being a devoted chocolate lover, my recommendation for this non-chocolate cake comes as a surprise for those who know me best. It is a wonderfully moist and delectable cake. This is a great recipe for utilizing the abundant zucchini that grows in Southern gardens. This bundt cake looks very pretty on a luncheon table or as a "friend" to a dip of homemade ice cream in a huge bowl.

4 eggs
3 cups sugar
1½ cups vegetable oil
1 teaspoon vanilla extract
3 cups grated zucchini
3 cups all-purpose flour
2 teaspoons cinnamon
1½ teaspoons baking powder
1 teaspoon baking soda
1 teaspoon salt
1 cup chopped nuts

. . . .

Preheat oven to 350°. Combine the eggs, sugar, oil, and vanilla. Add the zucchini. Slowly add the dry ingredients and nuts. Pour into a greased bundt pan or 2 loaf pans. Bake for 1 hour for a bundt cake or 40 to 50 minutes for loaf pans. Yields 10 to 12 servings.

Shirley Cothran Barret, Miss America 1975

The 1980s—From Traumatic to Tremendous

In stark contrast to the riotous youth revolution of the previous two decades, the 1980s were marked by historic victories for democracy. President Ronald Reagan and Soviet leader Mikhail Gorbachev paved the way for peace between the rival nations and freedom prevailed in Europe as Romanians overthrew their communist dictatorship and Germans dismantled the infamous Berlin Wall.

But it was also the "Me Decade," the affluent era of dripping-in-diamonds *Dynasty* and *Dallas* clans—and yuppies who longed to live like them. In a decade known for its melodramatic television soap operas, it wasn't surprising that the Pageant occasionally seemed to be running an ongoing "soap" of its own. The first episode took place in 1980, when in an effort to modernize the Pageant telecast, Pageant chairman Albert Marks announced that Bert Parks would no longer emcee the program. The move backfired, leaving officials inundated with protest letters from irate fans. Even Johnny Carson joined the fracas, initiating a "Bring Back Bert" campaign. Convinced that the Pageant needed a more youthful image, Marks refused to budge and replaced Bert with actor Ron Ely, known for his role as television's Tarzan. After two years in the royal hot seat, Ely abdicated, and in 1982, officials brought in Gary Collins, an actor and husband of former Miss America Mary Ann Mobley. Collins was a dignified and popular emcee until 1991 when he moved on to other projects, paving the runway for the current hosts, Regis Philbin and Kathie Lee Gifford, of *Regis and Kathie Lee*.

Kaye Lani Rae Rafko, Miss Michigan, is crowned Miss America 1988 by Kellye Cash. (AP/World Wide Photos)

A major milestone in Pageant history occurred in 1983 when judges awarded the Miss America crown to a black woman for the first time. The winner, New York's Vanessa Williams, was a huge success for nine months—until *Penthouse* magazine published nude photos she had posed for before her crowning, leading to her resignation. Her first runner-up, Suzette Charles, Miss New Jersey, served as National titleholder for the duration of the year, making her the Pageant's second black Miss America.

After the traumas of the decade subsided, the Pageant came under new leadership when Albert Marks, pageant chairman for a quarter century, retired in 1987, naming attorney Leonard C. Horn as his successor. Horn immediately initiated changes to continue the Pageant's evolution as a serious scholarship program designed to promote women. First, judging was improved. An Olympic judging system was adopted, eliminating comparison judging, the value of the swimsuit competition was halved to 15 percent and changed to "Physical Fitness in Swimsuit," the Miss America Organization and Foundation were established, and a Women's Advisory Council was created, comprised of women professionals. Miss America's scholarship was increased to $35,000, a fund was created to award scholarships to deserving female students at the college attended by the national winner, and Fruit of the Loom, a corporate sponsor, established a community service recognition program for contestants. Additionally, a $10,000 Woman of Achievement Award was created to aid women making significant contributions to society. Honorees have included Rosalyn Carter, Betty Ford, AIDS activist Elizabeth Glaser, Mary Davis Fisher of Family AIDS Network, and Nan Roman, vice-president of Programs and Policy for the National Alliance to End Homelessness.

The changes were in stark contrast to the "Me Decade" and defined the Miss America Pageant as an organization devoted to the education and advancement of American women.

*The Evening Gown Competition provides a pictorial of American fashion trends from decade to decade. In the 1980s, the event showcased glamorous styles popular in the Reagan/*Dynasty/Dallas *era. Susan Akin, who would become Miss America 1986, is second from right.* (Irv Kaar)

Greek Yogurt Cake

1 stick unsalted butter
¾ cup sugar
2 eggs
2 cups all-purpose flour
1 teaspoon baking powder
1 teaspoon baking soda
1 teaspoon cinnamon
1 cup yogurt or sour cream
1 teaspoon vanilla extract
1 cup chopped almond, pecans, walnuts, or filberts

Preheat oven to 350°. Cream the butter and sugar until fluffy. Blend the eggs into the sugar mixture. Sift the dry ingredients together and add to the creamed mixture alternately with the yogurt and vanilla. Fold in the nuts. Pour the batter into a 9 x 13-inch pan. Bake for 40 minutes or until a toothpick inserted in the center comes out clean.

Note: Traditionally, Greeks pour the following syrup over the cooled cake, but it is just as delicious served plain or with a dollop of whipped topping.

Syrup

1½ cups sugar
¾ cup water
1 tablespoon lemon juice
3 whole cloves
1 cinnamon stick
3 tablespoons brandy, rum, or whiskey (optional)

Stir all the ingredients together and bring to a boil. Boil for 10 minutes. Strain and pour over the partially cooled cake. Cut the cake in diamond or square shapes when cooled. Yields 24 servings.

Rena Michaelides, Miss New York State Pageant

Scarlett's Sister?

Arkansas' Elizabeth Ward won the 1982 Miss America title wearing a homemade gown her grandmother had sewn from the family tablecloth and punched with rhinestones. As she was escorted away in a limousine after her victory, the rhinestones' prongs snagged on the upholstery—and Miss America had to be carefully peeled from her seat.

Lo-Cal Lemon Pudding Cake

2 tablespoons margarine (not calorie-reduced)
¾ cup sugar
¼ cup self-rising flour
⅛ teaspoon salt
5 tablespoons fresh lemon juice
1 tablespoon lemon zest (grated peel)
3 egg yolks, well beaten
3 egg whites, stiffly beaten
1½ cups low-fat milk

Preheat oven to 350°. Coat a 1½-quart baking dish or 6 custard cups lightly with non-stick vegetable spray. Cream the margarine and sugar, add the flour, salt, lemon juice, and zest, and mix well. Stir in the egg yolks and milk. Fold in the beaten egg whites. Spoon the mixture into the baking dish or cups and place in a large pan filled with 1 inch of hot water. Bake until the custard is puffed and lightly browned, 45 to 50 minutes in a baking dish or 35 to 40 minutes in individual cups. Remove from the water and cool on a wire rack. Serve chilled with a touch of whipped topping if desired. This may be made the night before and refrigerated. Yields 6 servings.

Dorothy Kohrt Karr, Miss Illinois 1943

Bourbon Cake

¾ of a 12-ounce package chocolate
1 cup white raisins
1 cup black walnut pieces
2¼ cups sifted cake flour, divided
4 egg whites
1 stick butter
1 cup sugar
1 teaspoon baking powder
¼ teaspoon salt
½ cup milk
½ cup 100-proof bourbon

. . . .

Preheat oven to 350°. Grate the chocolate and set aside. Combine the raisins and nuts with ¼ cup of the flour so they are completely coated. Set aside. Beat egg whites until stiff peaks form and set aside. Cream together the butter and sugar until light and fluffy. Sift together the remaining flour, the baking powder, and salt. Add the dry ingredients to the creamed mixture alternately with milk and bourbon, beating well between additions. Fold in the beaten egg whites, then the grated chocolate, nuts, and raisins. (Reserve a little of the chocolate, raisins and nuts for garnish.) Pour the batter into 2 well-greased and floured 9-inch layer cake pans. Bake for about 25 minutes. Cool on a rack and then frost with Butter-Bourbon Cream Frosting. Frost the bottom layer, sprinkle with reserved raisins and half the reserved nuts. Frost top layer and decorate with reserved chocolate and remaining nuts. Yields 10 to 12 servings.

Butter-Bourbon Cream Frosting

½ stick butter
2 cups or more confectioners' sugar
2 tablespoons bourbon
1 or 2 tablespoons milk if necessary

. . . .

Cream the butter until soft and fluffy. Beat in confectioners' sugar and bourbon. If the frosting is too thin, add more sugar, and if it is thick, add milk.

Dottye Nuckols Lindsey, Miss Kentucky 1951

Hazel's Bourbon Cake

Every year just after Thanksgiving, my mother would bake this cake in our wood cookstove. She then kept it sealed, wrapped in aluminum foil, in a box in the attic. Every four or five days she would unwrap the cake and pour a tablespoon or so of Kentucky bourbon over it. The cake would then be served on Christmas Day.

2 sticks sweet butter
2 cups sugar
5 eggs, well beaten
2 cups all-purpose flour
1 teaspoon black pepper
½ teaspoon cinnamon
1½ teaspoons ground cloves
1½ teaspoons allspice
1 teaspoon baking soda
1 cup buttermilk
1 cup raisins
1 cup chopped walnuts
1 cup blackberry jam
1 3½-ounce can coconut

Filling

½ cup cake batter
1 cup firmly packed brown sugar
½ cup sugar
1 stick butter
½ cup milk
Kentucky bourbon

. . . .

Preheat oven to 325°. Cream the butter and gradually add the sugar. Cream until light and fluffy. Add the eggs. Sift the flour and spices twice. Dissolve the baking soda in the buttermilk and add it and the flour alternately to the egg mixture. Beat well after each addition. Lightly dredge the raisins and nuts with extra flour and add them to the mixture. Stir in the jam and coconut. Reserve ½ cup of the batter for the filling. Pour the remaining batter into 3 greased and floured 9-inch cake pans and bake for 40 minutes. Combine the first 5 filling ingredients in a saucepan and cook until thick. Cool and beat. Spread the filling between the layers and on the top and sides of the cake. Make the cake a few weeks ahead and moisten with bourbon every 4 or 5 days. Yields 10 to 12 servings.

Alice Chumbley Lora, Miss Kentucky 1960

Jackie's Heavenly Fruit Cake

Read through the entire recipe.
This is my gift at Christmas to family and friends throughout the country.

3 8-ounce packages pitted dates
1 pound candied pineapple
1 pound whole candied cherries, plus some for garnish
2 cups all-purpose flour (do not use cake or self-rising flour)
2 teaspoons baking powder
½ teaspoon salt
4 eggs
1 cup sugar
2 pounds (8 cups) pecan halves, plus some for garnishing
White corn syrup

. . . .

Assemble the ingredients and let stand at room temperature for 1 hour. Make no substitutions. All measurements are level. Use two 9 x 5-inch loaf pans or two 9-inch spring-form pans, or use one of each. Grease the pans well with butter or margarine and line the bottoms and sides with brown paper cut to fit. Then grease the paper. (If you have only one pan, let ½ the batter stand in the bowl while baking one cake. After removing the first cake, wash and dry the pan. Grease; line with brown paper and grease.)

Cut the dates and pineapple in coarse pieces. Place them in a large bowl. Add the cherries. Sift, then lightly spoon the flour onto a measuring cup. Level the top with a spatula. Put 2 cups of sifted flour back into the sifter. Add the baking powder and salt. Sift the flour onto the fruit. Mix the fruits and dry ingredients well by hand, separating the pieces of fruit so that all are well-coated with dry ingredients. Preheat the oven to 275°.

Use an electric mixer or rotary beater to beat the eggs until frothy. Gradually beat in the sugar. Add this mixture to the fruit mixture; mix well , covering all pieces of fruit. Add the pecans. Use hands to evenly distributed the nuts and make sure they are coated with batter. Pack the batter firmly into the pans with palms of hands. If necessary, rearrange the pieces of fruit and nuts to fill any empty spaces. Decorate with rows of whole cherries and pecan halves.

Bake the spring-form cakes for about 1¼ hours, loaf cakes 1½ hours. (The tops of the cakes, where batter is visible, should look dry, but will not be brown. If there is any doubt, leave the cakes in the oven a few minutes longer; a little extra baking does no harm.) Cool the pans on racks. Let them stand for about 5 minutes before turning out on the racks and carefully peeling off the paper. Turn top side up and brush with corn syrup. Cool. Yields 20 to 40 servings.

Note: To store the cake, wrap loosely in foil and store in an airtight container in a cool place. Stored this way, the cakes will keep for several weeks. If wrapped well and stored in a freezer, the cakes will keep indefinitely.

Jacquelyn Mayer Townsend, Miss America 1963

Pageant Premonition

When Debra Maffett won her state title on the way to the 1983 Miss America title, her mom had a nocturnal premonition of victory. On the night of the Miss California Pageant, Nonnie Maffett went to bed in her Cut n' Shoot, Texas, home. In the middle of the night she jolted awake and turned to her husband. "The strangest feeling just came over me," she said. "They just crowned Debbie Miss California!" The couple had just managed to get back to sleep when the phone rang. "Would you like to speak to the new Miss California?" the caller asked. Debbie had won. "The time they were crowning her was exactly the time I sat up in bed and told my husband she had won," Nonnie explains excitedly. "It was kind of eerie!"

Cheryl's Chocolate Chip Cake

1 18¼-ounce package yellow cake mix
1 3-ounce package instant chocolate pudding
½ cup vegetable oil
½ cup water
4 eggs
1 8-ounce carton sour cream
1 6-ounce bag chocolate chips

Preheat the oven to 350°. Combine all of the ingredients, except the chocolate chips. Gently stir in the chocolate chips. Bake in a tube pan for 1 hour. Yields 10 to 12 servings.

Cheryl Prewitt-Salem, Miss America 1980

Chocolate Pound Cake

3 cups sugar
2 sticks butter, softened
½ cup shortening
5 eggs
3 cups all-purpose flour
½ cup cocoa powder
½ teaspoon baking powder
¼ teaspoon salt
1 cup milk
1 teaspoon vanilla extract
Fudge Icing

Preheat oven to 300°. Cream the sugar, butter, and shortening on medium speed with an electric mixer. Add the eggs, one at a time, beating well after each addition. Sift together the flour, cocoa powder, baking powder, and salt. Combine the milk and vanilla. Reduce the mixer speed to low. Add the dry ingredients and milk alternately to the creamed mixture, beating well after each addition. Pour into a greased and floured 10-inch tube pan. Bake for 1 hour and 20 minutes. Cool for 10 minutes in the pan. Turn onto a rack or plate to cool completely. Frost with Fudge Icing. Let stand until the icing is thoroughly cooled and set. Yields 10 to 12 servings.

Fudge Icing

2 cups sugar
⅔ cup milk
1 stick butter
¼ cup cocoa powder
¼ teaspoon salt
1 teaspoon vanilla extract

Combine all of the ingredients except for the vanilla in a heavy saucepan. Bring to a boil and boil for 2 minutes, stirring constantly. Remove from the heat and add the vanilla. Beat by hand or with an electric mixer until creamy.

Note: For the microwave, combine all of the ingredients, except the vanilla, in a glass bowl. Cook on HIGH 4 to 5 minutes, or until the mixture boils, stirring twice. Boil on high for 2 more minutes. Add the vanilla. Beat until creamy.

Kayanne Shoffner Massey, Miss Georgia 1959

First Class Escape

Kaye Lani Rae Rafko, Miss America 1988, recalls the time she was trapped in luxury. After making an appearance on a particularly frigid day, a proud chauffeur drove her to the airport to leave for her next appearance. Thrilled to be escorting Miss America, he had freshly washed his limousine. "I started to jump out to catch my flight only to find that the doors wouldn't open," recalls Kaye Lani. "They were frozen shut! Since it was a small town, everybody was standing around waiting to see who was going to come out of this limousine. Well, the only escape for my traveling companion and myself was to climb through the moonroof." So as the crowd watched in delight, Miss America climbed through the car's roof to catch her flight.

Chocolate Lovers' Chocolate Cake

This dessert, made in the microwave, is a very rich cake and is great served with whipped topping.

1 18¼-ounce box chocolate pudding cake mix
1 8-ounce carton sour cream
4 eggs
½ cup vegetable oil
½ cup warm water
1 3½-ounce package instant chocolate pudding
1½ cups semisweet chocolate chips

. . . .

Combine all of the ingredients, except the chocolate chips. Do not use a mixer or overstir. Fold in the chocolate chips. Spray a microwaveable bundt pan with nonstick vegetable spray and sprinkle it with sugar. Pour the mixture evenly into the pan. Microwave at 50% power for 11 to 13 minutes. Microwave on HIGH for 4 to 6 minutes. Turn the pan several times while cooking. Let the cake stand in the pan for 15 minutes after removing it from the oven. Invert and turn out. Yields 8 to 10 servings.

Alison Lenee Boyd Traynowicz, Miss Nebraska 1984

Mississippi Pound Cake

3 cups sugar
2 sticks butter
6 eggs
3 cups cake flour
½ pint heavy cream
2 teaspoons vanilla extract

. . . .

Cream together the sugar and butter. Add the eggs one at a time, beating well after each addition. Add the flour and cream alternately. Beat well, then add the vanilla. Pour the batter into a greased tube pan. Start in a cold oven. Turn oven to 325° and bake for 1½ hours. Yields 10 to 12 servings.

Carla Haag, Miss Mississippi 1988

Survival Strategy

During her reign as Miss America 1985, Sharlene Wells discovered that even those approaching 100 years old aren't immune to Miss America's charms. At an autograph session in a mall, a ninety-six-year-old man approached her table with a stern expression. "It took him five minutes just to get from the end of the table to the middle where I was sitting," she recalls. When Sharlene smiled at him, he nearly shouted, "My doctor said that I needed a physical, but I told him that I don't need one if I can survive this handshake!" "Then he put his hand out," says Sharlene. "We shook hands and he just walked away." Cancel one physical.

Sponge Cake Cream

10 eggs, at room temperature
10 tablespoons sugar
10 tablespoons all-purpose flour
1 12-ounce container whipped topping
1 cup milk
1 3½-ounce package instant vanilla pudding mix

Preheat oven to 350°. Separate the eggs. Beat the egg whites until stiff. Add the sugar, 1 tablespoon at a time, until peaks form. Whisk the yolks and slowly add to the egg whites. Add the flour and beat slowly on low until the flour disappears. Grease a spring-form pan. Bake for 35 minutes. The batter can be baked in three 9-inch cake pans for 15 minutes. Cool quickly in the refrigerator and release from the pan. If baked in spring-form pan, slice into three layers. Add the milk to the instant pudding and beat for about 1 minute. Add the pudding to the whipped topping. Spread over the cake layers and chill. Yields 10 to 12 servings.

Maxine Waack Field, Miss Ohio 1948

Old-Fashioned Pecan Pie

3 eggs
2 tablespoons unsalted butter, melted
3 tablespoons all-purpose flour
¼ teaspoon vanilla
⅛ teaspoon salt
½ cup sugar
1½ cups real maple syrup
⅔ cup chopped pecans
1 tender pie crust, pre-baked for 4 minutes at 425°

Preheat oven to 425°. Beat the eggs. Blend in the butter, flour, vanilla, salt, sugar, and syrup. Add the pecans. Pour the mixture into the pie crust. Bake on the lowest oven shelf for 10 minutes. Reduce the oven temperature to 325° and move the pie up to the middle shelf for 40 to 45 minutes, or until the filling is set. Yields 6 to 8 servings.

Maria Beale Fletcher, Miss America 1962

Tender Pie Crust

1½ sticks unsalted butter, cold
1½ cups all-purpose flour
Dash of salt
3 to 7 tablespoons ice water (use more water at higher altitudes)

Take the *cold* butter and cut it into the flour and salt. Chill your hands under cold water and work the largest lumps into the loose flour gently using your fingers. When it is down to large grains, add the ice water a tablespoon at a time, sprinkling around the edges and collecting the mixture into a ball. Finally, make a ball with your hands, pressing together lightly. Wrap in plastic wrap or waxed paper and chill for 20 to 30 minutes. Divide the dough ball in half, leaving one half in the refrigerator. Roll the other on a lightly floured board. Flatten it at the start with the heel of your hand. Roll from the center outward. Strokes should be very light (for every extra teaspoon of flour you sprinkle on you decrease the final flakiness). Yields 2 pie crusts.

Maria Beale Fletcher, Miss America 1962

Texas Pecan Pie

The Texas state tree is the pecan tree.

½ cup sugar
1 cup light Karo syrup
3 tablespoons butter
3 eggs, well beaten
1 cup chopped pecans
1 teaspoon vanilla extract
⅛ teaspoon salt
1 9-inch pie crust, uncooked

Preheat oven to 350°. Combine the sugar and syrup in a saucepan; bring to a boil. Add the butter and stir until melted. Remove from the heat and stir in the remaining ingredients. Pour into the pie crust. Bake for 50 to 60 minutes. Enjoy!

Jo Thompson, Miss Texas 1987

Escalating Fashions

Ellie Ross, traveling companion to over a decade of Miss Americas, recalls the time she and Susan Powell, the 1981 titleholder, were scheduled for a dressy ladies luncheon in a Yonkers mall. As Susan slipped on a floor-length skirt, she realized she needed hosiery and suggested that they pick some up on the way. "Here's Susan in this long gown with this security man leading us down the escalator," says Ellie. "Well, as she was getting off the escalator, her gown got caught and it ripped all the way up until she had just a mini, mini, mini dress on! The poor security man yanked and yanked until he got it out and then we wrapped it around her. But it was hysterical!"

Sweet Potato Pie

2 egg whites
½ cup sugar
½ stick butter, melted
4 large sweet potatoes, cooked, drained, and mashed
1 teaspoon all-purpose flour (optional)

Topping

1 cup chopped pecans
1 cup firmly packed brown sugar
½ stick butter or margarine, melted
2 tablespoons all-purpose flour

Preheat oven to 350°. Beat the egg whites, sugar, and butter. Combine the egg mixture with the mashed sweet potatoes, and add the flour. Mix together and pour into a casserole dish. Combine the topping ingredients in a bowl. Pour the topping mixture onto the pie. Bake for 20 to 30 minutes, or until top is browned. Don't let it burn or bubble over! Yields 6 to 8 servings.

Cheryl Prewitt-Salem, Miss America 1980

Sensational Substitute

Sharlene Wells became a stand-in for Old Glory during an appearance at a major convention down south, when a state governor stood to lead the Pledge of Allegiance and realized there was no American flag present. "Without missing a beat," says Sharlene, "he told all five thousand people there, 'Everybody stand, place your hand over your heart, turn and face Miss America, and repeat the Pledge of Allegiance after me!' So I had five thousand people reciting the Pledge of Allegiance to me."

Shoo-Fly Pie

1¼ cups all-purpose flour
⅔ cup firmly packed brown sugar
Dash of salt
2 tablespoons butter
1 egg
1 cup molasses
¾ cup boiling water
1 tablespoon baking soda
1 9-inch unbaked pie crust

. . . .

Preheat oven to 400°. Combine the flour, brown sugar, salt, and butter to make crumbs. Set aside. Beat the egg in a bowl, add the molasses, water, and baking soda. Mix half of the crumb mixture with the liquid mixture. Pour into the pie crust and top with the remaining crumbs. Bake for 15 minutes. Reduce the heat to 350° and continue baking for another 30 minutes or until firm. Cool completely before serving. Yields 6 to 8 servings.

Lynne Grote Tully, Miss Pennsylvania 1977

Super Chocolate Mousse

For a great pie, use a ready-made pie crust. Add the following Chocolate Mousse filling, top with Stabilized Whipped Cream, and garnish with mint leaves and raspberries or strawberries.

1 6-ounce package semisweet chocolate chips
2 eggs
3 tablespoons hot coffee
2 tablespoons Kahlua
¾ cup scalded milk

. . . .

Combine all the ingredients in a blender and mix for 2 minutes. Chill until firm. This can also be served in parfait glasses. Yields 6 to 8 servings.

Stabilized Whipped Cream

4 tablespoons confectioners' sugar
2 teaspoons cornstarch
2 cups heavy cream, divided
1 teaspoon vanilla extract

. . . .

Combine the confectioners' sugar and cornstarch in a small saucepan. Gradually stir in ½ cup of the cream. Bring to a boil, stirring constantly, and simmer for a few seconds until the liquid is thickened. Scrape into a small bowl and cool to room temperature. Add the vanilla. Beat the remaining cream just until traces of beater marks begin to show. Add the cornstarch mixture, beating constantly. Beat until stiff peaks form. This can be stored up to 24 hours in the refrigerator. Yields 4 cups.

Susan Perkins Botsford, Miss America 1978

Donald Trump proudly welcomes the 1988 national contestants onto his yacht, the Trump Princess. (George Sorie)

Pennsylvania Dutch Shoo-Fly Pie

Filling

2 cups hot water
1 cup molasses
2 teaspoons baking soda

Crumbs

3 cups all-purpose flour
1½ cups sugar
1 cup shortening

3 9-inch pie crusts, unbaked

. . . .

Preheat oven to 450°. Combine the first 3 ingredients and mix well. Combine the next 3 ingredients in a separate bowl. Divide the filling into the 3 pie crusts, and top with the crumb mixture. Bake for 10 minutes; reduce heat to 350° and bake for an additional 25 minutes. Yields 24 servings.

Jennifer Lynn Eshelman, Miss Pennsylvania 1983

Grasshopper Pie

Crust

18 chocolate layer (Hydrox) cookies, crushed but not too fine
¼ cup melted margarine or butter

Filling

20 large marshmallows
½ cup milk
2 tablespoons green crème de menthe
2 tablespooons white crème de cacao
½ pint whipping cream, whipped

. . . .

Combine the ingredients for the crust and pat all but ¼ cup of this mixture into a 9-inch pie plate. Over hot water, in a double boiler melt the marshmallows and milk. Cool. Carefully stir the liqueurs into the cooled marshmallow mixture; then fold in the whipped cream. Pour into the pie crust and sprinkle the remaining crumbs on the top. Refrigerate overnight or put in freezer for 4 hours. Yields 6 servings.

Marilyn Van Derbur Atler, Miss America 1958

Mall Madness

On one occasion during her reign, Kaye Lani Rae Rafko, Miss America 1988, was in a shopping mall signing autographs for a long line of fans when the mall's alarm rang. A mall bank had been robbed. Moments later, police ran up to her and asked, "Have you seen a bank robber come this way?" "Not unless he stopped for an autograph," she replied.

Santa's Chocolate Pie

1 6-ounce package semisweet chocolate chips
¼ cup water
1 tablespoon instant coffee granules
Dash of salt
2 egg yolks, beaten
1 8-ounce jar marshmallow creme
1 teaspoon vanilla extract
⅛ teaspoon almond extract
2 egg whites, stiffly beaten
1 cup heavy cream, whipped
1 graham cracker pie crust

. . . .

Over hot water, combine the first 4 ingredients in the top of a double boiler; stir until blended. When melted, pour a small amount of the chocolate mixture into the beaten egg yolks. Blend and add the eggs to rest of the chocolate mixture. Cook for 5 minutes, stirring constantly. Remove from heat and stir in the marshmallow creme, vanilla extract, and almond extract. Chill. When cooled fold in the egg whites and whipped cream. Pour into the pie crust. Freeze at least 10 hours or overnight or until firm. Yields 6 to 8 servings.

BeBe Shopp Waring, Miss America 1948

Mud Pie

This is my mother Charla McMechan's recipe.

½ package chocolate wafers, crushed
½ stick butter, melted
1 quart cookies and cream ice cream, softened
1½ cups rich fudge sauce
Whipped cream
Toasted almonds

. . . .

Combine the chocolate wafers and melted butter in a mixing bowl or a food processor. Process or stir until combined. Press into a buttered 9-inch pie plate. Cover with the softened ice cream and return to the freezer until the ice cream is firm, for about 4 hours. Spread the fudge sauce on top and freeze overnight. To serve, cut into wedges and garnish with the whipped cream and toasted almonds. Yields 8 servings.

Note: For a nice touch, serve on a chilled plate.

Joni McMechan Checchia, Miss Indiana 1988

Kentucky Derby Pie

1 cup sugar
½ cup all-purpose flour
2 eggs, beaten
1 stick butter or margarine, melted
1 cup semisweet chocolate chips
1 cup chopped pecans
1 teaspoon vanilla extract
1 pie crust, unbaked

. . . .

Preheat oven to 350°. Combine the sugar and flour. Add the eggs and melted butter. Fold in the chocolate chips, pecans, and vanilla. Mix well. Pour into the unbaked pie crust. Bake for 35 minutes. Yields 6 to 8 servings.

Gwen Witten Upchurch, Miss Kentucky 1982

Peach Cobbler

6 to 8 large very ripe peaches or one 29-ounce can sliced cling peaches
2 cups sugar, divided
1 stick butter
1 cup self-rising flour
1 cup milk
Vanilla ice cream (optional)

. . . .

Pit, peel, and thinly slice the peaches. Place in a plastic bowl and pour 1 cup of the sugar over the peaches. Stir well, cover tightly, and chill for 2 hours. Preheat oven to 400°. Place butter in bottom of rectangular 3-inch-deep glass oven-proof dish. Place in oven until the butter melts. Combine flour, remaining sugar, and milk in a bowl. Mix well with a whisk. Pour into the buttered dish. Spoon the peaches onto batter mixture. If you are using canned peaches, add only a small amount of juice from the cans. Don't stir. Bake until the top becomes golden brown. Serve with vanilla ice cream on top. Yields 6 servings.

Mary Ann Mobley Collins, Miss America 1959

Fruit Cobbler

1 quart fruit (peaches, cherries, raspberries, etc., with about 1½ cups juice and sugar to taste)
1 stick margarine
1½ cups all-purpose flour
1½ cups sugar
2 teaspoons baking powder
1 cup milk

. . . .

Preheat oven to 375°. Place the fruit and juice in a 9 x 13-inch pan. Melt the margarine and combine with the remaining ingredients. Pour the mixture evenly over the fruit. Bake for 35 to 40 minutes, or until golden brown. Yields 8 to 10 servings.

Debra Barnes Miles, Miss America 1968

Florida Key Lime Pie

Just after the Civil War, one of the few foods available in the devastated South was sweetened condensed milk, a new product developed in 1858. Cooks squeezed limes grown in the Florida Keys into the condensed milk to complement the milk's sweetness, and accidentally hit upon a mixture firm enough to be a pie filling.

3 egg yolks and 1 egg white
1 14-ounce can sweetened condensed milk
½ cup lime or lemon juice
1 teaspoon grated lime rind
A few drops of green food coloring
1 9-inch baked and cooled pastry shell or graham cracker crust
1 cup sweetened whipped cream
Lime slices

. . . .

In a medium-size bowl with electric mixer, beat the yolks and egg white until thick and light colored. Beat in the condensed milk, lime juice, and grated lime. Add the green food coloring, if desired. Pour the mixture into the prepared pie shell. Chill for about 6 hours. When ready to serve, spread the unsweetened whipped cream over the filling and garnish with twisted lime slices. This pie also freezes beautifully. Yields 8 servings.

Kimberly Boyce, Miss Florida 1983

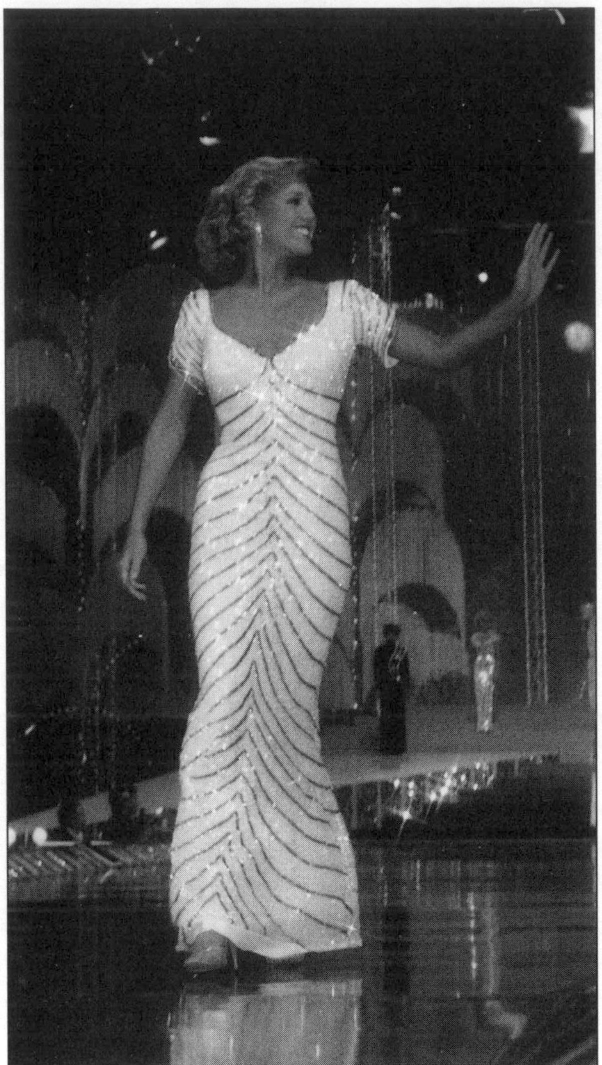

Kellye Cash, Miss Tennessee and grand-niece of country music legend Johnny Cash, proved that star quality runs in the family by walking off with the 1987 Miss America title. (Irv Kaar)

Grandma Hazel's "Impossible French Apple Pie"

The pie that makes its own crust. We lived with my grandmother until I was 5. The kitchen was the center of her household. While I have an enviable legacy of thousands of memories she created for me, none is more special than the smell of Grandma baking for Sunday dinner. It would take a whole cookbook to share all of her many pies. The most important ingredient is a grandmother's unconditional love!

6 cups sliced tart apples
1¼ teaspoons cinnamon
¼ teaspoon nutmeg
1 cup sugar
2 tablespoons butter, softened
¾ cup milk
½ cup Bisquick mix
2 eggs

Streusel

1 cup Bisquick mix
⅓ cup firmly packed brown sugar
3 tablespoons cold butter
½ cup chopped nuts

Preheat oven to 325°. Grease a 10-inch pie plate. Mix the apples and spices together, and place into the pie plate. Beat the remaining ingredients until smooth with a hand beater, approximately for 1 minute. Pour over the apples in pie plate and spread with the streusel. To make streusel, combine the Bisquick, brown sugar, and butter until crumbly. Add the chopped nuts and sprinkle on top of the apples. Bake for 55 to 60 minutes. A knife inserted in the center should come out clean when pie is done. Yields 6 to 8 servings.

Terry Meeuwsen Friedrich, Miss America 1973

Yankee Apple Pie

Crust
2 cups all-purpose flour
1 teaspoon salt
3/4 cup shortening
6 tablespoons cold water
1½ tablespoons shortening
½ cup all-purpose flour

Filling
8 apples (4 Cortlands, 4 McIntoshes)
¾ cup sugar
1 teaspoon cinnamon
1 tablespoon all-purpose flour
1 tablespoon butter
Milk

. . . .

Combine the 2 cups of flour and the salt in a medium bowl. Cut in the shortening with a pastry cutter or 2 knives. Sprinkle the cold water onto the mixture, 1 tablespoon at a time, stirring lightly with a fork. Form the dough into a ball and divide it in half. Roll out half to fit the bottom of a 9-inch pie plate. Put both the bottom crust and the second ball of dough into the refrigerator while you prepare the filling. Preheat oven to 350°. To prepare the filling, peel and thinly slice the apples. Combine the sugar, cinnamon, and 1 tablespoon flour with the apples, and fill the bottom crust with the mixture. Dot the top of the filling with the 1 tablespoon of butter. Roll out the top half of the dough and spread it with 1½ tablespoons of shortening. Sift the ½ cup of flour on top and lightly roll again. Wet the edges of the bottom crust and cover it with the top crust. Trim and press along the edge with a fork to seal. Brush the top with milk and slit the top a few times. Bake for 1 hour. Yields 6 to 8 servings.

Carol Norval Kelley, Miss Connecticut 1969

French Apple Tart

Crust
This tart requires two recipes of the following:
1¾ cups sifted white unbleached flour
¼ cup unsifted whole wheat flour
¾ teaspoon salt
½ cup vegetable oil
¼ cup skim milk

Filling
10 cups sliced pie apples
1½ cups sugar
2 teaspoons cinnamon
½ cup raisins

Glaze
1 cup confectioners' sugar
1 teaspoon margarine or butter, melted
1 tablespoon water
¼ teaspoon maple flavoring

. . . .

Preheat oven to 400°. Stir together the first 5 ingredients. Form a ball and roll out between two sheets of waxed paper. Fit into a 10 x 15-inch jelly roll pan. Make a second crust ready for use. Combine the next 4 ingredients and mix well. Place in the crust-lined pan and cover with the second crust. Slash the crust at least 8 times. Bake for about 45 minutes, or until apples are soft and crust lightly browned. Cool slightly. Spread with the glaze. To make the glaze, combine the remaining 4 ingredients and mix until smooth. The mixture will be thin. Cool the tart. Cut into squares and serve with Cheddar cheese. Yields 12 to 15 servings

Lee Anne Hibbert Stormer, Miss Washington 1975

Vermont McIntosh Apple Pie with Cheddar Cheese Crust

Crust

1½ cups all-purpose flour
½ cup shortening
1½ cups grated Cheddar cheese
4 to 6 tablespoons ice water

Filling

2 medium McIntosh apples, peeled, cored, and thinly sliced
1 tablespoon water
1 tablespoon brown sugar
1 tablespoon cinnamon
½ cup sugar
⅔ cup heavy cream
¼ cup grated rind and juice of one lemon
¼ cup sherry
3 eggs, well beaten

Meringue

⅓ cup confectioners' sugar
3 stiffly beaten egg whites

. . . .

Preheat oven to 400°. Combine all of the ingredients for the crust. Roll out and press into a 9-inch pie plate. Cook the apples in the water until soft. Add the brown sugar and cinnamon, then the sugar, cream, lemon rind and juice, sherry, and eggs. Pour into the pie crust. Bake for 15 minutes, then lower oven temperature and bake for an additional 40 minutes at 325°. Cool. Top with meringue.

For the meringue, fold the confectioners' sugar into the egg whites. Place the meringue on top of the apple pie and bake for 15 minutes or until browned. Yields 6 servings.

Lisa Mary Volkert, Miss Vermont 1978

Mountain State Apple Pie

During my term as Miss West Virginia 1981, I was invited to the Mountain State Apple Harvest Festival in Martinsburg, West Virginia, where I made several appearances throughout the weekend. My last official duty was to attend the Queen's Ball. The festival had arranged for a local man to be my escort at the dance; a year and a half later we were married. Every year in remembrance of my appearance at the Mountain State Apple Harvest Festival, I bake a delicious apple pie.

Pastry for 2-crust 9-inch pie
8 red Delicious apples, peeled, cored, and sliced
½ cup water
1 cup sugar, divided
2 tablespoons all-purpose flour
1 teaspoon ground cinnamon
Dash of ground nutmeg
2 tablespoons margarine

. . . .

Make your favorite recipe for a double crust pie pastry. Cook the apples on top of the stove in ½ cup of water until tender, adding ½ cup of the sugar. Drain. Preheat oven to 400°. Combine the remaining sugar, flour, and spices; mix with the apples. If the apples are too tart, add more sugar. Line a 9-inch pie plate with one of the crusts. Fill with the apple mixture; dot with the margarine. Adjust the top crust, cutting slits to vent steam; seal. Sprinkle with sugar. Bake for approximately 50 minutes or until done. Yields 6 to 8 servings.

Note: Fold strips of foil around rim of crust to prevent the edges from browning too quickly. Remove during the last ten minutes of baking.

Candy Cohen Reid, Miss West Virginia 1981

Peanut Butter Pie

4 ounces cream cheese, softened
¼ cup milk
½ cup confectioners' sugar
½ cup peanut butter
1 8-ounce container whipped topping
1 9-inch pie crust, prebaked
Chocolate syrup

Combine the cream cheese, milk, confectioners' sugar, and peanut butter and mix well. Fold in the whipped topping. Pour into the pie shell. Top with whipped topping and drizzle the chocolate syrup on top. Yields 6 servings.

Robin Meade Yeager, Miss Ohio 1993

Banana Split Pie

3 sticks margarine, divided
2 cups graham cracker crumbs
2 cups confectioners' sugar
2 eggs
5 bananas
1 20-ounce can crushed pineapple, drained
1 16-ounce container whipped topping
1 bottle maraschino cherries

Melt 1 stick of the margarine and mix with the graham cracker crumbs. Press into a 13 x 9-inch pan. Beat the remaining sticks of softened margarine with the confectioners' sugar and eggs for 15 minutes. Spread over the crust; cover with the sliced bananas. Spread on the pineapple; cover with the whipped topping. Sprinkle the top with the cherries (add chopped nuts, if desired). Refrigerate overnight. Yields 6 to 8 servings.

Dean Herman Maguire, Miss Florida 1981

Broadway Bound

One Miss America contestant told judges she wanted to star on Broadway. Figuring he would assess her morals, a judge asked her, "How far would you go to get that coveted role on Broadway?" "To New York," replied the contestant.

Banana Cream Pie

⅔ cup sugar
¼ teaspoon salt
3 tablespoons cornstarch
2 tablespoons all-purpose flour
2 cups scalded whole milk
2 egg yolks (or 1 whole egg)
1 teaspoon vanilla extract
2 bananas, sliced
1 8-inch baked pie crust

Combine the sugar, salt, cornstarch, and flour in the top of a double boiler. Combine the scalded milk with the beaten egg yolk, and add to the dry ingredients. Cook the mixture for 15 minutes, stirring constantly until thickened. Remove from the heat, cool, and add the vanilla extract. Place sliced bananas in pie crust. Pour thickened milk mixture over top. Yields 6 to 8 servings.

Dorothy Benham McGowan, Miss America 1977

Delicious Squash Pie

1 2-pound acorn squash
1 cup nonfat vanilla yogurt
1 cup firmly packed brown sugar
3 eggs, beaten
1 teaspoon cinnamon
1 teaspoon ground nutmeg
½ teaspoon salt
½ teaspoon ginger
¼ teaspoon mace
¼ teaspoon allspice
1 pie crust, prebaked for 4 minutes at 450°

Pierce the acorn squash 8 times with a sharp knife. Cook it in the microwave for about 10 minutes. Let it cool for 1 hour or so. Scoop out 1 cup of the cooked squash, reserving the second cup for a second pie! Preheat oven to 450°. Combine all of the ingredients, except the pie crust. Stir well. Pour into the pie crust. Set the pan on the lowest oven shelf for 10 minutes at 450°. Decrease the heat to 350° and move the pie up to the middle shelf for 40 to 45 minutes or until the filling is set. Serve the pie warm. Yields 6 to 8 servings.

Maria Beale Fletcher, Miss America 1962

Fifty women arrive in Atlantic City representing their states, but only one will become Miss America. In September, 1985, Susan Akin arrived as Miss Mississippi and left a week later as Miss America. (Irv Kaar)

Desserts

Chocolate Peppermint Dessert

1 stick margarine
1 cup confectioners' sugar
3 eggs, separated
2 squares unsweetened chocolate, melted
1 cup chopped nuts, divided
1 cup crushed vanilla wafers, divided
1 cup whipping cream
¼ pound hard peppermint candy, crushed
1 cup mini marshmallows

Cream the margarine and sugar together. Add the egg yolks and beat thoroughly. Gradually pour in the melted chocolate, beating constantly. Add ½ cup of nuts. Beat the egg whites until stiff, then fold into the chocolate mixture. Line an 8 x 8-inch baking pan with ¾ cup of the vanilla wafer crumbs. Pour the chocolate mixture into the pan and chill. Whip the cream and fold in the candy, remaining nuts, and marshmallows. Spread over the chocolate layer and sprinkle the remaining crumbs on top. Chill. Yields 9 to 12 servings.

Lynn Lambert, Miss Utah 1983

Chocolate Fluff

1½ sticks margarine
1½ cups all-purpose flour
¾ cup chopped pecans
1 cup confectioners' sugar
1 8-ounce package cream cheese, softened to room temperature
1 12-ounce container whipped topping, divided
2 3½-ounce packages instant chocolate pudding mix
3½ cups milk
1 teaspoon vanilla extract
Chopped pecans

Preheat the oven to 350°. Melt the margarine and allow it to cool. Combine the margarine, flour, and nuts, and press the mixture into a 9 x 13-inch baking dish. Bake for 20 minutes. Cool completely. Beat the sugar and cream cheese until smooth. Fold in 1 cup of the whipped topping. Spread over the crust and chill. Combine the pudding mix, milk, and vanilla and mix until thick. Chill, then spread mixture over the cream cheese mixture. Spread with remaining whipped topping and sprinkle with chopped pecans. Keep refrigerated. Yields 10 to 12 servings.

Andrea Lynn Patrick, Miss West Virginia 1983

Dirt

1 3-ounce box French vanilla pudding mix
1 1¼-pound package Oreo cookies
1 8-ounce package cream cheese, softened to room temperature
1 8-ounce container whipped topping

Prepare the pudding according to the package directions. Crush the cookies in a resealable plastic bag with a rolling pin. Combine the cream cheese with a little of the whipped topping until smooth. Fold in the remaining whipped topping and the pudding mix. Sprinkle ½ the cookie crumbs in the bottom of a 9 x 13-inch pan. Spread the pudding mixture over the crumbs. Top with remaining crumbs. Yields 10 to 12 servings.

Note: Have fun serving this! Garnish with gummy worms and a plastic shovel. You could even serve it out of a toy pail.

Kaye Lani Rafko Wilson, Miss America 1988

Crescent Cheesecake Dessert

2 10-ounce packages crescent rolls
1 8-ounce package cream cheese, softened to room temperature
1¼ cups sugar, divided
1 egg, separated
1 teaspoon vanilla extract
1 4-ounce package chopped pecans

Preheat oven to 350°. Line a greased 9 x 13-inch pan with 1 package of crescent rolls. Beat the cream cheese, 1 cup sugar, egg yolk, and vanilla together and pour over the crescent rolls. Layer the remaining crescent rolls on top of the filling. Beat the egg white until frothy, then spread over the rolls. Sprinkle the top with remaining sugar and the pecans. Bake for 25 to 30 minutes, or until golden brown. Chill and cut into squares. Yields 8 to 10 servings.

Lisa Somodi, Miss Iowa 1991

Cheesecake

Crust

1½ cups graham cracker crumbs
⅜ cup sugar (more if needed)
1 stick butter

Filling

3 8-ounce packages cream cheese, softened to room temperature
1 cup sugar
5 eggs
1 tablespoon lemon juice
1 tablespoon vanilla extract
½ teaspoon salt

Topping

1 pint sour cream
¼ cup sugar
1 teaspoon vanilla extract
⅛ teaspoon salt

Preheat oven to 325°. Combine the crust ingredients until they are completely moist and press them into a spring-form pan. Combine the filling ingredients with a mixer until smooth. Pour into the pan. Bake for 45 minutes or until a knife inserted in the center comes out clean. Cool the cheesecake for 15 minutes. Combine the topping ingredients and spread over top of cheesecake. Raise oven temperature to 425°. Bake for an additional 5 minutes. Cool and serve with strawberries, blueberries, or cherries. Yields 12 servings.

Terri Sue Liford, Miss Michigan 1992

Banana Yogurt Smoothie

1 cup plain nonfat yogurt
½ cup orange or apple juice
1 medium banana
Pinch of freshly grated nutmeg
1 or 2 ice cubes (optional)

. . . .

Place all of the ingredients in a blender and blend until smooth. It's thick, yummy, and filled with nutrients. Yields 1 serving.

Wendy Ann Mello, Miss Rhode Island 1993

Apple Pudding Dessert

This is a recipe from my grandmother

2 cups sugar
½ cup shortening
2 eggs, beaten
3 cups finely chopped or grated Washington State apples
1 cup chopped nuts
2 cups all-purpose flour
2 teaspoons baking soda
2 teaspoons cinnamon
1 teaspoon nutmeg
1 teaspoon salt

. . . .

Preheat oven to 350°. Cream the sugar and shortening together. Add the eggs. Sift together the dry ingredients and add to the mixture. Pour into a 9 x 13-inch pan. Bake for 30 minutes. Serve with ice cream or whipped topping. Yields 15 to 18 servings.

Teri Ann Plante, Miss Washington 1993

Apple Dumplings

Pastry

1 cup all-purpose flour
½ teaspoon salt
⅓ cup plus 1 tablespoon shortening, divided
¼ cup cold water

Syrup

½ cup sugar
1½ cups water
2 tablespoons margarine
¼ teaspoon cinnamon

Filling

2 baking apples
¼ cup sugar
2 teaspoons cinnamon
1 teaspoon butter, divided

. . . .

Combine the flour and salt. Cut ½ of the shortening into the flour with a pastry blender. Add the remaining shortening and cut until the crumbles are pea-sized. Gradually add the water, stirring constantly. Roll the dough out and cut two 7 x 7-inch squares for small to medium apples, or two 8 x 8-inch squares for larger apples.

Combine the sugar, margarine, cinnamon, and the remaining water in a saucepan and bring to a boil. Boil for 3 minutes, then remove the syrup from the heat.

Preheat oven to 425°. Core the 2 apples. Combine the remaining sugar and cinnamon and fill each apple with half of the mixture. Dot the top of each apple with ½ teaspoon of butter. Set each apple in the center of a square of pastry and bring the opposite corners of the pastry up to cover the apple. Seal with water. Place the apples in a baking dish and pour the syrup around them. Bake for 50 minutes. Serve warm with syrup. Yields 2 servings.

LaRonda Kaye Lundin, Miss South Dakota 1983

The shortest winner was the original queen, Margaret Gorman, at 5'1".

Gingerbread with Lemon Sauce

1 stick butter or margarine
½ cup sugar
2 eggs, separated
1 teaspoon ground cloves
1 teaspoon ground ginger
2½ cups all-purpose flour
1 cup molasses
1 teaspoon baking soda, dissolved in 1 cup boiling water

Preheat oven to 350°. Cream the butter. Add the sugar gradually, creaming until light and fluffy. Beat the egg yolks and add to the mixture. Sift together the flour and spices. Add alternately with the molasses and soda water; mix well. Beat the egg whites until stiff and fold into the mixture. Pour into a greased 9 x 9-inch pan and bake for 30 to 40 minutes. Serve with Lemon Sauce. Yields 10 to 12 servings.

Lemon Sauce

1 cup sugar
1 egg
Juice of 1 lemon
1 tablespoon butter or margarine

Combine all the ingredients and mix well. Cook over medium heat until thick. Serve with the gingerbread.

Burma Davis Posey, Miss Georgia 1968

Blueberry Dessert Salad

2 3-ounce packages black-raspberry-flavored gelatin
2¾ cups hot water
1 can blueberries, drained
1 can crushed pineapple, drained
1 8-ounce package cream cheese, softened to room temperature
1 8-ounce carton sour cream
½ cup sugar
½ teaspoon vanilla extract
Chopped pecans

Dissolve the gelatin in the hot water. Chill. When the gelatin is slightly congealed, fold in the blueberries and pineapple. Chill until firm. Cream the sour cream with the cream cheese. Pour in the sugar and vanilla and mix well. Spread on top of the gelatin. Sprinkle pecans over top. Yields 6 to 8 servings.

Kylene Barker, Miss America 1979

Pistachio Salad

1 8-ounce carton whipped topping
1 3½-ounce package instant pistachio pudding mix
½ to 1 cup chopped nuts
1 cup miniature marshmallows
1 7½-ounce can crushed pineapple with juice

Combine the first two ingredients. Stir in the remaining ingredients. Chill overnight before serving. This can also be frozen. Yields 6 to 8 servings.

Elizabeth Ward, Miss America 1982

The 1990s—Approaching a New Millennium

From the vantage point of the 1990s, it is clear that American women have progressed beyond anything contestants could have imagined in 1921. Women enjoy unprecedented success in business, education, politics, and the medical and legal fields, and Hillary Clinton has broken barriers as First Lady. The nineties are the decade of the well-educated, socially conscientious career woman.

As has been the case in each decade, the Miss America Pageant continues to reflect prevailing social standards and women's history. "It just seems like in every era of our society the 'right' Miss America steps forward with the 'right' thing to talk about," observes former Miss America Sharlene Wells Hawkes. "And those critics who say that Miss America is 'out of touch'—there's *no way* that Miss America is out of touch! Miss America is the common girl—just in an uncommon place. But she is always pertinent with what is going on with young women."

During the Pageant's 70th anniversary in 1990, beloved host Bert Parks was welcomed back to the stage by television host Gary Collins. (Terry Chenaille)

Two timely themes emerged as the decade's focus: increased educational opportunities for women and ethnic diversity. For instance, by 1991 the Pageant had its first official full-fledged female emcee, television personality Kathie Lee Gifford, who hosts with Regis Philbin. Furthermore, in 1990, for the first time in Pageant history, two black women, Debbye Turner and Marjorie Vincent, earned back-to-back Miss America titles. Marjorie was a third-year law student at Duke University, while Debbye used her pageant scholarships to earn her doctorate in veterinary medicine and become *Dr.* Turner, epitomizing the emphasis on education Lenora Slaughter envisioned half a century ago.

Community service has also evolved as a significant focus of the modern Miss America program, with its official platform program enabling each titleholder to use her year of service to champion a meaningful social cause. Contestants actively volunteer their efforts for worthy causes such as breast cancer awareness, increasing math literacy, and ending violence in schools. Since 1990, Miss Americas

During the Persian Gulf War, 1990 Miss America contestants, who were gathered in historic Philadelphia, sent their wishes to American military personnel stationed overseas. The eventual winner, Marjorie Vincent, of Illinois, is third from left. (C P News)

have addressed the issues of violence against women, improving education, AIDS prevention, and helping the homeless. Miss America 1995, Heather Whitestone, who won her coveted title despite being physically challenged, has used her national platform to share the message "Anything is Possible" to inspire young people to believe in themselves and achieve their potential even in the face of discouraging obstacles. Citing her mother's advice, "Remember, the last four letters in American spell 'I CAN!'" Heather is a living testimonial for everyone she meets that, indeed, "anything is possible."

Likewise, since 1921 the Miss America Pageant has been an example of how yesteryear's "impossibilities" become today's realities. As the nation approaches a new millennium, the Pageant has developed from a seaside bathing beauty parade into the world's largest private scholarship program for women, making available $24 million in scholarships annually. Her position as a treasured American institution has been demonstrated time and time again since Miss America first smiled her way into the nation's heart seventy-five years ago. The Miss America Pageant has matured gracefully through the nation's lighthearted eras and her darkest hours, and despite imitation from a slew of rival pageant wannabees. Yet she still reigns supreme. "It's an American institution," explains former Miss America Phyllis George, "a tradition which has gone on for [more than] seventy years. The Pageant has survived wars, depressions, social movements, scandals, crisis, and tough critics—and it's still here. They must be doing something right because fifty-five million people watch it and it's one of the top-rated shows every single year! It's a part of Americana that will continue," she remarks with confidence, "because America loves it."

Congratulations on your 75th anniversary, Miss America. Here's to a new century of grand American traditions.

Gorp

Gorp gets its name from my son, Bill, who at the age of 4 could not say the correct name. The recipe has been handed down by my mother and is always served for dessert at Christmas dinner.

1 16-ounce box vanilla wafers, crushed
2 cups confectioners' sugar
⅔ cup butter
4 eggs
1 pint heavy whipping cream
1 cup crushed, drained pineapple
1 teaspoon vanilla extract
Red and green candied cherries

. . . .

Cover the bottom and sides of an 8½ x 12-inch pan with ½ of the crushed wafers. Combine the confectioners' sugar and the butter. Add the eggs, beating them in one at a time. Spread the mixture over the crumbs. Whip the cream and fold in the pineapple. Add the vanilla and spread over the egg mixture. Cover with the remaining vanilla wafer crumbs. Decorate with cherries. Chill for 24 hours. Yields 16 servings.

Jacquelyn Mayer Townsend, Miss America 1963

Poached Raspberry Pears Ma Façon

6 cups water
2 cups sugar
8 firm Anjou or Comice pears, peeled whole and dropped in water mixed with lemon juice to prevent discoloration
2 10-ounce boxes frozen raspberries in syrup, thawed
2 teaspoons cornstarch
1 recipe Zabaglione sauce

. . . .

Bring the water to a boil. Add the sugar. Reduce heat to simmer and gently lower the pears into the saucepan. The syrup should cover the pears. Cover and simmer just until the pears are tender when gently pierced with a fork, about 30 minutes. Remove the pears immediately from the syrup. The syrup can be cooled then frozen for future use.

Place the raspberries in the saucepan and bring to a boil. Dissolve the cornstarch in 2 tablespoons of the hot raspberry syrup, then add to the berries. Cook until slightly thickened, stirring to keep the mixture smooth. (Syrup should coat a spoon.) Press the berries and syrup through a food mill or strainer to make the sauce. Let cool. Pour the sauce over the pears, making sure to cover them completely.

Cover and refrigerate, preferably overnight, turning once or twice to color the fruit a deep red. To serve, arrange the pears on separate dessert dishes or together in a large glass bowl. Spoon the sauce over top. Top chilled pears with hot Zabaglione Sauce and serve. Yields 8 servings.

Zabaglione Sauce

6 egg yolks
½ cup sugar
⅓ cup Marsala wine

. . . .

Beat the egg yolks over hot water in a double boiler until thick and pale in color. Gradually add the sugar and wine, beating constantly until foamy and almost tripled in volume.

Dorothy Benham McGowan, Miss America 1977

Behind the Crown

Carolyn Sapp, Miss America 1992, became the first Miss America to star in a movie during her year of service. The television movie, *Miss America: Behind the Crown* shared the story of how she survived and left an abusive relationship with her then-fiance, a pro football player.

Orange Baked Alaskas

1 quart vanilla ice cream, or lemon, lime, or orange sherbet
3 large seedless oranges
4 egg whites
½ teaspoon cream of tartar
½ cup sugar, or firmly packed brown sugar

Scoop the ice cream into 6 balls. Freeze until firm, at least 6 hours. Cut the oranges in half cross-wise; if necessary, cut a very thin slice from the bottom of each half so the oranges will stand upright. Remove the fruit and membrane from the orange shells. Cut the fruit into pieces and line the bottom of the shells with cut up fruit. Refrigerate.

Move the oven rack to the lowest position. Preheat the oven to 500°. Beat the egg whites and cream of tartar until foamy. Beat in the sugar, 1 tablespoon at a time; continue beating until stiff and glossy. Do not underbeat. Place the orange shells on an ungreased baking sheet; fill each shell with an ice-cream ball. Completely cover the ice cream with meringue, sealing it to the edge of the shells. Bake until the meringue is light brown, 3 to 5 minutes. Serve immediately. Yields 6 servings.

Note: Grapefruit can be substituted for the oranges.

Rebecca Jane Nyboer, Miss Alaska 1993

Yolande's Champagne Sherbet

1 liter bottle champagne (I recommend Korbel)
1 liter bottle rosé wine
1 quart soda water
1 cup Grand Marnier liqueur
2 10-ounce packages frozen crushed strawberries
1 10-ounce package frozen whole strawberries
1 20-ounce can crushed pineapple
1 cup firmly packed brown sugar
1 8-ounce bottle lemon juice

Combine all the ingredients and freeze until mushy, preferably in a hand freezer. Let sit until served. Can also be frozen in the ice compartment of the refrigerator, stirring occasionally. Delicious served in a punch bowl with rings of ice. Yields about 5 quarts.

Yolande Betbeze Fox, Miss America 1951

Original Pineapple Dessert

This recipe was designed for no-measuring ease!

1 20-ounce can crushed pineapple with juice
1 3-ounce package lemon-flavored gelatin (or desired flavor)
1 8-ounce package cream cheese, softened to room temperature
1 8-ounce container whipped topping

Bring the pineapple and juice to a boil. Dissolve the gelatin in the pineapple and add the cream cheese. Stir until the cheese melts. Chill until partially set. Fold in the whipped topping and chill overnight or until set. Yields 8 to 10 servings.

Jane D. Briggeman Sype, Miss Nebraska 1969

Coffee Mallow Tortini

1 cup mini-marshmallows
⅓ cup milk
1 teaspoon instant coffee powder
¼ cup toasted chopped almonds
2 egg whites
½ teaspoon vanilla extract
2 tablespoons sugar
½ cup whipping cream
Maraschino cherries
Slivered almonds

Heat and stir the marshmallows, milk, and coffee powder in a small saucepan until the marshmallows are melted. Cool. Add the chopped almonds. Beat the egg whites and vanilla to soft peaks. Gradually add the sugar, beating until stiff peaks form.

Whip the cream just until soft peaks form. Fold the egg whites into the coffee mixture. Fold in the whipped cream. Spoon the mixture into paper-lined muffin cups. Top each tortini with a maraschino cherry and additional toasted slivered almonds, if desired. Freeze until firm. Yields 8 medium or 12 small servings.

Marilyn Meseke Rogers, Miss America 1938

Arkansas Peach Crisp

Since my local pageant was the Johnson County Peach Festival and my parents are still growing peaches there, this recipe seemed a natural one for me.

7 peaches, peeled and sliced
Juice of 1 lemon
½ cup sifted all-purpose flour
¾ cup oats
½ cup firmly packed brown sugar
⅓ cup margarine

Preheat oven to 325°. Arrange the peaches in a 9 x 13-inch baking dish and sprinkle with lemon juice. Combine the flour, oats, and brown sugar. Cut in the margarine with a pastry blender. Press the mixture over the peaches. Bake for 30 to 40 minutes. Yields 6 servings.

Marilyn Morgan Bishop, Miss Arkansas 1971

Linzertorte

1 cup unblanched almonds
1 stick plus 2 tablespoons sweet butter
⅔ cup sugar
Grated rind of 1 lemon
2 egg yolks
⅛ teaspoon ground cloves
½ teaspoon cinnamon
1 cup all-purpose flour
1 cup raspberry jam
Confectioners' sugar

Grind the almonds with the steel blade of a food processor; set aside. Place the butter, sugar, and lemon rind in the food processor and, with the motor running, add the egg yolks, one at a time. Add the spices, flour, and almonds and blend. The dough will be soft. Chill. Preheat oven to 350°. Roll out ⅔ of the dough and line a 9-inch tart pan. Spread with raspberry jam. Roll out the remaining dough and cut into ½-inch strips to lattice the top. Bake for 35 minutes. Sprinkle with confectioners' sugar. This is best made 2 days in advance. Great with ice cream. Yields 10 servings.

Marian McKnight Conway, Miss America 1957

Fond Memories

Traveling companion Ellie Ross knows just how seriously little girls take Miss America. "One time, Susan Perkins (Miss America 1978) and I were going through an airport and this little girl came running over to say, 'Hi!' So Susan said, 'Hello,'—not being rude, but just saying hello. Well, the little girl started crying, 'Waaaaaa . . . you don't remember me!' Susan turned around and said, 'Oh, I'm sorry honey, where did we meet?' And she said, 'When they crowned you, you waved to me on TV!' "

Lemon Squares

Crust

½ cup confectioners' sugar
2 cups all-purpose flour
¼ teaspoon salt
2 sticks butter, softened to room temperature

Filling

4 eggs
4 tablespoons lemon juice
2 cups sugar
4 tablespoons all-purpose flour
Grated rind of 1 lemon
Confectioners' sugar

. . . .

Preheat oven to 325°. Combine the dry ingredients and cut in butter. Pat into the bottom of an 8 x 10-inch baking dish. Bake for 20 minutes. Remove from the oven and cool slightly. Combine the first 5 filling ingredients and pour into the crust. Bake for 20 to 30 minutes. Remove from oven. Sprinkle with confectioners' sugar. Cut into squares. Yields 8 to 10 servings.

Susan Powell, Miss America 1981

Bread Pudding

1 10-ounce loaf stale French bread, crumbled (or 6 to 8 cups any type bread)
4 cups milk
2 cups sugar
1 stick butter, melted
3 eggs
2 tablespoons vanilla extract
1 cup raisins
1 cup coconut
1 cup chopped pecans
1 teaspoon cinnamon
1 teaspoon nutmeg
Bourbon Sauce
Chantilly Cream

. . . .

Combine all ingredients, except for the Bourbon Sauce and the Chantilly Cream; the mixture should be very moist but not soupy. Pour into a buttered 9 x 12-inch or larger baking dish. Place in a cold oven. Turn the oven to 350° and bake for approximately 1 hour and 15 minutes, or until the top is golden brown. Serve warm with Bourbon Sauce and Chantilly Cream. Yields 10 to 12 servings.

Bourbon Sauce

1 stick butter
1½ cups confectioners' sugar
2 egg yolks
½ cup bourbon (or to taste)

. . . .

Cream the butter and sugar over medium heat until all of the butter is absorbed. Remove from the heat and blend in the egg yolks. Pour in the bourbon gradually to your own taste, stirring constantly. The sauce will thicken as it cools. Serve warm over warm bread pudding.

Note: For a variety of sauces, just substitute your favorite fruit juice or liqueur to complement your bread pudding.

Chantilly Cream

⅔ cup heavy cream
1 teaspoon vanilla extract
1 teaspoon brandy
1 teaspoon Grand Marnier liqueur
¼ cup sugar
2 tablespoons sour cream

. . . .

Refrigerate a medium-sized bowl and beaters until very cold. Combine the cream, vanilla, brandy, and Grand Marnier in the bowl and beat with the electric mixer on medium speed for 1 minute. Add the sugar and sour cream and beat on medium until soft peaks form, about 3 minutes. Do not overbeat. (Overbeating will make the cream grainy, which is the first step leading to butter. Once grainy you can't return it to its former consistency, but if this ever happens, enjoy it on toast!) Yields 2 cups.

Sharon Carnes Mesker, Miss Minnesota 1963

Easy Butter Crunch

The most difficult part of this recipe is cutting the butter crunch. The rest is a cinch. And the best part is that it is so delicious. I make this anytime I'm invited to a picnic or party because not only is it fast, but it is absolutely delectable. This is definitely not for pre-pageant contestants unless they have enough willpower to eat just one!

2¼ sticks butter, divided
Unsalted saltine crackers
1 cup sugar
1 12-ounce package semisweet chocolate morsels
1 to 1½ cups chopped walnuts.

. . . .

Soften 2 tablespoons of the butter and use it to grease an 11 x 17-inch jelly roll pan. Line the entire sheet pan with crackers. You may need to cut the crackers along the sides of the pan in order to make sure they fit and there are no gaps.

Preheat oven to 375°. Melt the remaining 2 sticks of butter with the sugar in a medium saucepan over medium-high heat, stirring constantly until the mixture becomes thick and bubbly. Just as the mixture takes on a pale brown color (the start of carmelization), immediately remove the pan from the heat and pour the mixture over the crackers. Working very quickly, spread the mixture evenly over all the crackers with a spatula.

Place the jelly roll pan in the center of the oven and bake for approximately 6 minutes, or until golden brown. Be sure the crackers have turned golden brown as this indicates that carmelization of the sugar mixture has occurred. Do not allow the crackers to get too dark as they may taste slightly burnt, but do not allow the crackers to stay too light as the carmelization will not be complete and this will cause the final taste to be diminished somewhat.

Remove the pan from the oven and sprinkle the entire bag of chocolate morsels over the crackers. Quickly fix any "unruly" crackers that may have moved or bubbled over from being in the oven. Place the pan back into the oven for another minute to melt the chocolate morsels. Again remove the pan and, using a spatula, spread the chocolate over the crackers. Sprinkle nuts over top and let cool thoroughly before cutting into 1½-inch squares. If you are in a hurry, put the pan in the freezer or refrigerator for about 30 minutes. Remove and let stand until the butter crunch reaches room temperature and then cut. Yields 20 to 25 servings.

Karyn Zosche-Sobieski, Miss New Jersey 1986

Special Banana Pudding

I am an adjunct professor in the math department at Carson-Newman College, but cooking has always been a hobby of mine. In 1985 my husband nearly died and returned home needing a special diet. I began to create dishes for him. This pudding is one of his favorites—low in fat and sugar.

1 3½-ounce package sugar-free instant vanilla pudding mix
1 cup skim milk
1 cup plain yogurt
1 8-ounce container whipped topping
1 7¼-ouncebox vanilla wafers
4 bananas, sliced

. . . .

Combine the pudding and milk. Stir in the yogurt. Fold in the whipped topping. Layer the bottom and sides of a 9 x 9-inch glass dish with vanilla wafers. Cover the wafers with sliced bananas. Cover the bananas with ½ the pudding mixture. Place another layer of wafers, then bananas, then pudding mixture. Sprinkle the top with crushed wafer crumbs. Yields 8 servings.

Robbie Robertson Pinkerton, Miss Mississippi 1966

Alabama Ambrosia

This dessert has been in my family for over three generations and is a "must" with Christmas dinner. It is always served with pound cake and Christmas cookies.

6 medium apples, peeled and grated
1 12-ounce can frozen orange juice concentrate, thawed
2 15-ounce cans crushed pineapple
1½ cups water
1 8- to 10-ounce package grated coconut
1 cup sugar
Maraschino cherries

. . . .

Combine all the ingredients, except the cherries. Mix well and chill. Serve in dessert dishes topped with a cherry. Yields 8 to 10 servings.

Patricia Bonner Burton, Miss Alabama 1962

Aunt Julia's Baked Rice Custard

This recipe is a family favorite. In fact, if Aunt Julia doesn't make her famous rice pudding for family reunions, we refuse to attend. This recipe is anything but fat-free, but a once-a-year splurge won't hurt that swimsuit figure!

1⅓ cups white rice (not quick or instant), uncooked
5 cups milk, divided
1 teaspoon salt
3 eggs
¾ cup sugar
1½ teaspoons vanilla extract
Nutmeg

. . . .

Combine the rice, 4 cups of milk, and the salt in the top of a double boiler. Cook over boiling water, stirring occasionally, for approximately 1 hour or until the rice is soft. Preheat oven to 350°. Butter a 2-quart casserole dish and place it in a pan with 1 inch of water. Combine the eggs, sugar, vanilla, and the remaining milk. Beat just until blended. Gradually add to hot rice. Mix well. Pour into the buttered casserole dish and sprinkle with nutmeg. Bake for 50 to 60 minutes or until a knife inserted in the center comes out clean. Remove from the oven and cool. Serve warm. Yields 6 to 8 servings.

Debra Renea Fries Baker, Miss Maryland 1991

Healthful Rice Pudding

Skim milk
1 can evaporated skim milk
1 cup cooked white rice
1 cup Egg Beaters (equivalent to 4 eggs)
½ cup yellow raisins
6 packets sugar substitute
⅛ teaspoon salt
2 teaspoons vanilla extract
Ground cinnamon

. . . .

Preheat the oven to 350°. Add skim milk to the evaporated milk to make 3 cups. Add the remaining ingredients except for the cinnamon. Pour the mixture into an oblong baking dish sprayed with nonstick vegetable spray. Bake for 40 minutes. Generously sprinkle cinnamon on top and bake for an additional 5 minutes.

Marilyn Van Derbur Atler, Miss America 1958

New Hampshire Maple Mousse

This recipe originally came from the wife of a marketing professor at New Hampshire College. Because it was a rich dessert, I have since made modifications to lighten it up.

1¼-ounce envelope unflavored gelatin
¼ cup cold water
1 8-ounce package light cream cheese, softened to room temperature
½ cup New Hampshire pure maple syrup
⅔ cup skim milk
1 cup whipping cream, whipped
½ cup ground pecans or walnuts
1 9-inch pie crust, baked and cooled

. . . .

Soften the gelatin in the water and stir it over low heat until dissolved. Combine the cream cheese and syrup. Blend well. Slowly add the milk and gelatin to the cream cheese mixture, blending well. Chill until slightly thickened, about 20 minutes. Fold in the whipped cream and nuts. Pour into a baked pie crust or lightly greased mold and chill until firm. Yields 8 servings.

Cathy Burnham, Miss New Hampshire 1975

Sponge Cake Layers for Trifle

This is a Christmas tradition in my family.

6 eggs, separated
2¼ cups sugar
4½ tablespoons cold water
3 cups self-rising flour (always use fresh flour)
1½ teaspoons vanilla extract

. . . .

Preheat oven to 400°. Beat the egg whites in a small bowl and set aside. Beat the egg yolks in a large bowl. Stir in the sugar and water, then the flour and vanilla. Fold in the whites and immediately pour into 3 cake pans. Bake for 12 minutes. This cake freezes well and makes a delicious strawberry or peach shortcake or trifle.

Trifle: Break the cake into bite-size pieces and layer cake, fruit, and whipped topping in a tall glass bowl.

Christmas Trifle: Alternate the cake pieces with egg custard or vanilla pudding with brandy mixed in, sliced almonds, and whipped topping. Yields 2 trifles, 12 servings each.

Trudy Riley Kearney, Miss North Carolina 1946

Banana Berry Mint Brownie Pizza

⅓ cup cold water
1 17-ounce package brownie mix
¼ cup vegetable oil
1 egg
1 8-ounce package cream cheese, softened to room temperature
¼ cup sugar
1 teaspoon vanilla extract
1 egg
Strawberry slices
Banana slices, dipped in lemon juice to prevent browning
2 squares semisweet chocolate, melted
Mint leaves

Preheat oven to 350°. Bring the water to a boil. Combine the brownie mix, boiling water, oil, and 1 egg. Blend well. Pour into a greased and floured 12-inch pizza pan. Bake for 20 minutes.

Beat the cream cheese, sugar, vanilla, and remaining egg at medium speed with an electric mixer until well blended. Pour over the crust and bake for 15 minutes. At this point your dessert should look like a cheese pizza with the brownie forming the crust.

Cool. Arrange the fruit on top, drizzle with melted chocolate and garnish with mint leaves. Yields 6 to 8 servings. (Can serve up to 12 if cut into small wedges.)

Lisa Desroches, Miss Massachusetts 1992

Funnel Cakes

1 egg
⅔ cup milk
1⅓ cups all-purpose flour
¼ teaspoon salt
2 tablespoons sugar
¾ teaspoon baking powder
1 teaspoon baking soda
Vegetable oil
Confectioners' sugar or molasses

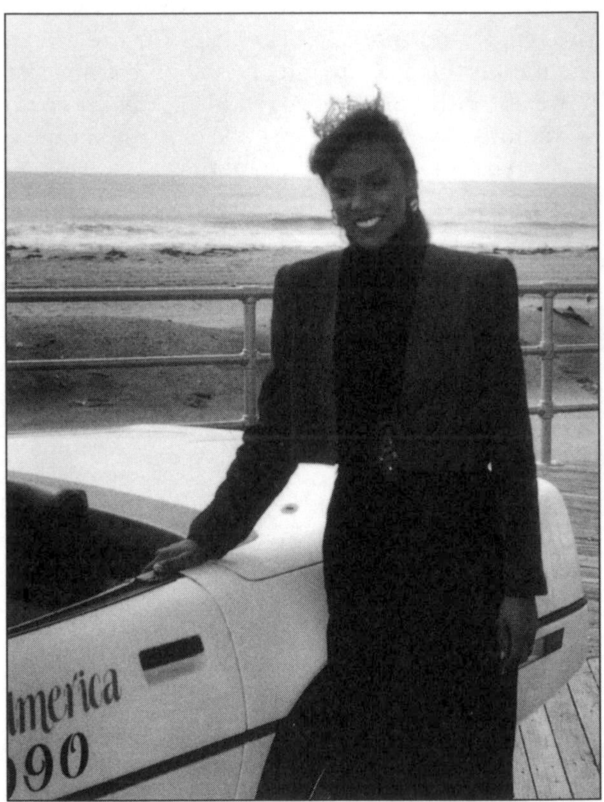

Along with the most coveted title in the country, Miss America wins a $35,000 college scholarship, $150,000 to $200,000 in appearance income, and a new sports car from Chevrolet, a longtime sponsor. Debbye Turner (1990) receives her new Corvette. (Irv Kaar)

Beat the egg and add the milk. Sift together the flour, salt, sugar, baking powder, and baking soda. Add the egg mixture and beat until smooth. Heat approximately 2 inches of vegetable oil to 375° in a skillet. Holding your finger over the bottom, pour some batter into a funnel with a ⅝-inch opening. Remove your finger, dropping the batter into the hot oil and swirling it into circles from the center out. Make each cake about 6 inches in diameter. Fry until golden brown. Drain on brown paper or paper towels and serve with confectioners' sugar or molasses. Yields 4 to 6 cakes.

Lynne Grote Tully, Miss Pennsylvania 1977

Frozen Soufflé Amaretto

4 macaroon cookies
6 eggs yolks
2 eggs
¾ cup sugar
¼ cup Amaretto liqueur
2 cups whipping cream, whipped
⅓ cup sliced almonds

. . . .

Preheat oven to 300°. Crumble the macaroons into coarse pieces. Reserve some of the crumbs for a garnish. Spread the remaining crumbs in the bottom of a shallow baking pan and dry in oven for 20 minutes, stirring once. Cool the crumbs. In a large bowl combine the egg yolks, whole eggs, and sugar. Beat at high speed with an electric mixer until thick and fluffy and sugar is dissolved. Continue beating, gradually adding liqueur. By hand, fold in the whipped cream and ¾ cup of the macaroon crumbs. Prepare six 6- to 8-ounce individual soufflé dishes or a 1-quart soufflé dish with a 2½-inch high buttered aluminum foil collar. Gently spoon soufflé into dishes and freeze at least 4 to 6 hours. To serve, top with additional whipped cream and sprinkle with macaroon crumbs and sliced almonds. For prolonged storage, wrap frozen soufflé in foil or seal in airtight containers. Yields 6 servings.

Amy Linder Beninato, Miss Massachusetts 1980

Doughnuts

When I was in 4-H as a little girl, our Hancock Happy Hoppers sold homemade glazed doughnuts to pay for a train trip to Kansas City. It was a very memorable and special trip for all of us.

2 eggs, well beaten
1 cup sugar
½ stick butter
4 cups all-purpose flour
½ teaspoon baking powder
1 teaspoon nutmeg
1 teaspoon salt
1 teaspoon baking soda
1 cup sour milk
Vegetable oil
Cinnamon and sugar

. . . .

Beat together the eggs, sugar, and butter. Add the flour, baking powder, nutmeg, and salt. Add the baking soda to the sour milk and add to the other ingredients. Mix well. Heat about 2 inches of oil to 350°. Drop the batter into the oil and fry, turning once, until browned. Drain on paper towels. Sprinkle with cinnamon and sugar. Yields 16 to 20 doughnuts.

Rebecca King Dreman, Miss America 1974

Spritz Cookies

2 sticks butter, softened
⅔ cup sugar
3 egg yolks
1 teaspoon vanilla or almond extract
¼ cup finely chopped almonds
2½ cups all-purpose flour

. . . .

Preheat oven to 400°. Combine the butter, sugar, egg yolks, and extract thoroughly. Stir in the almonds. Measure the flour by the dip-level-pour method or by sifting. Work in the flour. Using ¼ of the dough at a time, force the dough through a cookie press into desired shapes onto a greased baking sheet. Bake for 7 to 10 minutes, or until set but not brown. Yields 6 dozen cookies.

Debbye Turner, Miss America 1990

No Bake Peanut Butter Cookies

2 cups sugar
1 stick butter
4 teaspoons cocoa powder
½ cup milk
½ cup peanut butter
1 teaspoon vanilla extract
3 cups quick-cooking oatmeal

. . . .

Combine the sugar, butter, cocoa, and milk in a saucepan. Bring to a boil. Remove from the heat and add the peanut butter and vanilla. Mix well. Stir in the oatmeal. Drop the cookies by the spoonful onto a cookie sheet and chill until firm.

Kylene Barker, Miss America 1979

Pecan Cocoons from Mama Prewitt

2 sticks real butter
8 tablespoons sugar
2 cups sifted self-rising flour
2 cups chopped pecans
Confectioners' sugar

. . . .

Preheat oven to 275°. Cream the butter and sugar. Add the flour and nuts. Roll the dough into finger lengths. Bake for 40 to 45 minutes on an ungreased cookie sheet. When cool, roll in confectioners' sugar. Yields about 50 cookies.

Cheryl Prewitt-Salem, Miss America 1980

Puff Ball Cookies

1 stick butter
2 tablespoons sugar
1 teaspoon vanilla extract
1 cup pecan meats, measured, then ground
1 cup sifted all-purpose flour
Confectioners' sugar

. . . .

Preheat oven to 300°. Soften and beat the butter; blend in the sugar until creamy. Add the vanilla. Stir the pecans and flour into the butter. Roll the dough into small balls and place on a greased baking sheet. Bake for about 45 minutes. **Do not let them brown.** Roll, while still hot, in confectioners' sugar. Allow the cookies to cool in a bag of confectioners' sugar. Yields 2 to 3 dozen cookies.

Lee Meriwether, Miss America 1955

Chewy Oatmeal Cookies

¾ cup soft margarine
1¼ cups firmly packed brown sugar
2 eggs
1 teaspoon vanilla extract
1 cup all-purpose flour
¾ teaspoon baking soda
½ teaspoon salt
1 teaspoon cinnamon
¼ teaspoon nutmeg
2 cups uncooked oats
1 cup raisins
1 cup pecans

. . . .

Preheat oven to 350°. Cream together the margarine and sugar in a large mixing bowl. Add the eggs and vanilla. Beat until smooth. Add the flour, soda, salt, cinnamon, and nutmeg, and continue beating. Stir in the oats, raisins, and nuts. Drop by heaping teaspoons onto a greased cookie sheet. Bake for 12 to 15 minutes. Cool before storing. Yields about 48 cookies.

Jane Jayroe, Miss America 1967

Unbaked Cookies

As a child I was very allergic to wheat flour. An elderly lady in our neighborhood felt compassion for me, and devised several recipes without wheat flour.

30 dates, pitted
2 eggs, well beaten
1 cup sugar
1 tablespoon butter
1 teaspoon vanilla extract
4 cups oven-toasted rice cereal
Coconut
Pecan pieces

. . . .

In a saucepan, cook the dates, eggs, sugar, and butter, stirring constantly. Add the vanilla. Pour over the cereal. Stir lightly. Form into small balls and roll them in coconut and pecans. Place on cookie sheet to set. Yields 2 to 3 dozen cookies.

Debra Barnes Miles, Miss America 1968

The tallest Miss Americas were:
Bess Myerson, 1945—5'10"
Colleen Hutchins, 1952—5'10½"
Tawny Godin, 1976—5'10"
Kaye Lani Rae Rafko, 1988—5'10½"

Scottish Shortbread

This recipe was brought from Scotland by my mother.

4 sticks butter
1 cup confectioners' sugar
4 cups all-purpose flour

. . . .

Preheat the oven to 300°. Cream the butter and add the sugar a bit at a time. When the butter and sugar are creamed, add the flour a bit at a time. Knead the dough for 20 minutes. Add additional flour if necessary to prevent stickiness. Divide the dough and pat into 2 ungreased, 9-inch round pans and prick with a fork. Bake for 40 to 45 minutes. The kneading is the secret to good shortbread. Yields 16 servings.

Marjorie Kelly Shick, Miss Canada 1952

Molasses Sugar Cookies

¾ cup shortening
1 cup sugar
¼ cup molasses
1 egg
2 teaspoons baking soda
2 cups all-purpose flour, sifted
½ teaspoon cloves
½ teaspoon ginger
1 teaspoon cinnamon
½ teaspoon salt
Sugar

. . . .

Melt the shortening, add the sugar, molasses, and egg. Beat well. Sift the remaining ingredients, except for the sugar, together. Add to the creamed mixture, and mix well. Roll the dough into 1-inch balls and chill. Preheat oven to 375°. After chilling, roll balls in sugar and place on a greased cookie sheet 2 inches apart. Bake for 8 to 10 minutes. Do not overbake. Yields 2 to 3 dozen cookies.

Majorie Kelly Shick, Miss Canada 1952

Granola Bars

Trying to create original and healthy school lunches presents a problem. This snack bar is always a hit when tucked inside a lunch box.

1 cup corn syrup
1 cup crunchy peanut butter
1 teaspoon vanilla extract
1 cup dry milk
1 16-ounce box low-fat granola cereal
1 cup raisins
1 cup chocolate chips
Chopped nuts (optional)

. . . .

Bring the corn syrup to a boil. Add the peanut butter and stir until melted. Add the remaining ingredients and mix well. Line a 9 x 13-inch pan with waxed paper. Press the mixture into the pan. Cool for 30 minutes. Cut into bars. Wrap each bar individually and freeze for handy, nutritious snacks. Yields 2 dozen bars.

Shirley Cothran Barret, Miss America 1975

New Jersey's Finest Cookies

4 sticks butter
2 cups sugar
2 cups firmly packed brown sugar
4 eggs
2 teaspoons vanilla extract
4 cups all-purpose flour
5 cups finely powdered oatmeal (process in a blender)
1 teaspoon salt
2 teaspoons baking powder
2 teaspoons baking soda
2 12-ounce packages chocolate chips
1 8-ounce Hershey bar, grated
3 cups chopped nuts

. . . .

Preheat oven to 375°. Cream the butter and both sugars. Stir in the eggs and vanilla. Blend in the flour, oatmeal, salt, baking powder, and baking soda. Stir in the chips, grated chocolate, and nuts. Roll the dough into balls and place them 2 inches apart on a cookie sheet. Bake for 6 minutes. Yields 112 cookies.

Lynette Falls Bonacquisti, Miss New Jersey 1990

Whoopie Pies

2 sticks margarine
2 cups sugar
2 eggs
4 cups all-purpose flour
1 cup cocoa powder
2 teaspoons salt
1 cup buttermilk
2 teaspoons vanilla extract
2 teaspoons baking soda
1 cup hot water

Filling

2 teaspoons vanilla
2 egg whites, beaten
4 tablespoons all-purpose flour
4 cups confectioners' sugar, divided
2 tablespoons milk
1½ cups shortening

Preheat oven to 400°. Cream the margarine, add the sugar and eggs. Beat with a hand mixer. Sift together the dry ingredients except for the soda. Add the dry ingredients alternately to the creamed mixture along with the buttermilk and vanilla. Dissolve the soda in the hot water and add it last. Mix well. Drop by the spoonful onto a lightly greased cookie sheet and bake for 7 to 8 minutes. Cool the cookies on paper towels.

For the filling, add the vanilla to the egg whites along with the flour, milk, and 2 cups of sugar. Beat until creamy. Add the remaining sugar and the shortening. Beat until smooth and fluffy. Place a generous amount of filling between 2 chocolate cookies. Yields about 5 dozen cookies.

Lynne Grote Tully, Miss Pennsylvania 1977

Peanut Butter Temptations

This is a Fries and Baker family favorite. I can't go to either family's Christmas gatherings without these tasty treats.

1 stick butter
½ cup peanut butter
½ cup sugar
½ cup firmly packed brown sugar
1 egg
½ teaspoon vanilla extract
1½ cups sifted all-purpose flour
¾ teaspoon baking soda
½ teaspoon salt
1 bag Reese's miniature peanut butter cups

Preheat oven to 375°. Thoroughly cream together the butter, peanut butter, sugar, brown sugar, egg, and vanilla. Sift together the flour, baking soda, and salt. Blend into the creamed mixture. Shape into 1-inch balls and place in a muffin tin with 1 ½-inch cups. Bake for 10 minutes. Remove from the oven and quickly push the peanut butter cups in the center of each cookie (be sure to have the peanut butter cups unwrapped and ready). You have to work quickly!! Cool the cookies slightly in the pan then remove to a rack to cool completely. Yields about 2 dozen cookies.

Note: For those of us who cannot have chocolate, substitute plain peanut butter and carob. Once you remove the muffin tin from the oven, use a spoon to make an indentation for the peanut butter. Fill the dent with peanut butter while the cookie is still in the pan. Melt the carob until it is thoroughly soft and easy to work with. Top the cookies with the melted carob. (Key: melt the carob slowly and with a touch of margarine if it is sticking to the pan.) Presto.

Debra Renea Fries Baker, Miss Maryland 1991

There's Always the Swimsuit Competition . . .

The most unusual talents to win the Miss America title have been: trampoline, conducting the pageant orchestra, ventriloquism, a mock striptease, vibraharp, marimba, bass fiddle, imitating Marilyn Monroe, acting with a three-character costume, Tahitian dancing, and singing in Spanish while playing the Paraguayan harp.

Dakeita's Pageant Gooeys

When I was competing, dieting, and working out, I would allow myself one of these per week. It was about five minutes of heaven! I am now executive director of the Miss Western Piedmont Scholarship Pageant in North Carolina and these are a must for the local pageant. People come to judge and help out with the promise of a plate of Gooeys.

1 18¼-ounce box yellow cake mix
3 eggs
1½ sticks margarine, melted and divided
½ cup chopped pecans
1 16-ounce box confectioner's sugar
1 8-ounce package cream cheese, softened to room temperature
1 teaspoon vanilla extract

Preheat oven to 350°. Combine the cake mix, 1 egg, and 1 stick of margarine. Pat into the bottom of a greased 9 x 13-inch pan or glass dish. Sprinkle the nuts over top. Combine the remaining ingredients and pour over the nuts. Bake for 45 minutes or until golden brown. Cut into squares. Yields 2 dozen bars.

Dakeita Vanderburg-Horton, Miss Connecticut 1983

Nebraska Cornflake Wreaths

18 large marshmallows
5 tablespoons margarine
1 teaspoon green food coloring
¾ teaspoon vanilla extract
2½ cups cornflakes
Redhots candies

Melt the first 4 ingredients in a double boiler, stirring constantly until marshmallows are melted. Add the cornflakes (not crushed). Drop onto waxed paper and quickly form into small wreaths, adding the redhots to look like holly. Chill until set. Yields 1½ to 2 dozen cookies.

Jane D. Briggeman Sype, Miss Nebraska 1969

Mexican Wedding Cookies

So tender and rich they melt in your mouth.

1 stick butter
½ cup shortening
1 teaspoon vanilla extract
2 cups all-purpose flour
1 cup chopped walnuts
6 tablespoons confectioners' sugar

Preheat oven to 400°. Cream the butter, shortening, and vanilla; stir in the flour and walnuts. Mix well. Shape into small balls and place on an ungreased cookie sheet. Bake for about 10 minutes. Roll the cookies in confectioners' sugar while still warm. Store overnight before serving. Yields 3 dozen cakes.

Dot Morris, Miss America Pageant Committee

Chocolate Chip Cookies

2 sticks butter, softened to room temperature
2 sticks margarine, softened to room temperature
2 cups sugar
2 cups firmly packed brown sugar
4 eggs
2 teaspoons vanilla extract
4 cups all-purpose flour
5 cups finely powdered oatmeal (processed in a blender)
1 teaspoon salt
2 teaspoons baking powder
2 teaspoons baking soda
1 24-ounce bag chocolate chips

. . . .

Preheat oven to 375°. Cream the first 4 ingredients together. Add the eggs and vanilla and mix well. Combine the dry ingredients and add them to the creamed mixture. Stir in the chocolate chips. Place golf ball-sized rolls of dough 2 inches apart on an ungreased cookie sheet. Bake for 6 minutes. Yields 112 cookies (but you'll have no trouble getting rid of them!).

Note: You can also add a grated 8-ounce chocolate bar and 3 cups chopped nuts.

Carolyn Sapp, Miss America 1992

Pensacola Cookies

This is one of my favorite cookies. My mother would make them for me when I came home from appearances during my reign.

¾ cup shortening
1 cup sugar
2 eggs
2½ cups all-purpose flour
½ teaspoon baking soda
¼ teaspoon salt
¾ cup orange juice
1 cup shredded coconut

. . . .

Preheat oven to 400°. Cream the shortening until it is soft. Add the sugar gradually and beat until light. Add the eggs and beat until very light and fluffy. Sift the dry ingredients, and add alternately with the orange juice, beating smooth after each addition. Add the coconut. Drop by teaspoons onto a baking sheet. Bake for 10 to 12 minutes. Yields 6 dozen small cookies

Maryann Olson, Miss Florida 1991

Oatmeal Chocolate Fudge Cookies

During my year as Miss Florida, these cookies made great nutritious snacks. I love sweets and these were a special treat and a quick pick-me-up.

2 cups sugar
3 to 4 tablespoons cocoa powder
½ cup milk, evaporated or plain
2 teaspoons vanilla extract
2 tablespoons margarine
½ cup peanut butter
2 cups quick-cooking oatmeal (or 1 cup oats and 1 cup nuts)

. . . .

Combine the first 3 ingredients, boil for 1 minute, and remove from the heat. Add the margarine, peanut butter, vanilla, and oatmeal. Cool for 5 minutes. Drop the dough onto waxed paper from a teaspoon. You are finished! Let the cookies set and then enjoy! Yields 2 dozen cookies.

Nicole Padgett, Miss Florida 1993

Battle Between the Hair Colors

Brunettes are nearly twice as likely to win the Miss America title as blondes. Here's the hair color breakdown:

Brunettes—44
Blondes—20
Redheads—1
Auburn—3

Original Graham Crackers

Dr. Sylvester Graham was well known where I grew up in Stafford Springs, Connecticut, for his promotion of good health. He toured the country, lecturing on the virtues of "unbolted" (sifted) flour. Dr. Graham's zeal for dietary reform is far surpassed, though, by his recipe for that great American favorite, the graham cracker. Here is his original recipe.

½ cup butter or margarine
⅔ cup firmly-packed light brown sugar
2 cups graham flour
½ teaspoon salt
½ teaspoon baking powder
¼ teaspoon cinnamon
⅓ cup plus 1 tablespoon water

. . . .

Cream the butter and sugar well. Blend together the remaining ingredients and add them to the creamed mixture alternately with ⅓ cup plus 1 tablespoon water. Work the mixture well with your hands. Let the dough stand for 30 minutes. Preheat oven to 350°. Roll out onto a floured board to ⅛-inch thickness. Cut in 2-inch squares or rounds and place on greased cookie sheets. Bake for 12 minutes. Yields 3 dozen crackers.

Carol Norval Kelley, Miss Connecticut 1969

Deer Cookies (Animal Crackers)

I often use reindeer cookie cutters to make deer cookies because they remind me of my childhood in Nevada. In honor of Heather Whitestone, Miss America 1995, and the thousands of other people in the U.S. who are hearing impaired, my daughters and I shall be making lots of these cookies using a cutter shaped like a hand with the index and ring fingers cut out to make "I Love You" in sign language.

2 sticks butter or margarine
1½ cups sugar
1 egg
½ cup sour cream
1 teaspoon vanilla extract
4 cups all-purpose flour
1 teaspoon baking powder
½ teaspoon baking soda
½ teaspoon nutmeg
½ teaspoon salt

. . . .

Beat together the butter, sugar, and egg. Add the sour cream and vanilla. Combine the flour, baking powder, soda, nutmeg, and salt. Add this to the first mixture and blend well. Press the dough into a bowl, cover with plastic wrap, and chill for several hours. Take one-quarter of the dough and roll it between lightly floured sheets of plastic wrap. (Keep the remainder of the dough in the refrigerator.) Preheat oven to 375°. Roll the dough out to ¼-inch thickness. Use a reindeer cookie cutter to cut out the deer cookies. Place the cookies on a lightly greased cookie sheet and bake for 8 to 10 minutes or until golden on edges. Yields about 3 dozen cookies.

Nancy Bowen Tadie, Miss Nevada 1960

In 1983, twenty-five former Miss Americas gathered in Atlantic City. Left to right (back row): Vonda Kay VanDyke, 1965; Deborah Bryant, 1966; Jane Jayroe, 1967; Judi Ford, 1969; Laurel Schaefer, 1972; Rebecca King, 1974; Shirley Cothran, 1975; Susan Perkins, 1978; Kylene Barker, 1979; Cheryl Prewitt, 1980; Susan Powell, 1981; Elizabeth Ward, 1982; Donna Axum, 1964; Jacquelyn Mayer, 1963; (front row): Marian Bergeron, 1933; Marilyn Meske, 1938; Jean Bartel, 1943; BeBe Shopp, 1948; Evelyn Ay, 1954; Debra Maffett, 1983; Lee Meriwether, 1955; Sharon Ritchie, 1956; Mary Ann Mobley, 1959; Lynda Mead, 1960; Maria Fletcher, 1962. (Irv Kaar)

Easy Lemon Squares

1 18¼-ounce box Duncan Hines Lemon Supreme cake mix
1 stick margarine, melted
1 egg, beaten
1 16-ounce box confectioners' sugar
1 8-ounce package cream cheese, softened to room temperature
2 eggs, beaten

Preheat oven to 350°. Combine the cake mix, margarine, and 1 of the eggs. Press the mixture into a greased 9 x 13-inch pan. Combine the remaining ingredients and spread over the first layer. Bake for 30 to 45 minutes. Cool in the pan, then cut into small squares. Yields 16 to 20 servings.

Gail Bullock Odom, Miss Georgia 1973

Peanut Butter Balls

1 stick margarine
1 18-ounce jar peanut butter
1 16-ounce box confectioners' sugar
3 cups Rice Krispies, crushed with a rolling pin
1½ pounds Candiquik milk chocolate or white chocolate, melted

Cream the margarine and peanut butter. Add the sugar and mix well. Stir in the Rice Krispies and mold into small balls (about 1 inch). Set aside. These can be refrigerated until a later time. Dip the balls in the melted chocolate and set on waxed paper to cool. Store the candy in the refrigerator or freeze. Yields approximately 160 balls.

Debbie Bryant Berge, Miss America 1966

So Close . . .

California holds the record for producing the most first runners-up—nine—followed by South Carolina, Ohio, and New York, with four each.

Pride of Iowa Cookies

These cookies have special memories for me. This recipe comes from the Iowa Historical Society. The cookies were made by my fifth grade class and teacher and served to parents and friends who gathered for the Iowa-Heritage Program presented by our class at the Corse Elementary School in Burlington, Iowa. I sang my first solo on a public stage at this program.

1 cup firmly packed brown sugar
1 cup sugar
1 cup shortening
2 eggs
1 teaspoon vanilla extract
2 cups all-purpose flour
1 teaspoon baking soda
½ teaspoon salt
3 cups oatmeal
½ cup nuts
1 cup coconut

. . . .

Preheat oven to 350°. Cream together the sugars, shortening, eggs, and vanilla. Combine the dry ingredients and stir into the creamed mixture. Mix well. Add the oatmeal, nuts, and coconut. Drop by the teaspoonful onto a greased cookie sheet. Bake for 10 to 12 minutes, or until lightly browned. Yields 4½ dozen cookies.

Kerri Lynne Rosenberg Burkhardt, Miss Iowa 1990

Quick Cookies

1 18¼-ounce box cake mix
2 eggs
½ cup vegetable oil
½ to 1 teaspoon vanilla or almond extract, or any other flavoring (optional)
1 cup chocolate chips, nuts, or raisins

. . . .

Preheat oven to 375°. Combine all of the ingredients. Drop the dough by the teaspoonful onto an ungreased cookie sheet. Bake for 10 to 12 minutes. Allow the cookies to cool slightly before removing them from the cookie sheets.

Mary Shelby Bauer, Miss Passaic, New Jersey 1927

Popcorn Balls

¾ cup firmly packed brown sugar
¾ cup sugar
½ cup dark Karo syrup
½ cup water
3 tablespoons vinegar
¼ cup butter or margarine
¼ teaspoon baking soda
6 quarts popped popcorn

. . . .

Cook the sugars, syrup, water, and vinegar until it spins a thread; then add the butter. When the soft ball stage is reached (234°), remove from the heat and beat in the baking soda. Pour the hot syrup over the popped corn. Use wet hands to press the corn into balls of uniform size. Yields 2 to 3 dozen balls.

Jane Jayroe, Miss America 1967

Original New Orleans Pralines

1¼ cups sugar
¾ cup firmly-packed dark brown sugar
½ cup milk
½ stick butter (not margarine)
1 teaspoon vanilla extract
2 cups chopped pecans

. . . .

Combine the sugars and milk. Cook to 238° (soft ball stage). Remove from the heat and add the butter. Stir until the butter has melted. Beat until the mixture has the consistency of condensed milk and a dullish color. Stir in the vanilla. Add the pecans and mix well. Mixture will begin to harden quickly, so pour immediately onto waxed paper to cool. Yields 2 dozen.

Bobbie Candler, Miss Louisiana 1982

Aunt Bill's Brown Candy

This is not only a sinful, wonderful, fat-ladened treat, it is also a delightful Christmas tradition in our family. This recipe really requires two people to make: one to pour and one to stir. It's no wonder we have such fond memories of making this candy. It requires a kitchen full of family love and warmth.

6 cups sugar, divided
1 pint heavy cream
1 stick butter
¼ teaspoon baking soda
1 tablespoon vanilla extract
1 pound shelled pecan pieces

. . . .

Pour 2 cups of the sugar into a heavy iron skillet and place over low heat. Stir with a wooden spoon and keep the sugar moving so that it will not scorch. It should be the color of light brown sugar syrup when finished. As soon as the sugar has started to heat in the skillet, pour the remaining 4 cups of sugar together with the cream into a deep kettle and set them over low heat to cook slowly. As soon as the sugar in the skillet has melted, pour it into the kettle of boiling sugar and cream, keeping it on very low heat and stir constantly. The real secret to mixing these ingredients is to pour a very fine stream from the skillet. It is helpful to have two people working at this point, one pouring and one stirring. Continue cooking and stirring until the mixture forms a firm ball when dropped into cold water (248°). After this test is made, turn off the heat and immediately add the soda, stirring vigorously as it foams up. As soon as the soda is well mixed, add the butter, allowing it to melt as you stir. Remove the mixture from the stove, but not to a cold place, for about ten minutes. Then add the vanilla and begin beating. Using a mixer, beat until the mixture is thick and heavy with a dull appearance instead of the previous glossy sheen. Add the broken nut meats and mix in thoroughly. Pour into a greased pan and cut into squares when slightly cooled. Yields 6 pounds.

Jane Jayroe, Miss America 1967

Royal Record-Holders

The states with the most Miss Americas are:
California (6), Ohio* (5), Pennsylvania (5), and Mississippi (4).

*Ohio's first Miss America, Mary Campbell, won the title in both 1922 and 1923. Thus the state has five Miss Americas, but six Miss America *titles*.

What's In a Name?

A crown, perhaps. The most successful Miss America names are Susan and Deborah, with three Miss Americas named Susan and four named Deborah, Debra, Debbye. Then again, there are Miss Americas with unusual names: Neva, Vonda, Tawny, Jacque, Kylene, Kaye Lani Rae, Venus, Jo-Carroll, and Leanza.

Date & Nut Confection—A Colorado Treat

I remember holidays in the late 1920s and early 1930s when my mother would take me to visit a special cousin who owned a farm near the little town of Greeley, Colorado, 50 miles north of Denver. This was one of her homemade holiday treats. Many years have passed, and with fond memories of childhood I have continued to make it for our family.

1 cup diced dates
½ cup nuts
Pinch of salt
1 cup sugar
1 teaspoon baking powder
4 egg whites, beaten
Whipped cream

Preheat oven to 300°. Combine the first 5 ingredients. Fold the egg whites into the mixture. Pour into a buttered dish. Bake for 20 minutes. When cool, serve with whipped cream. Yields 6 to 8 servings.

Charlene Woods Faber, Miss Colorado 1941

Aunt Mary Dec's Tea Squares

Bottom crust

¾ cup shortening
2 egg yolks, well-beaten
⅓ cup sugar
1½ cups sifted all-purpose flour
1 teaspoon vanilla extract

Top crust

2 egg whites, beaten until stiff
2 teaspoons all-purpose flour
¼ teaspoon baking powder
1½ cups firmly packed brown sugar
1 cup chopped nuts
½ teaspoon salt
1 cup moist shredded coconut
1 teaspoon vanilla extract

Preheat oven to 350°. Blend all of the ingredients for the bottom crust and spread them in a 9 x 9-inch pan. Bake for 12 minutes or until golden brown. Combine all of the remaining ingredients and spread over the partially baked crust. Bake for 20 minutes. Yields 20 squares.

Pamela Jo Hoff, Miss Rhode Island 1983

Index